ENERGY AND TRANSPORT

SAGE FOCUS EDITIONS

Energy and Transport
Historical Perspectives on Policy Issues

edited by

GEORGE H. DANIELS
MARK H. ROSE

SAGE PUBLICATIONS
Beverly Hills / London / New Delhi

For information address:

SAGE Publications, Inc.
275 South Beverly Drive
Beverly Hills, California 90212

SAGE Publications India Pvt. Ltd.
C-236 Defence Colony
New Delhi 110 024, India

SAGE Publications Ltd
28 Banner Street
London EC1Y 8QE, England

Printed in the United States of America

Library of Congress Cataloging in Publication Data

Main entry under title:

Energy & transport.

   (Sage focus editions ; 52)
   Bibliography: p.
   Includes index.
   1. Energy policy—United States—History—
Addresses, essays, lectures.   2. Energy consump-
tion—United States—History—Addresses, essays,
lectures.   3. Transportation—United States—
History—Addresses, essays, lectures.   I. Daniels,
George H.   II. Rose, Mark H., 1942-
III. Title: Energy and transport.
HD9502.U52E446   333.79   82-5642
ISBN 0-8039-0786-9   AACR2
ISBN 0-8039-0787-7 (pbk.)

FIRST PRINTING

For
Donielle, Amy Claire,
and Lolly Isa

Contents

Acknowledgments

Every scholarly undertaking is the result of immense efforts by persons and agencies. Our financial support for the conference on which this work is based was excellent, and for this we must thank the Michigan Council for the Humanities, the National Endowment for the Humanities, the Sohio Corporation, and Michigan Technological University. At Michigan Tech, Dean William Powers, Vice President Calvin Gale, and President Dale F. Stein took time off from busy schedules to entertain our plans and to locate funds. John H. Winslow, the Head of the Department of Social Sciences and the Program in Science, Technology, and Society, first thought of the idea of a conference. He provided encouragement and counsel, and also stood ready to remove obstacles. John G. Clark, Arthur M. Donovan, and Joel A. Tarr wrote excellent papers that focused our thinking on key issues in the areas of energy, transport, and public policy. These efforts led up to a conference at Michigan Tech in September 1981, where early versions of these papers were presented. The conference also included four critics and six members of a Panel, whose respective tasks were to comment on the papers and to provide an overview of the findings. Although their remarks could not be published, it is important to acknowledge in print their efforts, which in every case were taken into account in revising the articles in this anthology: Arthur M. Donovan, Mark S. Foster, Ellis W. Hawley, Volker Hartkopf, Jack M. Holl, Daniel F. Leskinnen, Chester W. Lewis, Albro Martin, Thomas O. Mathues, William Turney, and Richard H.K. Vietor. Two others who were helpful in special ways should be mentioned at this point. Larry Lankton read portions of the manuscript and offered useful suggestions, and many of Melvin Kranzberg's insightful comments during the Conference have helped to guide the editorial work. That scholarship is a collective effort is a cliché, but it is also true. In the final analysis, the people who participated in this collaborative undertaking deserve joint credit for whatever contribution the edited version may make.

–George H. Daniels
Mark H. Rose

Introduction

GEORGE H. DANIELS

MARK H. ROSE

Beginning in the early 1970s, social commentators and social critics, as well as business, governmental, and labor leaders, noted the long lines at service stations, the inability to secure natural gas for homes and factories, and the mounting importation of foreign oil. Their uniform conclusion was that home heating, domestic appliances, the automobile, and the truck were consuming excessive quantities of fuel. These developments were of recent origin, or so ran the popular reasoning, and only adjustments in personal habits would resolve the contemporary "crisis." Despite the ready availability of information about earlier crises—for example, the recurring crises of 1914-1922 that led federal officials to mandate fuel conservation in order to overcome coal shortages caused by a combination of factors, including increased demand and an overburdened railroad network, and the severe shortages of natural gas between 1947 and 1950 that slowed housing construction and led to the imposition of another mandated conservation program—we have continued to look upon fuel abundance as being the natural order of economic affairs, requiring no particular systematic action by either private or public agencies.

Society has accepted imbalances as only temporary inconveniencies that could be explained in terms of the familiar myths of American politics: Malevolent men and women representing large interests had obstructed the workings of the system for personal gain, and they continue to do so. Only those who supported the public's interest could rescue us temporarily from these forces of evil. Such simplistic analysis has prevailed because the public has only begun to understand the significance of energy and transport sources in shaping the social, geographic, and historical dimensions of American life. Thus, general knowledge of the historical and contemporary roles of business, the farm, cities and communities, transport facilities, and politics in general in the production and consumption of energy is fragmentary.

Policy makers have fared no better in dealing with the energy dilemma. They routinely entertained pleas for additional solar, oil, natural gas, nuclear, or coal production, but no sooner had they decided upon one option (as they liked to label such decisions), than they were besieged with evidence that it had been the wrong one. Thus the option of fostering growth through the unlimited mining of coal was stopped when environmental groups proved successful in limiting western coal production and in securing the imposition of air quality standards. Equally difficult has been the path of the solar advocate, who seemed a few years ago to be on the inside track with policy makers. This source of energy, presumed to be clean, cheap, and abundant, has faced such obstacles as high innovation costs and the political and economic commitment of society to fossil fuels—which, in turn, are often polluting, expensive, and exhaustible.[1] The net result in policy circles has been that each governmental unit, especially at the federal level, has taken as its cause one or two energy solutions, either nuclear, solar, natural gas, oil, or coal, depending upon its mandate, and has not even made an effort to think in terms of an overall "fuels policy." Consequently, what has emerged is vast confusion, a deadlock in legislative arenas, and a public who has no choice but to rely upon a certain amount of myth in order to comprehend changes in energy and transport matters.

The confusion in policy and legislative circles has resulted not only from the partial view taken by each agency, but from an inability to fix general goals. Basically, three ideas have informed government and business relations in general, and energy policy in particular, a fact made clear by historian Ellis W. Hawley.[2] Government officials and many in the business community have endorsed the idea of unlimited development. In this scheme, government only cleared the obstacles to energy development by building roads and regulating unequal markets. Others in the policy community, again with their allies in business, preferred the prospect of a government-business partnership. Economic planning, and especially the elimination of waste, were the desired goals, creating an economy of abundance. The third approach, often the favorite of corporate leaders but also appealing to many in government, looked to business groups to plan among themselves for energy and transport development.

While enthusiasts for these diverse ideas argued among themselves, the nation passed through a succession of "crises." Never did any point of view achieve a national consensus, in part because the focus of the argument constantly shifted. First, there was the series of coal famines; next, attention shifted quickly to perceived shortages of oil, then to an oil glut during the 1930s, and then to the steady abundance of the post-World War II years. As promising as the American experimental efforts were to produce synthetic liquid fuel by coal hydrogenation up to 1952, few in government or business saw much reason to tamper with the market and administrative mechanisms that were providing gasoline for all who could afford it at a quarter a gallon.[3] By the 1970s, then, Americans faced the third energy and transport crisis of the century. Because the proponents of no single approach had managed to achieve a consensus, neither government nor business could mobilize a national consensus behind a unified approach to the energy shortage. In brief, policy was the outcome of its own history.

Scholars have tended to reproduce this shortcoming, failing to provide a general and useful explanation of energy production, transport, and consumption. The reasons for such weakness are complex, but they are clearly rooted in the nature of the work and organization or scholarly activity. The particular problem here seems to flow from the failure of the social sciences to examine the link between energy resources and transportation for its effect on values and public policy. Why this should be the case requires some explanation, for earlier scholars seemed conscious of the importance of the relationship. By 1900, those who studied the economic, urban, and political aspects of American society had identified emerging ties between energy and transportation. In 1908, the planners of a conference of state governors and their aids included as topics on their agenda the electrification of railroads, the electric propulsion of ships, and generally the idea of an "interdependence of industries . . . including transportation."[4] In 1933 a report to the President's Research Committee on Social Trends stressed the transport and energy developments that had stimulated economic growth in the nineteenth and early twentieth centuries by successive reductions in the costs of manufacture.[5] The report on urban developments to the President's Committee demonstrated the importance of transportation and energy in defining the spatial organization and functional arenas of urban centers, and also documented the out-migration of business and residents between 1900 and 1930. At the beginning of the Depression decade, in fact, researchers for the President's Committee relied upon data for utility service as well as commutation patterns to define the extent of the metropolis itself. The city that appeared in their report was "the child of modern facilities for transportation and communication," the latter including the public utilities that provided light, heat, and power.[6] As urban areas increased in size, observers concluded that manipulation of transportation and energy facilities could help create new and more livable cities.[7]

As this brief sketch indicates, until the 1930s, no matter how much observers of American energy and transport disagreed about the appropriate paths of national development, all agreed on the importance of treating both as one unit for the analysis of cities and the economy. After 1930, scholarly work on energy and transport diverged sharply from its original base in the accounts of participants. While on-site observers from 1900 through 1930 had placed the two together and brought them front and center in their analyses, the newer scholarship, especially after 1960, treated energy and transport as independent factors and often left the impression that energy was inconsequential. Only rarely have books published since World War II placed transport and energy together and projected them into the broader contexts of urban, economic, and industrial change; still more rare were those scholars who brought the public policy dimension to the fore; only a few, moreover, have attempted a holistic treatment, one tying energy and transport to social, economic, and political change. Standard treatments of the trolley and then the automobile and its associated complex of highways recognize their roles in facilitating (and often leading) urban change and overlook the cheap coal and petroleum that allowed the system to operate. None take account of federal or state energy policy or the complex oil and coal businesses in explaining that underlying energy component. Nor has it been customary to prepare explanations of the place of transport and energy as factors in the development of the contemporary economy, the functioning, organization, and arrangement of cities, interregional competition for firms, jobs, and taxes, or of their importance in state and federal legislatures.[8]

Several textbooks explain changes in urban form, politics, and social and economic organization. Again, each of the authors calls attention to the significance of the trolley and later the automobile for the changing form and social morphology of the city, ignoring, however, the conversion and distribution of energy resources which underpinned the trolley and highway networks. Similarly, a majestic, two-volume account of techniques and technologies in the physical growth of Chicago contains only one reference in the index to electric generation and does not list natural gas, gasoline, or energy systems in general.[9]

Scholars of transportation have concentrated on the role of the railroads and other transporters in carrying coal and oil, and on the social, economic, and political developments following the arrival of new transport systems such as airlines and automobiles. Several historians have also directed their attention to bargaining in the political arena prior to 1920 between shippers, railroad leaders, and politicians. Consumption of energy resources by locomotives, steam ships, and airplanes, as well as the prodigious appetite of millions of automobiles for gasoline, has received scant attention. Curiously, only one scholar has undertaken work on the forbidding complex of technologies and the legal, political, social, and economic issues surrounding pipelines, the one energy transporter which requires comparatively modest energy inputs.[10]

Scholarship, of course, is a social act, one linked to patterns on the national scene, to the subculture of those who train, finance, manage, and reward practitioners, and to the more intimate milieu of the disciplines and organizations that house scholars. In part, the material abundance of American life explains the direction of scholarship focused on energy and transport. Because the nation's immense energy endowment and well-developed rail and highway networks, scholars, one supposes, turned to the politics of transport and energy in an attempt to understand the administration and legislation affecting prices and delivery.[11] Only rarely did an assessment of consumption enter into this picture.

Specialization of scholarly activity, including teaching, has also reduced the chances of considering energy and transport as a single problem. In fact, the thrust of research in every field of inquiry has been toward the creation of new, ever smaller units of analysis. The ward and district loomed large for political analysis; the inventor and his context for technologically oriented studies; and, say, the trolley and its significance for residential location choices for urban geography. Equally influential in shaping scholarship has been the virtual absence of unifying mechanisms—professional associations, funding agencies, and journal and monographic series treating and insisting upon the treatment of energy and transport in unison. The net result, up to the present time, has been fragmentary policy and fragmented scholarship, rendering impossible the task of coordinated planning and the achievement—even by senior scholars—of a sense of the whole.[12]

Despite the lack of integration, the fundamental ideas for a reconsideration of energy and transport are in place, and have been for quite some time. Coal, electricity, and petroleum facilitated the growth of transportation networks and the subsequent decentralization of American cities.

Coal influenced the creation of the centralized, high technology manufacturing firm, and the building of central electric firms and the erection of long-distance transmission lines demanded the skills of those who could solve technological problems, assemble immense capital resources, and manage large businesses. In short, the policy and scholarly dimensions of energy and transport mandate attention to the culture of energy and transport, to their organizational frameworks, and then to their consequences. The core idea is that the interaction of values, technologies, and decisions shaped the power and transport technologies, the firms that housed them, and also created the framework within which social change—consequences—took place. A good beginning would be to link energy and transport studies and policy analysis in a vital relationship with the actual workings of transportation, business, economic and urban affairs, politics, and the history of technology. In turn, this work will require moorings in professional associations and in the popular imagination, an immense increase in data and theoretical platforms, and several practical and successful applications. This is the need that the contributors to the present volume have begun to fill.

George Basalla, for example, in the first contribution to this collection, argues persuasively that Americans have historically viewed their energy sources in terms of certain persistent myths which have likewise colored their view of successive transportation forms utilizing the energy. According to the myth, the emerging energy source is seen to be without any faults; it is infinitely abundant, and it has the ability to effect utopian changes in society. In each case, the myth persists until the new energy has been developed to the point that its drawbacks become apparent and its failure to establish a utopia has been reluctantly recognized. The discarded myth then finds a new life with the discovery of yet another new source of energy. And so the cycle continues, with only the myth remaining unaltered while different energy sources enter and leave the public spotlight. Warren Belasco, also pursuing mythical associations connected with different energy/transportation forms, shows how in the early twentieth century certain social-cultural variables contributed to a pervasive movement away from mass, collective transportation and toward private, individualistic travel. This changing attitude was partly explained by the simple fact that an economical means of private transportation had only recently become available, but it was also associated with the growing tendency to criticize the steam engine as a polluter of air and a destroyer of a valuable natural resource, and, on the other hand, with the view of the internal combustion engine as a clean alternative to steam.

As Belasco's chapter clearly shows, important social transformations are implied by energy transitions. In this case, the myths of energy and the ideal of being able to control transport fixed the framework for the development of energy and transport systems. Martin Melosi goes even further, arguing that the study of energy transitions is the key to under-standing the economic, technical, and even the social development of a nation. But at the same time, his study of the nineteenth century transition from wood and waterpower to coal reinforces Basalla's argument by showing that Americans did have preconceived notions about the benefits of a single energy source that made a transition to a new source difficult.

Joel A. Tarr and Kenneth E. Koons look at another aspect of the fuel transition process—the various factors affecting rates of conversion to new technologies—and are also concerned with the relation between transport and environmental regulations. Even though there were a variety of both economic and environmental incentives for the railroads to replace their coal burning locomotives, their position as prime haulers of coal balanced the losses due to inefficiency, and thus provided a disincentive to rapid conversion. Railroads did institute a number of procedures aimed at reducing waste, in part with a view toward achieving greater economy in their operations, and also in order to reduce the smoke nuisance in cities. But the technological inertia of the railroad networks, according to Tarr and Koons, precluded in the minds of the railroad leaders the option of switching to diesel power or diesel electric locomotives in large numbers until after World War II.

Simultaneously with the transitions came the creation in both public and private sectors of agencies capable of meeting the demand for energy and transport. Large oil firms and their trade associations, along with state and federal officials, created a vast organizational network. One approach emphasized in these pages is the organizational complexity of operations and the inability of different interests to agree upon a common policy—laissez faire, government planning, or corporate planning. A second point equally worth remembering is that millions of private choices, based on the values of the culture, served as the foundation for the creation of these organizations.

August W. Giebelhaus points to the emergence of the automobile as a significant force in American life and explores the development of the large, integrated oil firms which took up the challenge of finding oil, refining it, and distributing gasoline to an increasing number of motorists. Using the experiences of the Sun Oil Company of Pennsylvania as a vehicle to explore the relationship between the growth of the modern oil industry and patterns of economic development at the local, regional, and national levels, he concludes that the major oil company has played a role as both initiator and respondent to demographic and economic changes in the United States during the twentieth century. While individual firm decision-making has indeed reflected the interests of the public as expressed by the market forces in the economy, it has also played a part in stimulating and encouraging the growth of a nation wedded to petroleum in what was once an economy of energy abundance. In effect, Giebelhaus shows that one role of the large firm is to encourage a still greater degree of dependence on its energy product.

Joseph A. Pratt explores another dimension of the petroleum industry—the role of its trade association, the American Petroleum Institute. Founded in 1919, partly in the hope that the pattern of successful government—industry cooperation developed during World War I could be continued indefinitely, API leaders sought to promote the interests of the petroleum industry by collecting data that would prove useful, by establishing industry-wide specifications, and by representing the industry before governmental bodies. The API helped to promote the development of the member oil companies in matters of mutual interest, and also fostered cooperative relationships between government and business by acting as a liaison.

At first glance, it appears that the petroleum industry matured effortlessly, almost through the workings of the proverbial invisible hand, and that government and business easily found common areas of understanding. But Giebelhaus and Pratt also highlight the conflicts—between large and small producers, between the integrated and wildcatting firms, between differing interpretations of the public interest—thus showing the basic point that the shape of the firms and their relationships with one another and with the government were always contingent upon judgments and decisions in their social, economic, political, and geographical contexts.

John G. Clark investigates the efforts of government officials during the years between World Wars I and II to create a national energy policy. In a word, they failed, largely because they were as confused and divided as everyone else about the most appropriate directions for national policy. Responding to the pressures of their constituencies, agencies charged with managing coal excluded petroleum and gas, gas-oriented agencies overlooked coal, and so forth; none was successful in dealing with the periodic gluts and famines that characterized energy sources and the transport and other industries dependent on them. The net result, up to 1940, was a contradictory and ambivalent energy policy, one which never satisfied competing interests and never provided stable prices and profitability for contemporaries or later generations. It was simply a "politics of factions," in which the government bestowed favors and legal authority upon various groups in proportion to their ability to bring the proper symbols of legitimacy to Washington.

Jack M. Holl examines federal energy policy from World War II through 1973 and reaches conclusions similar to Clark's. Holl shows that federal energy policy was limited in scope, cautious, and badly fragmented along regional and technological lines. But it was President Richard M. Nixon, according to Holl, who began to shape a coherent federal program even before the crisis of 1973. This new program involved the creation of federal agencies charged to deal with energy for the nation as a whole. But this program was blocked in Congress, where neither consistent economic principles nor scientific/technical knowledge appeared to have any bearing on the fragmented decision process.

It is the question of the role of knowledge and of principle, and of the bearing of both on the formation of policy, that Edward W. Constant examines at the state level. Specifically, he considers the evolution of the Texas Railroad Commission's prorationing policy and its relationship to reservoir engineering. From his study it is clear that where important economic interests are directly involved, even such hallowed principles of the law as due process can be interpreted, and such sacroscant notions as the virtue of free market forces can be replaced. The intricate and laborious process by which a changing scientific information base can be assimilated into legal decisions again exemplifies the connection between organized—and persistent—interests and public policy. In this case, the federal court of appeals finally accepted the role of an expert commission dependent upon changing scientific knowledge, deciding in favor of the "fruitful empiricism of a continuing administrative process." Constant closes with the disturbing conclusion that such public controversies as he describes may be inherent in the effort to manage twentieth century technological systems founded upon dynamic and esoteric scientific knowledge.

It is clear from the work of the scholars we have discussed that during the twentieth century, Americans adjusted their politics, cities, households, and legal institutions to accommodate the emerging complexes of transport and energy and the private and public agencies that managed them. It is well known that the trolley, and later the automobile, facilitated household and industrial decentralization, leading to the creation of urban centers spread across thirty or even fifty miles. Less well known are the responses of urban planners who occasionally attempted to coordinate transport and energy developments in the midst of frenzied urban growth and change. Eugenie Ladner Birch argues that their history is essentially one of response to popular demand, not enlightened leadership. Only the rare planner ever understood the significance of energy and transport for urban growth and rapid social-spatial change, and none were able to cope adequately with these essential factors. The recommendations that were accepted, in fact, can best be seen as a demand-generated response to the observed consumer preference for private vehicular transportation. Anything that did not coincide with the agenda of the political and economic decision makers and with the thrust of popular preferences—that is to say, anything beyond the familiar solution of radial arteries and expressways— was rejected as city after city took on the same appearance, and the same problems were created for the present generation.

The next two chapters return to the theme of energy transitions and force us to consider certain implications of differing energy systems. First, using an exhaustive national study of the records of household energy consumption from 1900 to 1980, Bonnie Maas Morrison questions the notion that a return to some of the fuel sources of the past (wood and coal in particular) might help to resolve the present energy problems. Her figures, in fact, make it clear that total energy consumption on a per household level has actually decreased since a peak in 1907. Whatever the solution to our present energy crisis may be, it is clearly not to be found, she says, in an uncritical "conservation" effort at the household level. The implication is that system-wide planning directed toward specific problem areas will be required.

The study by Corlann (Corky) Gee Bush narrows the focus still further. Using information collected in the Palouse region of eastern Washington and northern Idaho, she argues powerfully that changes in energy and transportation technology have dramatically different effects on men and women, at least in rural settings, and she naturally raises the question whether this may not be true generally. On the farms, the transition to modern energy and transportation technologies has resulted in making a woman's traditional role less "crucial" to the survival of the family unit at the same time the man's traditional role has become more crucial. Thus, there has been no transformation in roles but in the meaning attached to them, and as Bush observes, the public policy consequences of the changes are profound, for everything from the health of the individual to the health of entire communities is affected.

Thus, at the same time that we become broader in our interests, we must also become narrower in our conclusions. We can no longer speak of the "impact" of the transition from wood to coal or from coal to oil in general, but must distinguish between changes at the household level, at the industrial level, and, so one gathers, in type of use. Burning coal in a moving locomotive is certainly not the same in its implications as burning coal in an electricity generating plant equipped with scrubbing facilities in its stacks.

In the final chapter in this volume, Langdon Winner assesses what he describes as the "Grand Consensus" among contemporary energy policy analysts. Without arguing that a different model would be better, Winner notes that all current debate among experts takes place within the framework of economic growth, in which efficiency, measured in terms of output per unit, is the only relevant variable. In adopting this framework, of course, analysts have simply been reflecting dominant attitudes in their society, for the idea that freedom and social well-being could be achieved through sheer abundance has been an almost unquestioned tenet of American political thinking. The result, he says, is that questions about the quality of human associations as affected by the social organization of energy will simply not be raised, and we will continue to ignore the social and political dimensions of the structure of energy systems. The fact is, so Winner concludes, that the building of each new energy system involves a partial reconstruction of society, and a determination to submit to the needs of the "regime" it represents.

These chapters contain many different implications for scholarship and policy. Do they lend support to the idea of a return to that mythical era of free markets, to government regulation and planning, to a wholesale turnover to corporate officials of all transport and energy activities? Probably not. Taken individually or even as a group, they may be of little help to the private or public policy analyst who must make judgments for the next six months, or five years, and be judged in turn by the results. While they lack that complex of variables and cost-benefit analyses now deemed necessary in the policy sciences, these studies, among the best that the scholarly community has provided, are useful for comprehending that mix of technology, politics, and values that has shaped the current energy and transport dilemmas. The point is not that policy makers should proceed without the sort of studies that appear in this volume—they do so at their peril, and at ours. The real need, it appears, is to link broader studies of energy and transport to the routines and reports of those located in policy circles. Until that happy moment, policy will continue to be shaped by the realities of technologies, values, and earlier decisions, and yet policy makers will speak knowingly of printouts and formulas and "politics," and will render judgments based upon hunches, prescriptions, organizational resources and politics, and the passions of the moment.

Whatever their utility for policy makers may be, the articles will be valuable to members of the scholarly communities. The writers express the "state of art" in a developing field of social and historical research. Their findings will have an immediate importance in the education of today's students. A second contribution of these chapters is to provide an immensely useful framework for future research that, in time and in its turn, will be linked to policy. One important theme that policy analysts can recognize here is that if they are to be successful, they must understand the degree to which the landscape of energy and transport development has molded their work. To remain successful in a democratic society, policy makers must comprehend the manifold and virtually unstoppable consequences of technological change for social, urban, political, and economic life. The alternative, these chapters clearly suggest, is to simply ratify without comprehension the decisions of whatever "regime" that, in some fashion, manages to deliver the goods.

NOTES

1. Richard H.K. Vietor, "Comment," Symposium on Power, Transport, and Public Policy in Modern America, Michigan Technological University, September 25, 1981; see also his *Environmental Politics and the Coal Coalition* (College Station, TX, 1980).

2. "Comment," Symposium on Power, Transport, and Public Policy in Modern America, Michigan Technological University, September 25-27, 1981, see also his *The New Deal and the Problem of Monopoly* (Princeton, NJ, 1966).

3. Arnold Krammer, "An attempt at transition: the Bureau of Mines synthetic fuel project at Louisiana, Missouri," in Lewis J. Perelman et al., eds., *Energy Transitions: Long-term Perspectives* (Boulder, CO, 1981), 90-99.

4. Newton C. Blanchard et al., eds., *Proceedings of a Conference of Governors in the White House, Washington, D.C., May 13-15, 1908* (Washington, D.C., 1909), 292, 308.

5. F. G. Tryon and Margaret H. Schoenfield, "Utilization of natural wealth: mineral and power resources," Report of the President's Research Committee on Social Trends, *Recent Social Trends in the United States*, Vol. I (New York and London, 1933), 60, 66-67.

6. R. D. McKinzie, "The rise of metropolitan communities," 444, 453, 494; and see also Malcolm M. Willey and Stuart A. Rice, "The agencies of communication," 167-183, both in ibid.

7. Lewis Mumford, *Technics and Civilization* (New York and Burlingame, 1963), 238-239.

8. See for example, Paul Barrett, *Straphanger's Dream: Transportation Policy and Planning in Chicago, 1900-1930* (Philadelphia, forthcoming); Charles W. Cheape, *Moving the Masses: Urban Public Transit in New York, Boston, and Philadelphia, 1880-1912* (Cambridge, 1980); Mark H. Rose, *Interstate: Express Highway Politics, 1941-1956* (Lawrence, KS, 1979). An exciting exception is Fred W. Viehe, "Black gold suburbs: the influence of the extractive industry on the suburbanization of Los Angeles, 1890-1930," *Journal of Urban History* 8 (November, 1981), 3-26.

9. David R. Goldfield and Blaine A. Brownell, *Urban America: From Downtown to No Town* (Boston, 1979), 205-208, 379-381; Zane L. Miller, *The Urbanization of Modern America: A Brief History* (New York, 1973), 79-80; Gerald D. Nash, *The American West in the Twentieth Century: A Short History of an Urban Oasis* (Englewood Cliffs, NJ, 1973), 84-86, 90-92, 233-234; Carl W. Condit, *Chicago, 1910-1929: Building, Planning, and Urban Technology* (Chicago, 1973); and also his *Chicago, 1930-1970: Building, Planning, and Urban Technology* (Chicago, 1974).

10. K. Austin Kerr, *American Railroad Politics, 1914-1920: Rates, Wages, and Efficiency* (Pittsburgh, 1968); Albro Martin, *Enterprise Denied: Origins of the Decline of American Railroads, 1897-1917* (New York and London, 1971); Arthur M. Johnson, *The Development of American Petroleum Pipelines: A Study in Private Enterprise and Public Policy, 1862-1906* (Ithaca, 1956).

11. For the role of economic abundance in shaping American life, see David M. Potter, *People of Plenty: Economic Abundance and the American Character* (Chicago and London, 1954).

12. The explanation of the absence of interest by contemporary scholars in energy and transportation as a unified theme is intellectually difficult, demanding as it does an account of a non-event. Additional work in the sociology of knowledge and specific research in the social history of the humanistic disciplines would contribute to our understanding of the patterns of research choice, and perhaps explain as well this particular lacuna.

PART 1

Ideology and Culture

1

Some Persistent Energy Myths

GEORGE BASALLA

Traditionally, technology has been placed in opposition to the irrational, emotional, or mythic elements that constitute a large part of man's social and intellectual experience. The assumption is made that technology is a form of objective knowledge and that its practitioners are dispassionate, neutral observers who carefully weigh the facts and coolly draw their conclusions.[1] According to this view, the technologist is the unprejudiced, rational servant of a public susceptible to whims and fancies that are not always in its best interest. Thus, the engineer designs nuclear weapons because he is asked to do so by "politicians and generals"; he builds—or at least has built—unsafe, inefficient automobiles because the public demanded them; and he pollutes the environment by manufacturing products that customers, swept by fads, believe they need.

This outlook will be challenged by a description and analysis of the energy myths that all of us, both inside and outside the technical community, have lived with and by for the past two centuries. According to these myths, any newly discovered source of energy is assumed to be without faults, infinitely abundant, and to have the potential to affect utopian changes in society. These myths persist until a new energy source is developed to the point that its drawbacks become apparent and the failure to establish a utopian society must be reluctantly admitted. That is to say, the myths persist until skies darkened by coal smoke must be acknowledged as a problem or until the real threat of a nuclear accident (Three Mile Island) forces society to concede that coal or uranium are not the miraculous substances they were once thought to be.

At this point, one might suppose that society would emerge from its difficulties sadder but wiser and treat the next new energy source differently. Unfortunately, this is not the case. The latest form of energy is not handled in a more restrained fashion. Instead, the recently discarded energy myths are resurrected and bestowed upon the newcomer. And so the cycle continues, with only the myths remaining unaltered while various sources of energy enter and leave the public spotlight.

Before exploring the nature of the modern energy myths associated with coal, hydropower, nuclear power, and solar energy, I wish to offer three general remarks applicable to my entire discussion. First, it is much easier to recognize the myths clustering about older energy sources than it is for us to acknowledge that such myths are a part of the way we respond to currently fashionable ones. Hence, it is less difficult for us to find fault with the naive progressive ideas the nineteenth century held about coal and the steam engine than it is to admit that we might be similarly infatuated with solar energy today.

The second general remark is that the myths described here are not the sole creation of scientists, engineers, and their business associates. Although energy myths often serve (and are exploited by) these persons, they are generated by a much wider group of men and women. The fantasies attached to energy use and production are shared by technologist, capitalist, and the general public alike.

The third remark comes in the form of a warning. Energy myths are particularly dangerous because they blind us to the realities of new energy sources by promising a golden land of the future and ignoring the real problems of today. In every case to be discussed in this essay, the promise of some novel source of energy has not been realized, while the difficulties it has generated have been far greater than ever imagined.

Coal (The Steam Engine)

The energy myth cycle begins with the age of coal early in the nineteenth century, even though other energy sources (wood, for example) had served mankind much earlier. The relatively late date at which coal made its entrance into man's economic and social life might account for the fact that it became the center of attention in a way that wood never was. Wood, as fuel, dates to the early history of man, whereas coal entered the scene sometime in the seventeenth century.[2] In any case, prior to the nineteenth century one searches in vain for the energy myths covered in this essay.

The Middle Ages had witnessed a great power revolution, one that was recognized by historians writing in the twentieth century. The waterwheel, windmill, and effective harnesses for horses and oxen were all first extensively used in western Europe during the Middle Ages.[3] No medieval

thinker, however, ever claimed that these new power sources had transformed the social or economic life of the time. No medieval thinker would
have claimed that water, wind, and horsepower could account for the
cultural and spiritual achievements of his day. Such claims could only be
made after science and technology had undergone some revolutionary
changes.

Modern energy myths had their origins in the Scientific Revolution of
the seventeenth century and the Industrial Revolution of the eighteenth
century. The appearance of modern science, and the subsequent identification of scientific and technical advancement with human progress, provided the kind of intellectual environment in which a newly introduced
power source would be dealt with differently than it had been in earlier
times. The Scientific Revolution created a world view in which the
concept of energy could be formulated and then applied to situations
beyond the realm of the physical sciences.

In the seventeenth century, Sir Francis Bacon listed the great inventions
that had altered the course of civilization: the compass, gunpowder, and
the printing press. With the rapid growth of science and technology, it was
an easy matter to extend Bacon's original list by adding new inventions.
The Industrial Revolution of the eighteenth century provided an obvious
addition to that list: the coal-fueled steam engine, a mechanically ingenious device that produced large amounts of power and had noticeable
social and economic effects. The final phase occurred in the nineteenth
century when a theoretical understanding of the steam engine in terms of
energy exchanges became part of the physicist's knowledge of the
universe.[4]

In Great Britain, where the steam engine first appeared, it was admired
as a bringer of enlightenment and utopia to the nation. The British viewed
it as a device that was bound to raise civilization in their land to new
heights. One British writer claimed that just as man was the noblest work
of God, so the steam engine was the noblest work of man. Why did the
steam engine deserve such acclaim? Because it was largely responsible for
the physical, intellectual, and moral advancement of mankind in the
nineteenth century. In fact, the steam engine was such a potent civilizing
agent that some writers even speculated that ancient Greek culture could
have been driven to greater heights if steam power had been available to
the Athenians![5]

Such sentiment was not confined to England. It could be found
wherever coal-fueled, steam-powered industrial civilization flourished. In
1876, the American people celebrated the centenary of their independence
in Philadelphia. They celebrated it with a great exhibition and much

political oratory; yet all of this paled in comparison to the central symbol of American progress: a huge, 1400-horsepower Corliss steam engine that stood 40 feet above its platform and supplied power to the machinery on display. To this day, the Corliss engine remains the single best-known feature of the commemoration of American independence. Its message: A nation able to build a huge steam engine must be a great and powerful one.[6]

Steam engines require coal in order to provide power. Therefore, it occurred to some that the exhaustion of the coal supply would mark the end of steam-powered civilization. In mid-century, when this pessimistic verdict was heard by the American patent commissioner Thomas Ewbank, he quickly dismissed it. All the world, he said, was a workshop, a gigantic factory with Almighty God as its supervisor. Because it was God's responsibility to see that his factory was well stocked with the necessary raw materials, it was heretical to suppose that He would not have had the foresight to provide his workshop with so basic a commodity as coal. After all, how could man carry out his assigned tasks on earth without coal?[7]

For most of the nineteenth century coal was seen as an ideal, inexhaustible, and utopian source of energy. By the third quarter of the period, however, critical voices gained public attention. The distinguished British economist Stanley Jevons wrote a long, detailed book on the coming coal shortage. He envisioned a poverty-stricken, culturally bereft England barely able to exist on a rationed coal supply.[8]

There was also growing concern over the social, cultural, economic, and environmental implications of coal-based industry. The steam engine had not brought heaven to earth. Industrial cities filled with slums, peopled by poor, hard-working laborers, and poisoned by pollutants discharged from factories were not urban utopias. Smoke abatement and reform movements were initiated in American and European industrial centers, and those who could afford to move left the smoky cities to live in the countryside or the suburbs.

By the end of the nineteenth century, coal had lost most of its mythic associations. It had come to be regarded as a source of problems and not as the utopian solution to perennial social troubles. The advent of hydropower early in the twentieth century and the theoretical promise of atomic power at about the same time opened the way for a shift of the energy myths away from coal and the steam engine to the hydroelectric dam and to hypothetical "atomic-powered engines." Coal continued to serve useful purposes in the economy and in society. It is not that its usefulness had ended, but that coal was no longer considered to be the ultimate supplier of energy for a better world.

Hydropower

At the time when coal shortages and pollution were first becoming social concerns, hydroelectric plants were being built, and their enthusiastic supporters were advancing extravagant claims in their behalf. During the 1920s, interest in hydropower grew in engineering circles and in the American West, where the idea of cheap energy was linked to the exciting prospect of rapid commercial and urban development. The promotion of hydropower as the solution to man's energy needs hit its peak in the 1930s and 1940s in the United States and then subsided rather quickly.

At the end of the nineteenth century, three developments converged to make possible, and to accelerate, the building of giant dams and hydroelectric plants. They were: (1) accumulated dam-building experience which permitted construction of bigger, better, and safer dams; (2) the invention of efficient water turbines; and (3) the development of large electrical generators.[9]

All of this was revolutionary and exciting because the building of dams was now joined to the production of electricity which, in the late nineteenth and early twentieth century, was seen as a perfect, almost magical, form of energy. Electricity was a form of energy that entered the home or factory swiftly, silently, and cleanly. It was believed that electricity was certain to lead to the decentralization of industry and to the establishment of a utopian society. These beliefs were part of the electrical mystique which had enormous popularity, including among its followers such diverse men as Lenin and Henry Ford.[10]

Given the electrical mystique, to build a dam was to engage in an activity that transcended mere commerce and industry. It was an activity guaranteed to alter the nature of society, uplifting morals and culture and stimulating economic growth. Of course, electricity could also be generated by steam power. Steam engines or turbines could turn generators as well as the force of falling water. But steam power used coal, a valuable natural resource; it spewed out polluting smoke; and it left a residue of ashes.

As opposed to steam power, hydropower wasted no natural resources and was nonpolluting. Furthermore, hydropower was virtually inexhaustible, for as long as one dammed large streams and rivers, the water would flow continually through the turbines. These are the reasons why hydropower in the early twentieth century came to be called "white coal," "clean coal," or "super power."[11] It was *superior* because it harnessed the water cycle in nature in order to produce energy in its finest, even spiritual, form—electricity. But there was still more to be said in praise of hydropower. The same dams that made possible a continuous, free, and infinite source of power also controlled flood waters, prevented soil erosion, stored water for irrigation, aided inland water transportation, and created new recreational areas for fishing and boating.

The only problem was that hydropower necessitated regional, rather than local, development and high initial investment for dam construction. The solution was intervention by the federal government. So the United States, in the midst of a great economic depression, built Hoover and Grand Coulee Dams in the West and 32 dams of the Tennessee Valley Authority in the Southeast. TVA hydroelectric plants and dams were expected to reclaim the lands of a 7-state region and elevate the entire valley to a new economic and social level. Thus the myth of clean superpower and its utopian possibilities became part of a gigantic federally funded project.

The success of TVA has often been told. It accomplished so many of its goals that it was proposed as a model for river valley development outside the United States. In 1944, Vice President Henry A. Wallace argued for the building of TVAs throughout the world because, as he said, "River valleys are much the same everywhere." A decade later, TVA-type projects were proposed as the answer to Communist encroachment in India, Egypt, and much of Africa. Even as late as the 1960s, when the United States was involved in the Vietnamese War, there was a proposal to win the hearts of the South Vietnamese people with hydroelectric dams by creating a Mekong River Delta Authority.

TVA had its triumps and influences, but it was also a victim of its own successful production of cheap electricity. As the population grew, and as heavy energy-using industrial and military facilities were drawn to the area, hydroelectrical generation was supplemented more and more by coal-burning steam plants. The steam plants were part of the original TVA scheme because, in practice, dams could not fulfill the simultaneous functions assigned to them by their overly enthusiastic supporters. They cannot simultaneously provide irrigation water, generate power, control floods, and facilitate recreational activities.

By 1980, only 20 percent of TVA electricity was generated by water power. Of that electricity, 10 percent came from nuclear plants and 70 percent from steam plants burning coal obtained by strip mining. That is how the TVA became the single largest consumer of coal in the nation. So much for the dream of white coal and superpower.

The TVA, in attempting to serve public, industrial, and governmental interests, had become a despoiler of the environment it was created to save. Because its founders were mesmerized by the myth of clean, cheap, socially transforming electrical energy, they made it available for wasteful purposes—the heating of households—and generally created demands that could not be met by hydropower alone.[12]

In 1980, on a nation-wide basis, hydropower accounted for about 3.5 percent of our energy needs. It is not expected to increase appreciably in the future, for the best dam sites have already been utilized. As for the energy myths that accompanied hydropower in its heyday, they were appropriated by the partisans of inexpensive, nonpolluting, and safe nuclear power.[13]

Atomic/Nuclear Energy

Any account of atomic energy must begin prior to World War I, because it was then that scientists began their study of the nucleus of the atom and speculated about the great power hidden therein. In 1911, British chemist Frederick Soddy, who won the Nobel prize in 1921 for his work on isotopes, began the process of mythicizing atomic energy. It was Soddy's contention that if man could liberate the energy locked in the heart of the atom, he would have an inexhaustible supply of power at his command that could be used to transform society. He prophesied that the atomic-powered world of the future would reach such a peak of perfection that it could only be compared with our first paradise, the Garden of Eden. Early twentieth-century man, living as he did in a coal-burning society, might find it difficult to comprehend the glories of the coming atomic utopia. This was because the gulf that existed between 1911 and that glorious future was every bit as great as the one that separated the culture of our cave-dwelling ancestors from that of pre-World War I Europe.[14]

Soddy recognized the fact that the power of the atom could be used destructively in war as well as constructively to build a utopia. His scientific work and his prophetic statements were seized upon by science fiction author H. G. Wells. Wells explored the pessimistic strain in Soddy's thought by writing a novel, *The World Set Free* (1914), in which the atom was first used in a devastating world war. Only when man saw his folly did he end the war and use the atom for peaceful purposes. The book concluded with a cultural renaissance spawned by atomic power, but it opened with a very bleak picture of the horrors of atomic warfare.[15]

The World Set Free might well stand as a symbol of the ambiguous response of Western men and women to atomic power. The choice was utopia or oblivion, the Garden of Eden or Armageddon. More pertinent to this essay than the Wellsian dichotomy, and more subtle also, is the question of the harmful consequences of the peaceful uses of atomic energy. In our day, that question has settled on radiation hazards and the disposal of radioactive wastes.

"Radioactive poisons," as products of atomic fission, were mentioned as early as May 1940 in a report of the National Academy of Sciences. However, in August 1945, when the first post-Hiroshima book on atomic energy appeared (*The Atomic Age Opens*), the public was assured that although the disposal of these "poisons" was "a troublesome problem," scientists had solved it. That such a complex subject could be dismissed so casually is a result of two factors: first, the failure by technical experts to realize the nature and extent of the issue; second, the power of the energy myth to perpetuate the idea that so new and wonderful a source of energy must be without any faults.

Having handled the question of radioactive waste disposal, the authors of *The Atomic Age Opens* went on to paint a rosy picture of the coming age of the atom. It would be one in which coal and petroleum would go unused and in which all non-atomic fuels and explosives would become antiquated. In this energy-rich world, existing hydropower dams would be abandoned and electrical power lines become as obsolete as the stagecoach was in 1945. And then, in order to give the general public some feeling for the vast amounts of energy soon to be theirs, the authors calculated the atomic power residing in ordinary things. This was a practice dear to the hearts of journalists and scientists of the 1940s and 1950s. Here are some typical examples. One pound of water contains enough energy to heat 100 million tons of water from freezing to boiling. A handful of snow has the potential to heat a large apartment house for a year. The energy in a small paper railroad ticket is sufficient to run a heavy passenger train several times around the earth.[16]

Optimistic appraisals of the wonderful age of the atom continued to be issued ten years later when a group of distinguished Americans were asked by *Fortune* magazine to predict the shape of American life 25 years hence—in 1980. In keeping with the title of the book recording these forecasts—it was called *The Fabulous Future*—many predicted utopian times for Americans.

David Sarnoff, chairman of the Radio Corporation of America, took it for granted that long before 1980, atomic-powered ships, submarines, aircraft, and automobiles would be commonplace. Each American home and factory would have its own compact reactor producing all the electricity needed in an average human's lifetime. In defense of Sarnoff, it should be noted that the 1950s and 1960s saw a number of schemes offered by scientists and inventors for prototype nuclear aircraft and automobiles. Such vehicles were to be powered by atomic reactors that would outlast airframes or chassis.

The final example drawn from the pages of *The Fabulous Future* are the forecasts of John von Neumann, mathematician and member of the

Atomic Energy Commission. He predicted with great confidence that by 1980, electricity would be produced so cheaply (by nuclear power) that it would not be worthwhile to meter its use in home or factory. Electricity in 1980, he wrote, would be as free as air was in 1955. As for coal and petroleum, chemists would be given the task of finding new uses for them as raw materials for the chemical industry, since they would no longer be needed as energy sources.[17]

In all this euphoria there were few who discussed radioactive wastes, the dangers of radiation, or the possibility of a dangerous accident at a nuclear generating plant. It is not true to claim that these matters were deliberately concealed by those who were aware of them. All of these issues had been raised publicly by scientists, but layman and nuclear expert alike were caught in the grips of a myth that portrayed atomic energy as perfect, inexhaustible, and utopian in its social implications.

By the early 1970s, though, many had become disillusioned with nuclear energy, divested it of its myths, and came to regard it as an enemy of all life on earth. During the preceding decade, the medical and genetic implications of the testing of nuclear weapons in the earth's atmosphere had been brought to public attention by test-ban activists. Simultaneously, environmentalists attacked nuclear generating facilities as unsafe and as producers of waste materials that would contaminate the earth for centuries to come.[18]

At its first appearance, atomic energy was believed to offer two possibilities for mankind: utopia or oblivion. Even after Hiroshima and Nagasaki, the prospect of an utopian atomic future was not diminished. By 1970, however, the possibilities had become oblivion or oblivion. Peace or war, the atom in its latest interpretation leads only to destruction. In the midst of this deeply pessimistic assessment of the future of nuclear power, the energy myths have been transferred to solar energy.

Solar Energy

The energy of the sun was crucial to man's survival long before he invented the steam engine or even built the first water wheel. The sun warmed his body, nurtured his crops, and dried his food for preservation. Because the sun supplies heat and life to all plants and animals, and because the sun is the heavenly body responsible for day and night as well as the seasons, it has always held a very important place in religious, mythological, and mystical thought. There it was honored as the source of all creative and propagative energy.[19]

The world-wide significance of the sun in religion, philosophy, art, and literature can only be alluded to here, since every culture, no matter how primitive or civilized, has made extensive symbolic and metaphorical use of it. Nor will it be possible to discuss the resurgence of solar symbolism during the Renaissance and its various manifestations in artistic representations and scientific thought. One quotation from the works of a well-known Renaissance scientist must serve as an illustration of that development. In 1543, Nicolas Copernicus published his book on the heliocentric astronomical system. After rejecting geocentric astronomy and replacing it with a sun-centered universe, Copernicus wrote these words in praise of the sun:

> In the middle of all sits Sun enthroned. In this most beautiful temple could we place this luminary in any better position from which he can illuminate the whole at once? He is rightly called the Lamp, the Mind, the Ruler of the Universe. . . . So the Sun sits as upon a royal throne ruling his children, the planets which circle round him.[20]

This quotation is not intended to be read as proof that the Polish astronomer was a sun-worshipper. Nor should the other allusions to solar symbolism and mythology be taken to imply that the modern members of the International Solar Energy Society are followers of a religious sun cult. However, anyone studying the ideology of solar energy must be aware of the fact that there exists an ancient and pervasive solar mythology which has influenced all subsequent responses to the sun. No other form of energy has come to us with the rich symbolic overtones associated with the sun.

The sun, for all of its mystical associations, is our nearest star and the provider of free energy for our use. The possibility that that energy might be captured efficiently by some technological means, and the sun tamed, intrigued technologists of the nineteenth century and continues to fascinate them today. As might be expected, these persons, like all others who first explored a new energy source, succumbed to the extravagant promises of the energy myths. To take a nineteenth century example, John Ericsson, designer of the iron-clad *Monitor,* became concerned about an imminent coal shortage and invented a solar engine for use in the sunnier parts of the earth. He introduced his invention in a predictable fashion. Beginning with the statement that "a great portion of our planet enjoys perpetual sunshine," he went on to claim that the uses of his new solar engine would be beyond computation because "the source of its power is boundless." From this he concluded that no one could "foresee what influence an inexhaustible motive power [would] exercise on civilization."[21]

In 1963, a century after Ericsson's optimistic remarks were first recorded, D. S. Halacy wrote an early and popular work on *The Coming Age
of Solar Energy*. He concluded his book with:

> As we stand on the threshold of the age of solar energy, a new age
> of plenty made possible by the most "noble" form of energy, how
> fortunate it is that "none are hid from its heat."

Earlier in the same volume, Halacy offered the "gee-whiz" equivalents of
solar energy that were encountered earlier in the popularization of atomic
energy. Here are two of them: When the sun is directly overhead, a single
acre of land receives about 4000 horsepower, an amount equal to the
power developed by a large railroad locomotive. And, in less than three
days the earth receives a total amount of solar energy equal to all the
energy already stored in its fossil fuels.[22]

Having already met the energy myths as they were applied to coal,
hydropower, and nuclear energy, the reader knows well what to expect in
the case of solar power. It is infinitely abundant, we are told, absolutely
pollution-free, and democratically distributed, since sunlight falls upon all
of God's children. However, because the Third World countries happen to
get more sunshine than Europe and America, there is a bit of a bias in
favor of those needy nations. Above all else, solar energy costs nothing. As
an advertisement for a solar collector announced in 1913: "Sunshine, like
salvation, is free."

Solar energy lends itself to decentralization so that we can turn our
backs on greedy power companies and generate electricity on the roofs of
our houses for domestic purposes. In using the sun's energy we will not
deplete any of our natural resources, nor will we create a need for
technologies far more sophisticated than the ones currently available. Solar
energy cannot possibly harm living things, since the sun has nourished
living beings from the first day they emerged into its light.

There is still more to be said in praise of the sun. It is the *ultimate form*
of energy because all fossil fuels were created by it and because it is the
final source of all the heat and light in our solar system. Just as man's
search for energy must stop with the sun, the absolute supplier of all
energy, so must the yearning for a perfect society cease when solar energy
has transformed ordinary communities into utopian ones. It is appropriate
that one of the better known utopias of the Renaissance was called the
City of the Sun. Then as now, cities of the sun are bound to be perfect
places.

To the believer who would argue that these are not solar energy *myths* but *truths,* the historian can only reply that such claims and hopes have appeared in the past and that invariably they have been exposed as naive and unrealistically optimistic. The energy of the sun will be utilized, but it will not be done soon; it will be more costly than we can imagine; it will not be without environmental problems; and it will not form the basis for a new utopian way of life.

NOTES

1. Edwin T. Layton, *The Revolt of the Engineers* (Cleveland, 1971), ch. 3.

2. John U. Nef, *The Rise of the British Coal Industry* (London, 1932).

3. Lynn White, Jr., *Medieval Technology and Social Change* (London, 1962), 79-103.

4. George Basalla, "Energy and civilization," in C. Starr and P. Ritterbush, eds., *Science, Technology, and the Human Prospect* (New York, 1980), 39-52.

5. John Farey, *A Treatise on the Steam Engine,* Vol. 1 (London, 1827), v; John Timbs, *Wonderful Inventions* (London, 1868), 186-187.

6. Howard Mumford Jones, *The Age of Energy* (New York, 1971), 142-144.

7. Thomas Ewbank, *The World a Workshop* (New York, 1855), 73.

8. William Stanley Jevons, *The Coal Question* (London, 1865).

9. Norman Smith, *Man and Water: A History of Hydrotechnology* (New York, 1975), 137-212.

10. James W. Carey and John J. Quirk, "The mythos of the electronic revolution, I and II," *The American Scholar* 39 (Spring, 1970), 219-241; (Summer, 1970), 395-424.

11. Guy E. Tripp, *Super-Power as an Aid to Progress* (New York, 1924).

12. Thomas K. McCraw, "Triumph and irony—the TVA," *Proc. IEEE* 64 (Sept. 1976), 1372-1380.

13. Earl T. Hayes, "Energy resources available to the United States, 1985-2000," *Science* 203 (Jan. 19, 1979), 237.

14. Frederick Soddy, *Science and Life* (New York, 1920), 22-24; Frederic Soddy, *Wealth, Virtual Wealth and Debt* (New York, 1926), 49-68.

15. Herbert G. Wells, *The World Set Free* (London, 1914).

16. Editors of Pocket Books, *The Atomic Age Opens* (New York, 1945), 202-203.

17. Fortune, *The Fabulous Future* (New York, 1956), 17-18, 36-37.

18. Spencer Weart, "Nuclear fear: a preliminary history," unpublished manuscript, 1982.

19. William T. Olcott, *Sun Love of All Ages* (New York, 1914); John N. Cole, "Giving Old Sol his due," The New York Times, Dec. 1, 1979 (Op-Ed page).

20. Nicolas Copernicus, *De Revolutionibus, Preface and Book I,* translated by J. F. Dobson and S. Brodetsky (London, 1947), 19.

21. Ken Butti and John Perlin, *A Golden Thread: 2500 Years of Solar Architecture and Technology* (New York, 1980), 77.

22. D. S. Halacy, *The Coming Age of Solar Energy* (New York, 1963), 239, 18.

2

Cars Versus Trains

1980 and 1910

WARREN J. BELASCO

In 1970, automobiles accounted for 85 percent of all domestic intercity passenger traffic, and railroads for less than 1 percent. Following the energy shortages of the 1970s, Americans began to appreciate the economic and political implications of that statistic. A study published in 1974 by the Congressional Office of Technology Assessment estimated that a fully loaded diesel-powered passenger train carried one passenger almost six times as far on a gallon of oil as an average, standard-sized, fully loaded automobile. Writing in the *EPA Journal* for March 1980, Amtrak President Alan Boyd drove the point home: Given the fact that intercity private car travel consumed over 15 percent of our oil supplies, "any reasonable transition from the consumption of petroleum by automobiles to more efficient means of travel will pay big dividends." To illustrate the railroad's energy-saving potential, Boyd pointed to Japan's Shinkansen High Speed Line—a 663-mile route through a dense population area much like our own Northeast Corridor. In 1977, using 4.4 million barrels of crude oil, Japan's electrically powered, state-of-the-art trains carried 124 million passengers at speeds up to 100 miles per hour. If those passengers had made the trip by car, they would have used 20.6 million barrels of gasoline or, given current refining technology, 46 million barrels of crude oil—almost the same amount of oil imported into the United States every week. In 1980, that oil would have cost over $1.2 billion; that year, the Shinkansen "Bullet Train" earned a profit of $1.35 billion.[1]

For Amtrak President Boyd, the solution seemed clear: more maintenance, more track, and more rolling stock (Amtrak had only 1200 revenue passenger cars, while the British, French, and Germans had over 15,000 each, and the Japanese 26,000). Above all, he implied, we needed more public support for a well-planned, well-subsidized national transportion program. In November 1980, however, it became clear that this vital support was lacking. Indeed, in electing Ronald Reagan, Americans chose an administration committed not simply to encouraging the existing car system, but to *restoring* the status quo before the energy crisis. By way of supporting the automobile industry, President Reagan wanted to repeal numerous safety and environmental regulations, raise the 55 mile per hour speed limit, and roll back gasoline mileage deadlines. To insure a steady supply of gasoline, the new president proposed to aid the oil companies and to defend Middle Eastern oil fields with a massive military buildup. At the same time, he would curtail the already meager subsidies to alternative energy programs and to rail transport—both intercity and urban. A Herblock cartoon dated March 15, 1981 caught the regressive thrust of the new program: A crowded, diesel-powered train (labeled "Transportation Systems") sat stalled on the tracks, blocked by the genial first executive who, waving a giant "Stop" sign, shouted: "Let's see some good old individual initiative—everybody get out and drive a car."[2]

While many questioned the wisdom of the New Beginning, few could doubt its consistency. In a word, it was a triumph of nostalgia. In virtually every area—from arms control and automobiles to welfare and worker safety—Reaganism invoked visions of an earlier Golden Age of American power, prosperity, and stability. Tired of economic complexity, bureaucratic incompetence, and a growing sense of individual helplessness, Americans chose a program oriented toward "free" competition, decentralization, and self-reliance. Or, as poet-musician Gil Scott-Heron put it in his masterful jazz poem, "B Movie," the former screen actor promised an easy return "to the days when movies were in black and white—and so was everything else."[3]

Although historians dispute whether such a simple time ever existed, in terms of transportation policy the Reagan program echoed a longstanding preference for cars over trains. In fact, the New Beginning revived not 1970 or 1950, but 1910, for in many ways the Reagan proposal to dismantle Amtrak, Conrail, and other rail transport programs in the name of old-fashioned principles recalled the original case made against trains by the first generation of motorists. When the newly motorized, affluent travelers of the early 1900s abandoned rails for roads, they too did so for libertarian, nostalgic reasons. What big government was to the neoconservatives of 1980, the railroad was to early motorists: a seemingly arrogant, impersonal, monopolistic establishment. What automobile tourist Theodore Dreiser wrote about trains in 1916 could easily have been election rhetoric in 1980: "At best, railroads [government agencies] have become huge, clumsy affairs, little suited to the temperamental needs and moods of the average human being." If the railroad—novelist Frank Norris's encroaching "octopus"—was the restrictive present, the car promised a nostalgic return to a simpler age of benign individualism, primitive struggle, and family solidarity. For the modern problems represented by the rail-based urban-industrial complex of 1910, the automobile offered pastoral solutions: country drives, wilderness camping, suburban homesteads.[4]

Thus, in the early fantasy stage of automobiling, few worried about the social costs of individualized transport, for cars were frankly portrayed as being refreshingly regressive. In the 1920s, when mass production put almost half of the population on the road, this nostalgia became institutionalized in mass culture. Through the 1930s, touring literature continued to describe car travel as a revival of premodern experiences. As rail revenues fell and equipment deteriorated, few travelers or policy makers regretted the decline of a once-comprehensive passenger rail network. By the 1970s, even the non-nostalgic, non-libertarian had little choice but to drive. From this long-term perspective, therefore, the Reagan policy simply ratified an ideological decision made in a period when travelers did have a choice between rail and road.

In the most general sense, the roots of this anti-rail ideology predated even the railroad. Almost from the beginning of the Industrial Revolution in eighteenth-century Europe, certain artists, intellectuals, and social critics decried the costs of economic and technological progress: a loss of individuality, spontaneity, local color, community, roots, family cohesiveness, contact with nature, spirituality. In the romantic reaction against modern science and reason, we can trace roots of modern consciousness itself—a deeply ambivalent attitude toward modern life. To "think modern" is to doubt modernity. In romanticism lay also the roots of radical ideologies of left and right. In attacking bourgeois materialism, dehumanizing technology, and alienating urban conditions, both socialists and archconservatives invoked visions of premodern Golden Ages.[5]

The European criticism mounted with the rail-based era of steel and steam that began in the 1830s; take, for example, Charles Dickens's description in *Dombey and Son* (1848) of the devastating impact of railway building on the landscape of central London. In America, however, where industrial growth lagged and where personal mobility seemed easier, relatively few writers and artists experienced the initial sense of ambivalence that came with the railroad in the 1830s. When Nathaniel Hawthorne and Henry David Thoreau meditated on the discordant sound of rail locomotives screeching by Sleepy Hollow (1844) and Walden Pond (1845), their concerns were not widely shared. The nostalgia wave did not really hit a wider segment of the population until the very end of the nineteenth century. And when the harsh economic and environmental realities did hit home, the reaction did not produce powerful, European-style collectivist movements. In part, the American political system was able to absorb and co-opt elements of radical protest. Also, just at the moment when many Americans were beginning to feel boxed in by modern conditions, ingenious businessmen were devising new, apolitical channels for privatistic resistance.[6]

For cultural historians chronicling this response to industrialism, 1893 was an important year. In 1893, the nation began one of the worst economic depressions of its history; central to the panic was the specula-tive nature of railroad capitalization, and within two years the entire rail network was on the brink of collapse. Also in 1893, historian Frederick Jackson Turner bemoaned the passing of the geographic frontier in "The Significance of the Frontier in American History." And in that same year, Charles and Frank Duryea drove the first American-built, gasoline-powered automobile in the streets of Springfield, Massachusetts.

For many Americans, the economic collapse of the 1890s hammered home a most unwelcome message: With its complex industrial capitalist economy and with its increasingly disgruntled farmers and workers, the United States was becoming all too European. Photographs and drawings in middle-class-oriented magazines and newspapers portrayed social condi-tions that rivalled the worst scenes of Dickens's novels. Moreover, southern and eastern European immigrants seemed to be introducing strange and possibly dangerous ideas into crowded, filthy slums; middle-class writers complained of a loss of vigor among the once robust, native-born bour-geoisie; and members of the upper class openly aped decadent aristocratic manners and styles.[7]

Turner's paper—first delivered at the Chicago World's Fair in 1893, the 401st anniversary of Columbus's initial voyage—attempted to explain this unhappy trend. Perhaps, he speculated, the turning point had come in 1890 when, according to the Superintendent of the Census, the western "unsettled area" had become "so broken by isolated areas of settlement" that there could "hardly be said to be a frontier line." Statistically this was not a very significant change, since "unsettled" was defined as containing fewer than two people per square mile; obviously, there was (and still is) a good deal of open land available. Yet, metaphorically, the "end of the frontier" implied an end also to distinctly American advantages: the safety valve for labor unrest; the democratic frontier community; and, perhaps most important, the spiritual opportunity for "perennial rebirth" through primitive struggle with raw nature. By constantly confronting the hostile wilderness, Turner argued, Americans had developed "intellectual traits of profound importance": "coarseness and strength"; a "practical, inventive turn of mind"; a "restless nervous energy"; a "dominant individualism"; and, above all, a freedom-loving "buoyancy and exuberance"—all of which now seemed threatened by geographic, economic, and social consolidation. Although Turner was too careful to offer a detailed forecast, his closing reference to the ancient Greeks was a scarcely-veiled warning to contemporaries worried about the decline and fall of *fin de siècle* America:

> What the Mediterranean Sea was to the Greeks, breaking the bond of custom, offering new experiences, calling out new institutions and activities, that, and more, the ever-retreating frontier has been to the United States directly, and to the nations of Europe more remotely. And now, four centuries from the discovery of America, at the end of a hundred years of life under the Constitution, the frontier has gone, and with its going has closed the first period of American history.[8]

In announcing the closing of the frontier, Turner's mood was implicitly pessimistic, if not apocalyptic. Yet the Republic survived and even flourished. Was Turner wrong in looking to the frontier experience as a central source of national strength? Not entirely. Recent historians have suggested that Turner was too narrowly literal in his definition of the frontier. By concentrating strictly on western growth, he missed the potential for overseas (and extraterrestrial) expansion. Moreover, he may have underestimated the ability of Americans to develop new frontiers that were more ritualistic than geographic, more oriented to the *process* of movement than to a specific *place*. Perhaps this "perennial rebirth," this "fluidity of American life," this New Beginning, could be experienced in recreation—during leisure time—rather than literally on self-sufficient pioneer homesteads. After all, the word "recreation" came from the Latin root meaning "to create anew," to start over again. Was this renewal process not the key to frontier mobility? Recognizing the safety valve nature of recreation, political reformers at the end of the century incorporated the park and playground movement into their programs. At the same time, businessmen began to develop alternate, commercially viable opportunities for such regenerative movement, e.g., Wild West shows, motion pictures, primitivist ragtime and jazz, sporting events, national park tours, bicycles, and, of course, automobiles.[9]

After 1910, the automobile began to enjoy mass appeal as an instrument of nostalgic recreation. By that time, mass production techniques were reducing car prices, and a rudimentary infrastructure of dealers, car clubs, and services enabled ordinary motorists to undertake longer trips. An indispensable part of this infrastructure was the vast body of motor literature that provided guidance to novice travellers: pamphlets, magazine articles, newspaper columns, auto club journals, literary accounts of early transcontinental car trips, as well as advertisements for cars and supplies. Some writers were hired publicists for automotive interests—especially car makers, oil companies, and camping goods manufacturers. Yet it would be wrong to dismiss all motor literature as narrowly proprietary, for many other writers were enthusiastic amateurs and journalists who simply wanted to share their experiences and insights with fellow motorists. Their perspective was more broadly *ideological*; that is, their values reflected the middle-class market that dominated modern mass-media culture and that was essential to the success or failure of a transportation system. These were the travelers for whom automobile and railroad companies competed, and these were the voters who would shape transportation policy decisions in the 1920s and 1930s.[10]

Unfortunately for railroads, the first motorized generation tended to see the automobile as a panacea for the modern social and cultural problems that had disturbed the generation of the 1890s. To a remarkable degree, early motor literature—whether proprietary or ideological—developed a single central theme: Car touring was a preindustrial experience, a return to the simpler, more robust age eulogized by Frederick Jackson Turner. And, to the railroads' chagrin, these car enthusiasts frequently crystallized their arguments by contrasting motor and rail travel. While to the more optimistic generation of the 1870s and 1880s the train had represented the path to a glorious future, by the early 1900s it came to symbolize the all-too-alienating present.

In searching for a historical metaphor for automobile travel, some writers likened cars to intercity stagecoaches: Both were slow and inefficient; both traveled primitive highways; and both represented autarchic alternatives to modern mass travel. Clearly, the automobilists' memory of the stagecoach was much romanticized—but that was precisely the point. For *World's Work* editor Henry Norman, coaching was associated with independence and pageantry—"a fine, manly age, full of splendid horses and vigorous men, redolent of romance and gay with color." The same nostalgic fascination with coaching had colored Charles Dickens's critique of trains in the 1840s. The car/stage metaphor also offered a splendid romantic irony: The railroad had supplanted the coach, but now cars would replace railroads! As Norman predicted in 1903: "The stagecoach will be avenged upon the railway by the motor."[11]

Other writers likened cars to archaic gypsy vans, prairie schooners, and peddlers' wagons. Whatever the metaphor, these self-styled "motor vagabonds" agreed that the railroad was decidedly unromantic. In sheer bulk, the train, pulled by a massive, noisy, smoke-belching steam engine epitomized the dehumanizing direction of modern technology. Owned and operated by a distant, quasi-monopolistic corporation, the train reminded individuals of their relative insignificance in the modern business world. Cars, on the other hand, were small and vulnerable. From the start, motorists named their vehicles after pets and people—usually female. No haughty, mysterious, anonymously controlled supermachine, the car was a friend—helpful but humble. More reliable and powerful than a horse, more personal and approachable than a train, the automobile seemed to restore a human scale to machinery that had been lost with the onset of the steel age.[12]

Motoring emancipated travelers from dictatorial railroad timetables. The schedule was one frame of reference against which the car's responsiveness to individual needs could be measured and appreciated. In earlier years, rail timetables had fostered and symbolized a useful standardization, group discipline, and centralization in a chaotically developing society. Standard Time, for example, was an 1883 product of railroad modernization and was hailed as a great reform, allowing people within a broad region to live and do business by the same time. There was also a certain pride in the fact that train schedules were man-made. Arriving exactly on time—say 8:42—on some "crack" intercity express, was taken as a sign of American technological mastery over bad weather, hard terrain, and personal vagaries. By the early 1900s, however, auto advocates suggested that modern life demanded too much conformity to centralized agencies. The rail bureaucracy's authority to set time could seem especially arbitrary and onerous in smaller towns, where trains might stop only in the middle of the night. Why, rural residents asked, should they be so inconvenienced by the dictates of New York and Chicago?

By allowing more personal schedules, motoring restored local initiative. Motorists could start out at their own convenience—usually in the morning—and rather than having to go to some far away rail depot, or to some dark, monumental, possibly dangerous downtown railroad station, they simply started from their own doorstep. While the train passenger had to rely on a host of salaried, frequently sullen rail employees—clerks, conductors, porters, engineers—the driver was his own station master, engineer, and porter, with no one's time to make except his own. The amateur, independent nature of automobile personnel further strengthened the car's contrast with modern problems: no troublesome labor disputes and strikes.

Like the stagecoach or gypsy van, the car followed a more "natural" schedule than the through train which plowed through time and space without regard for weather, scenery, or darkness. Driving stopped at mealtimes and at night. Moreover, bad weather, poor roads, washouts, or a fellow motorist stranded ahead were unpredictable events that intervened and forced even the most scheduled tourist to stop, take a breather, meet fellow tourists, and take in the view. In a sense, the car freed motorists not only from the centrally-set rail timetable, but also from their own internal, work-disciplined scheduling. Faced with a washed-out bridge, the tourist simply had to shrug his shoulders and be patient. Even an interruption, then, could seem a bracing return to the days when life was more in tune with natural rhythms.

Some motorists complained that in addition to being too scheduled, train travel was too fast. Describing the view from the train as a "blur," passengers resented being "whirled through" at sixty miles an hour, with no time to stop and take in a particularly nice scene, and no time to stretch legs and smell flowers. Motor travel was much slower. Given bad roads, low speed limits, and frequent mechanical breakdowns, pioneer motorists averaged under twenty miles an hour. Early observers took this lack of speed to be an advantage. Perhaps the leisurely car trip would counter the modern tendency to sacrifice reflection for velocity. To be sure, with better roads cars went faster, but even as they speeded up (and as deteriorating trains slowed down), drivers still valued the option of being able to slow down and stop at their own convenience.

Not only did railroads dictate when and how fast you went, they channeled you along defined routes. To a generation concerned about being fenced in, this limitation added to the sense of claustrophobia. While trains were bound to under 300,000 miles of inflexible track, motorists had almost three million miles of road—mostly dirt, but passable—to choose from. Drivers discovered that there was more than one way to get from town to town, and that local people themselves were unsure of the way, so conditioned were they to rail patterns. Strictly goal-oriented, railroads traveled the flattest, easiest grades. But cars could travel off the beaten track. By choosing their own routes, motorists gained an insider's private access, the pioneer's exceptional view. The valley-hugging train may have been faster, but the motorist climbed to the highest spots—alone. "The motor car can be induced into localities inaccessible to railroads," wrote one explorer in 1913, "and the delights of getting into the primitive, away from the toots and hoots and howls and clangings of up-to-date confusion is immense."[13] Cars seemed to break the train's monopolistic hold over American geographical consciousness.

In an era of heightened, "See America First" nationalism, drivers experienced a different—and suitably more nostalgic—America from that seen from the rail car window. Train travelers saw, firsthand, the economic and environmental dislocation created, to a great extent, by rail-based modernization: factories, warehouses, tenements, slums. Even in smaller towns, trains invariably passed through the poorest areas; in rural areas, rail passengers witnessed the discarded equipment and trash that farmers often abandoned near the tracks. Automobile tourists, on the other hand, could enter cities by the best streets—Main Street instead of Front Street. Or they could avoid cities altogether. Traveling along quiet, picturesque rural lanes, they viewed the seemingly timeless pastoral calm, the human scale, of premodern villages and well-tended farms—well-tended in the front yards at least.

Catering to the motorists' preference for the "historic," local civic clubs established signs pointing out Revolutionary and pre-Civil War events and icons. This was a period of widespread historical renovation—old mills, colonial houses, battlefields, and, in the 1920s, Williamsburg. Antiquarians refurbished old inns for the motor trade or sought to convert dilapidated roadhouses and commercial hotels into "wayside taverns" suggestive of coaching days. Following the lead of Henry Ford's nostalgic excavation of the Wayside Inn in Sudbury, Massachusetts—and his restoration of the Clinton Inn at Greenfield Village—roadside entrepreneurs turned farm-houses into picturesque tearooms with names like Ye Ragged Robin, Sign of the Olde Tea Pot, and The Tally-Ho. Architects designed gasoline stations to look like Tudor cottages. It was, in fact, in this pervasive longing for coaching-era experiences that we can find the roots of the countless "inns," "shoppes," and "huts" of the modern roadside strip.

In early automobile touring, the physical experience of driving strength-ened the sense of nostalgia. This was perhaps the most important contrast with train travel. Like the Victorian parlor, the rail coach was consistently warm—overheated in winter, poorly ventilated in summer. The result was a fairly well-insulated ride. Motoring, on the other hand, was a step backward. Touring in an open car, with meager springs and little padding, on rough roads, was an arduous, bumpy, drafty ordeal. But writers turned difficulty into virtue. The Lincoln Highway guidebook of 1915 warned that the journey was "still something of a sporting trip, and one must expect and put up cheerfully with some unpleasantness, just as you would on a shooting trip." The easy train trip was too soft, too effete, too familiar. "Those who want luxury and ease should take a deluxe train," the guide sneered. "To those who love the wide spaces, who enjoy exertion in the clear ozone of the great out-of-doors, the trip is a delightful outing."[14] Like overpampered Victorian dandies, rail passengers sat passively while all the work was done for them and could do nothing if the train was delayed. In motoring, however, drivers might have to build log bridges, dislodge tree stumps, drain ditches, and pull each other out of the mud. Motoring thus answered Theodore Roosevelt's call for a revival of the "strenuous life" that had supposedly preceded *fin de siècle* decadence; and by forcing travelers to roll up their sleeves and work together to overcome road obstacles, motoring seemed to revive the cooperative democracy of Turner's idealized frontier.

The opportunity to take camping equipment along doubled the sense of return. Millions of tourists bought tents, stoves, and cots, and camped in public parks, farmers' fields, or on roadside shoulders. Like gypsies, cowboys, and rough riders—all popular heroes of the day—auto campers experienced regenerative hardship. Forced to devise ways to cook, clean, and perform everyday domestic chores, motor vagabonds lived simply, resourcefully, and independently. At a time when growing specialization seemed to threaten individual autonomy, auto camping offered training in traditional values of self-help and all-around dexterity. As in so many areas of the nostalgic car culture, here, too, the eccentrically old-fashioned Henry Ford took a major mainstreaming role. Ford's well-publicized auto camping trips with John Burroughs, Thomas Edison, Harvey Firestone, and, in the 1920s, Warren Harding, helped to make "motor hoboing" a respectable activity. Typical news photos depicted Ford chopping wood, cooking over a campfire, or clowning around in Stetson, chaps, and spurs.

To be sure, not all motorists found roughing it spiritually uplifting. For many travelers, the problem with trains was not that they were too comfortable, but that they were quite uncomfortable. For these people modernity had brought not an excess of softness, but an absolute decline in basic amenities and social civility. Train travel was often portrayed as a disagreeable, even dangerous social experience. Passengers competed for the more comfortable lower berths and window seats, and fought over whether windows should be raised or lowered. Separated at night by thin curtains, they tried to sleep to a chorus of whispers, coughs, and snores. In the morning they lined up to use the common washroom. Fresh air reformers worried about contagious "microbes" exchanged in unduly intimate sleepers and coaches. Such dangers were particularly worrisome to those traveling with children. Genteel coach passengers complained of malodorous salamis and ripe bananas consumed by those unable to afford eating in the dining car. Lower-class travelers, for their part, resented the obvious disdain of haughty conductors, tip-hungry porters, and snobbish middle-class coachmates. Etiquette manuals advised female travelers against unguarded acquaintances with salesmen in the next seat; Travellers' Aid Society officials warned that ingratiating strangers could be con artists or white slavers. Among themselves, railroad executives agreed that too many ticket clerks took bribes, too many conductors were unconscionably rude, and too few porters understood middle-class sanitary standards. In all, the population of the rail car seemed like that of the city: at best, diverse and colorful; at worst, "unscreened" and hostile. In the case against rail coach society, we can see traces of the Mass Society critique itself: By serving the "crowd," mass institutions leveled tastes, reduced individuality, and imperiled health.

Motoring, however, fostered more selective relationships. On the road, motorists met other motorists, especially at large mudholes, washed-out streams, crossroads garages, and camping sites. As tourists exchanged information and helped each other out of the mud, they experienced a small-town sense of camaraderie. Writers described such contacts as remarkably democratic, but this was largely a middle-class democracy. Occasional encounters with lower-class motorists could be pleasant, too, mainly because motoring allowed a degree of personal anonymity and privacy not possible on the train. Such protective anonymity was reinforced by the closed sedan and new commercial facilities that evolved in the 1920s—especially separate tourist cabins and self-service restaurants.[15]

In addition to resisting modern herding, motoring seemed to restore old-fashioned family solidarity. Modern life, numerous writers agreed, threatened family vitality. While the commercial octopus kept fathers in the office, schools raised the children. Large corporations dictated what families ate and wore; transit companies determined where they could live; and mass magazines propagated values. Anxious to find ways to cement home ties, middle-class Americans looked to recreation as a way to save the family. According to the emerging companionate family ideal, the family that played together stayed together. Yet train travel did not serve such recreational needs. In addition to being too expensive, rail coaches were considered environmentally and socially unsafe for children, and rail-oriented commercial hotels favored travelling businessmen while discriminating against women. Rail-based summer resort colonies were too crowded, too expensive, and too Victorian.[16]

Motor travel promised to revive what one writer called the "free cooperation of individualized family life."[17] Six or eight hours a day might be spent in the car, a cramped, intimate space. Planning trips ahead of time and reliving them afterwards bolstered cohesiveness. Auto campers enjoyed special restorative benefits. Life in a small, flimsy tent put a premium on harmony and cooperation. Setting up camp, preparing and eating three meals, sitting around the evening fire; these were all done together. Even as auto camping declined in popularity in the late 1920s, the nostalgic nature of family touring remained a major influence on car-oriented roadside businesses. Operators of tourist homes, tea rooms, and cabin camps all understood that traveling families wanted homey, feminine touches that contrasted sharply with the overly commercial, masculine atmosphere of rail coaches, downtown hotels, and conventional restaurants.[18] The ultimate product of the "save the family" movement was, of course, the suburban ranch, the twentieth-century equivalent of Frederick Jackson Turner's pioneer homestead: the new safety valve, a quasi-pastoral retreat from high pressured urban life.

In retrospect, the ironies are obvious. Americans may have welcomed the car because it offered a return to premodern values and experiences, yet the car was a decidedly modern and modernizing commodity. Its manufacture, sale, and service revitalized American business. As the automobile industry became central to the health of industrial capitalism, it quickly replaced the railroad as the key to economic growth. At the same time, car use spread city life and influence to previously isolated rural areas. Indeed, the car culture itself soon created immense new problems and laments—traffic, pollution, urban decay, rural disorder, suburban blandness—and these in turn created opportunities for other nostalgia-based retailed revolts. The modern business system thus profited from discontent with the problems created by the modern business system.

The recent evolution of roadside marketing illustrates this self-perpetuating entrepreneurial process. One of the primary appeals of early motoring was its unregulated, almost anarchic flavor. The first roadside services were appropriately unsupervised and heterogeneous. But what seemed quaintly eclectic and pluralistic in the 1920s began to seem disorderly and dangerous in the 1930s. Yet motorists still wanted a premodern atmosphere. Meeting this demand for safe, standardized food served in a conservatively colonial setting, Howard Johnson created the first successful franchise scheme. His orange-roofed New England Town Hall restaurants won widespread acclaim and served as models for post-war restaurant and motel chain expansion. By the early 1960s, however, with the development of placeless, nationally homogeneous suburbs, many Americans began to look for fragments of the non-WASP Old World. Out of the research for roots arose such "ethnic" chains as Pizza Hut and Taco Bell (both of which were bought up by Pepsi Co in 1977.)

As such chains proliferated in the 1970s, some Americans came to regret losing the intimacy, coherence, and convenience of the town center. To a large extent, the automobile had destroyed that center, but the car culture also created its own substitute: the enclosed suburban mall. Catering to a deepseated longing for an aesthetically integrated, well-planned village environment, these malls did about half ($300 billion) of America's retail business in 1977. In plan and ambience, these malls frequently emulated the Main Street, USA, model of America's master suburban mythmaker: Walt Disney. Inside these malls were franchised natural foods stores, do-it-yourself crafts shoppes, old-timey ice cream parlors, ethnic food stands, and, of course, the ubiquitous jeans boutiques. The jeans business was in itself a case study in retailed revolt. Dominating that business was the world's largest apparel manufacturer, Levi Strauss, Inc., a company that had parlayed its cowboy-farmer-bohemian image into a $2.5 billion-a-year empire.

But even the mammoth regional shopping centers could not rest easy, for in the late 1970s a new antithesis emerged: the successful historical renovation of Boston's Quincy Market by one of the nation's leading mall developers, James Rouse. The anti-suburban nature of these neo-Victorian downtown projects was deceptive, however, for like the initial anti-modernist thrust of the early 1900s, historic preservation served primarily upper middle-class shopper-tourists. And large-scale corporate interests were able to adapt handily, even along the now-maligned roadside strip: Witness McDonald's mansard roofs, Wendy's plastic Tiffany lamps, and, most striking, the parlor car motif of Victoria Station's franchised steak houses.[19]

Given the co-optive ingenuity of modern capitalism, it is not at all surprising that since 1980 Ronald Reagan has been able to invoke premodern values as a way to rationalize corporate consolidation. Nostalgia is clearly a powerful business tool. Behind Reagan's call for more old-fashioned individual initiative lies a program that may benefit many large corporations, especially the oil companies. Yet it is by no means clear that co-optation serves long-term economic interests. In recent years, the economic benefits of such adaptive behavior have come increasingly in low-productivity service and fashion industries that are inherently unstable and contribute little to long-term industrial growth. The current crisis in Detroit illustrates what happens in industries that focus on superficial imagery instead of basic needs.

Moreover, the underlying dissatisfaction with modernity remains because the essential causes have not been solved: workplace alienation, family disorder, community fragmentation, environmental decay, political powerlessness, spiritual emptiness. The dissatisfaction may in fact increase, for each new co-optive response raises expectations that are harder and harder to satisfy. Nostalgia is a double-edged sword. In defense of ancient values and virtues, people may be driven to conserve resources, develop humane technologies, and perhaps even to overthrow governments.

NOTES

1. Office of Technology Assessment, *Energy, The Economy, and Mass Transit* (Washington, DC, 1975), 23; Alan S. Boyd, "Passenger trains and energy conservation" *EPA Journal* (March 1980), 9; "Japanese bullet train studied for use here," *Washington Post*, November 5, 1981.

2. Boyd, "Passenger trains and energy conservation," 37; Washington Post, March 15, 1981.

3. Gil Scott-Heron, "B-Movie," *Reflections,* Arista Records, 1981.

4. Warren James Belasco, *Americans on the Road: From Autocamp to Motel, 1910-1945* (Cambridge, 1979), 19. Much of the following analysis is drawn from this book.

5. The literature on the romantic reaction to modernity is immense. For starters: Raymond Williams, *Culture and Society, 1780-1950* (London, 1958); *The Country and the City* (New York, 1973). For a longer-run overview of nostalgia as a central force, see Anthony Brandt, "A short natural history of nostalgia," *Atlantic* (December 1978), 58-63; Fred Davis, *Yearning for Yesterday: A Sociology of Nostalgia* (New York, 1979); Jackson Lears, *No Place of Grace: Antimodernism and the Transformation of American Culture, 1880-1920* (New York, 1981).

6. Raymond Williams, "Introduction," *Dombey and Son* (Harmondsworth, Middlesex, England, 1970), 11-34. On Hawthorne and Thoreau's reaction, see Leo Marx, *The Machine in the Garden* (New York, 1964), 227-265. For the American 1890s: John Higham, "The reorientation of American culture in the 1890s," in John Weiss, ed., *The Origins of Modern Consciousness* (Detroit, 1965); Larzer Ziff, *The American 1890s: Life and Times of a Lost Generation* (New York, 1966).

7. Neil Harris, ed., *The Land of Contrasts, 1880-1901* (New York, 1970).

8. Frederick J. Turner, "The significance of the frontier in American history," *Annual Report of the American Historical Association* (1893), 190-227.

9. George W. Pierson, *The Moving American* (New York, 1973); James J. Flink, *The Car Culture* (Cambridge, 1975).

10. Unless otherwise noted, the following is drawn from Belasco, *Americans on the Road,* especially 7-69.

11. Henry Norman, "The coming of the automobile," *World's Work* (April 1903), 3308.

12. Belasco, *Americans on the Road,* 19-39.

13. Helen Lukens Gaut, "Motoring up the Pacific coast," *Motor Life* (September 1913), 7.

14. Lincoln Highway Association, *Complete Official Guide* (Detroit, 1915), 11, 25.

15. On the developments of the 1920s-1930s, see Belasco, *Americans on the Road,* 71-173.

16. Ibid., 41-69.

17. Joseph W. Stray, "We go a-motor hoboing," *Motor Camper and Tourist* (December 1924), 412.

18. Belasco, *Americans on the Road,* 129-173.

19. Belasco, "Toward a culinary common denominator: the rise of Howard Johnson's, 1925-1940," *Journal of American Culture* 1 (Fall 1980), 503-518; Robert L. Emerson, *Fast Food: The Endless Shakeout* (New York, 1979); William Severini Kowinski, "The malling of America," *New Times* (May 1, 1978), 33-55; Belasco "Mainstreaming blue jeans: the ideological process," unpublished manuscript.

3

Energy Transitions in the Nineteenth-Century Economy

MARTIN V. MELOSI

In writing the energy history of the United States, scholars have been strongly influenced by a useful device—the energy transition—as a way of periodizing and evaluating the development and use of energy sources over an extended period of time. The concept is based on the notion that a single energy source, or group of related sources, dominated the market during a particular period or era, eventually to be challenged and then replaced by another major source. By tracing the rise and fall of dominant energy sources, scholars hoped to determine the role of energy within the American economy and possibly within society at large.

As a historical tool, the energy transition has much to recommend it. In the broadest sense, the concept can provide a necessary focus for understanding the evolution of human material culture, economic growth and development, and possibly, social organization. Utilized too narrowly, it is simply a convenient device for parceling energy history into manageable chunks with little relationship one to the other. Possibly the best use for the energy transition is to view it as a process rather than as a contrived barrier separating energy eras. Studying the energy transition for its intrinsic historical value offers some intriguing possibilities. As a mechanism of change, the energy transition influences and is influenced by the technical, economic, political, environmental, and social forces which also shape society.

In the past, scholars have employed the concept of the energy transition quantitatively, to measure changes in energy consumption, or qualitatively, to evaluate the impact of new sources of energy on various aspects of American life. The quantitative approach yielded a simple periodization

TABLE 3.1   Percentages of Aggregate Energy Consumption for Wood, Coal, and Oil

Year	Wood	Coal	Oil
1850	90.7	9.3	——
1885	47.5	50.3	.7
1910	10.7	76.8	6.1
1930	6.1	57.5	23.8
1955	2.6	28.7	40.0

Source: Based on Sam H. Schurr and Bruce C. Netschert, *Energy in the American Economy, 1850-1975* Baltimore, 1960), 36.

of energy history based on peaks and troughs of wood, waterpower, coal, petroleum, and natural gas usage. One widely accepted model traced the energy history of the United States between 1850 and 1955 through cycles of supply and demand with particular attention to increases in energy consumption. It recognized two major energy transitions during the period: from wood to coal in the nineteenth century, and from coal to petroleum in the early twentieth century. The use of wood (and to a lesser extent wind- and waterpower) dominated the United States until the mid-1800s, with wood consumption peaking in 1885. Beginning in 1850, coal was established on a commercial basis, and by 1885 coal mining became a major industry. Coal, in terms of national consumption, dominated the energy market from the mid-1880s through World War I. At that point coal began to suffer a relative decline, while petroleum (and later natural gas) became more popular as a fuel and began to undermine coal's dominance. Petroleum usage moved through several stages of its own before supplanting coal. In its "kerosene period" in the years after 1869, it became a major illuminant; in the 1890s it passed into its "fuel oil period"; by the turn of the century it became an important internal combustion engine fuel (see Table 3.1).[1]

This quantitative periodization is a convenient way to emphasize broad patterns of consumption and has been used as background for an economic analysis of contemporary and future energy requirements. Yet this approach in and of itself does not sufficiently explain why and how energy choices are made. Factors such as shifts in availability, technological advances, changes in the nation's output of goods and services, and shifts in consumer preference are not adequately explored but subordinated to the period of the transitions.[2]

Many scholars have accepted the quantitative approach to energy transitions uncritically and with little consideration to the causes and effects of those transitions in general. The qualitative approach, on the other hand, offers greater opportunity for understanding the impact of energy sources on society. Some studies have drawn very broad distinctions between what has become the "traditional" energy eras. For example, several writers have emphasized that energy use in the United States shifted from "renewable" (wood, windpower, waterpower) fuels to fossil or "non-renewable" (coal, petroleum, natural gas) fuels. This focus provides a good perspective for evaluating the results of energy transitions, namely resource depletion, environmental impact, changes in habits of consumption, alterations in governmental policy, and so forth.

The renewable/non-renewable perspective, however, has been used only in a cursory manner and has yet to produce much in the way of substantive historical analysis. Instead, academics, journalists, and social commentators have used it as a counterpoint in studies focusing on "energy strategies," "energy futures," "alternative energy paths," and "energy forecasting."[3] Future projectors have raised some thought-provoking ideas, such as the speculation that a potential long-term transition to a solar-based system could produce ominous societal consequences—possibly a return to feudalism and energy sources based on territoriality.[4] This kind of speculation, while relying on an evaluation of historical trends, deals only tangentially with the significance of past transitions.

Although the qualitative approach to energy transitions has been primarily a response to the current "energy crisis" and the search for alternative fuels, the energy transition as process has begun to attract some attention from historians. One useful approach is to examine how economic factors, which influenced the transition from one source of energy to another, are conditioned by non-economic factors in producing change. For example, a recent study of the rise of petroleum in the United States argued that not only did oil have a competitive edge over coal in terms of lower price, but also in terms of the structure of the industry. Oil companies developed superior technology for exploiting their resource—effective production and marketing techniques, more reliable transportation (rails and pipelines)—and were able to promote their product as a more versatile fuel than coal. Oil's economic advantage was tied not so much to the development of national markets as to the rapid acquisition of new markets, especially in the emerging "sunbelt" region of the South and West.[5] This type of analysis expands the use of the energy transition by examining the mechanism for change. It also raises questions about the nature of fuels as competing, rather than complementary, energy sources. Might one conclude, for example, that Americans were locked into a mind-set which accepted a dependence on a single energy source? If so, this can affect the definition of the energy transition.

Another fruitful approach is to emphasize the evolutionary as opposed to the revolutionary aspects of the energy transition. Specifically, older sources of energy (muscle power, renewable resources) are not replaced totally by newer sources (fossil fuels, atomic power). Instead, they are supplemented, complemented, or slowly displaced according to use. Simply calculating the total consumption of an energy source gives little sense of the stages of transition, and creates artificial thresholds through which society apparently passes from one energy era to another. Energy eras, therefore, might best be viewed as the accumulation of many smaller transitions.

America's first major energy transition, which took place in the nineteenth century, is an excellent example of this evolutionary process. Over the course of several decades, muscle power and renewable fuels continued to be employed for several tasks despite the rise in the use of anthracite and bituminous coal as industrial, and then domestic, sources of energy.[6] The factors which helped to perpetuate the use of older sources and the experience of newer ones provide some useful avenues of inquiry about the nature of transitions.

In *Energy in the United States,* the authors offer a simple explanation for the first major energy transition:

> It was not until the continuing cutting down of forests had raised the price of wood and removed its sources further and further from the emerging centers of population and industry that coal came to be accepted more widely.... What gave it the crucial push was the use of bituminous coal for two rising segments of the modern economy—steel manufacture and steam generation. This made coal the preferred industrial fuel and assured it a leading role among the energy sources.[7]

Although widely accepted at one time, this view depends too heavily on national patterns of consumption and fails to take into account the more complex nature of the energy transition. First and foremost, America's first major energy transition spanned the nineteenth century, especially between 1820 and 1885. It was clearly an evolutionary rather than a revolutionary process because: (1) the United States of the early- to mid-nineteenth century was dominated by local, regional, and sectional interests; thus, the transition from one energy source to another depended on local availability, local use, and local preference; (2) the transition was more than a change from wood to coal; it was a transition from wood, waterpower, and windpower to anthracite and bituminous coal, i.e., from an array of "renewable" resources to two quite unique fossil fuels located in different sections of the country and possessing different properties as fuels; (3) variables other than the depletion of wood resources led to the transition, including available transportation, market factors, technological changes, and head-on competition between the various types of fuels. The emergence of a new form of transportation or a new industrial process, however, did not necessarily mean a change in energy source. The question of the adaptability of the energy source to changing conditions influenced its continued use.

Wood had long been considered "the fuel of civilization." In America, wood fuel has the longest history of any energy source. However, to identify wood with preindustrial, or even primitive, cultures would be erroneous. Aside from its obvious importance as a cooking and heating fuel, fuel wood was a major element in the United States in the development of locomotives and steamboats, in the growth of a charcoal-fired iron industry, and in the emergence of stationary steam engines.[8] The development of motive steam power would have been delayed in the United States without abundant and accessible wood supplies. Because of the need for dependable means of transportation to connect the expansive North American continent, inventors in the United States produced viable steamboats as early as 1812. American steamboats were soon the state-of-the-art, and their obvious source of power, wood. Even when coal began to replace wood in steamboats operating in the East (by the 1840s), fuel wood remained in high demand throughout the West. On the Great Lakes and in the Atlantic, where accessibility to wood or coal was rare, sailing vessels dominated for several more years.[9]

As land transportation by rail proved more versatile than river and lake transportation, wood also played a dominant role as the chief energy source. (However, the limited geographical distribution of waterways more than the abundance of wood influenced the growth of railroads in the United States.) By the 1850s, well before the use of coal became widespread, there were almost 9000 miles of track in the United States, with most locomotives driven by wood-burning steam engines. Of course, the longevity of railroad transportation in the United States, especially when compared with the steamboat, suggested that railroads would outlive their dependence on wood. The bulkiness of the energy source and its depletion in the East led to the shift to coal by 1870, except in Maine and the Far West. Yet wood had provided the impetus to power-driven land transportation as it had for water transportation.[10]

It takes little debunking to convince people that fuel wood was crucial to home heating and transportation in the nineteenth century, but the process of large-scale industrialization has long been associated with coal. Yet the initiation of large-scale manufacturing, factory production, and resource extraction was first carried out in the United States with wood and waterpower. Before the coking process revolutionized the production of iron, charcoal was an essential ingredient. Especially valuable as a fuel for iron-making and glass-making, charcoal was also an ingredient in gunpowder, printer's ink, and black paint. It was used to purify liquids, insulate ice houses, and sometimes found its way to the medicine cabinet. Despite its high cost, the manufacture of charcoal-iron expanded during the early nineteenth century as producers learned the basics of maintaining their lumber supplies through tree crop rotation. By mid-century, one-half of all iron produced in the country was being smelted with charcoal.[11] Even after charcoal became prohibitively expensive and difficult to obtain, it was preferred for some processes. Charcoal-smelted iron was tough, malleable, and had a high capacity for welding, which made it especially popular in the West for many agricultural purposes.[12]

Waterpower also remained an important source of energy for some industrial uses throughout the nineteenth century. Grist mills or textile mills nestled in a tranquil rural setting come to mind when we think of waterpower. In many traditional interpretations of the first major energy transition, waterpower was considered a local energy source which was rapidly eclipsed in the early years of the Industrial Revolution by more modern sources of energy. That assumption has been discredited in recent years. Improvements in stationary waterpower in the nineteenth century have been unfairly overshadowed by the better-known applications of steam power to locomotives and steamboats. The successful adaptation of steam power to transportation, however, did not lead to its universal adoption as an energy source. Not until the 1880s did steam provide the foundation for industrial expansion in the Unites States.[13] Furthermore, steam power was highly concentrated in only a few industries—such as saw-milling—and provided the main power source for very few in the early nineteenth century. Since the cost of steam power was higher than waterpower, industries used it only when they needed freedom of location away from waterways.[14] Stationary steam power, therefore, was above all an urban phenomenon, where ready access to waterpower was absent but interest in manufacturing great.[15]

Conversely, the newer watermills situated in predominantly rural areas were not the old country watermills in nostalgic paintings. Watermills began to take on more than local roles, especially powering large commercial mills and industrial factories. As waterpower expert Louis Hunter states: "Although the basic elements remained much the same—dams, millponds, races, wheels—the scale, complexity, and refinement of detail in design and operation found in such major hydropower installations as those of the New England textile centers bore slight resemblance to the water mills in which they had their origins." The importance of waterpower to burgeoning industry is no better illustrated than with the Merrimack River, which runs 110 miles through New Hampshire and Massachusetts. The "hardest working river in the world" provided approximately 80,000 horsepower to 900 mills and factories in 1880, and was largely responsible for the success of its three leading textile centers, Lowell, Lawrence, and Manchester. The dramatic shift of manufacturing to major urban areas by mid-century clearly undercut the importance of waterpower, but its earlier vitality and that of wood suggests the importance of a range of viable energy choices even in the early years of the American Industrial Revolution.[16]

What ultimately led to the increasing use of fossil fuels in the United States was the transformation of the country from a rural, agrarian, decentralized society into an urban, industrial, national culture. Coal did not bring about that transformation, but in the long run it adapted more successfully to it than the renewable sources of energy which were much more territorially bound and less versatile. While renewable sources held on to a portion of the industrial and domestic energy market, the increasingly urban-based industrial economy, the rapidly expanding national railroad network, and the highly concentrated population came to depend more completely on coal. In short, coal was appropriate for the times.

In explaining why coal (and later petroleum) supplanted wood as a major energy source, an expert on fuel wood argues that wood never sustained a broad national industrial economy throughout the history of humankind. Furthermore, in an industrialized economy, wood was too valuable a commodity to be wasted as a fuel.[17] This is at best an incomplete explanation of the first major energy transition. It is true that only a fraction of the fuel utilized in the United States until 1870 went for industrial purposes, but wood continued to supply the lion's share of energy used at the time—if primarily for home heating. We must look elsewhere for a more plausible set of reasons for the emergence of coal as the dominant energy source in the country.

The actual dependence on coal in America took many years, but after certain barriers were overcome, coal grew quickly though selectively in importance. Opportunities to exploit coal go back to the colonial period, but the nature of fossil fuels provides a partial answer for why coal remained a relatively obscure energy source until the nineteenth century. Simply put, in most parts of the country it was more difficult to locate, mine, and transport coal than it was to chop down a stand of trees. In an agriculturally based society, clearing the land of trees offered a double bonus: space for building your home and planting a crop as well as fuel for the fireplace. Prejudice against the use of coal also grew out of an ignorance or a disregard for its commendable properties: high heat content, relative compactness, and exceptional versatility. Also, in the case of anthracite, coal burns cleanly. From a broader perspective, Americans had established an intricate wood-based energy system by the nineteenth century: fireplaces made for wood-burning, a charcoal-based iron industry, steam boilers adapted for wood, and supporting institutions within the economy which acquired and marketed fuel wood. Many jobs—wood-cutting, cording, operating wood depots—depended on the commodity. The reluctance to abandon wood, therefore, was built upon a practical foundation. Not only would vested interests be threatened, but new techniques for mining, transporting, marketing, and utilizing coal would have to be developed. Forces of change would have to be formidable or at least develop in a local environment receptive to the change.

Some authorities argue that the conditions were right in the early to mid-nineteenth century to affect a major change in power source. A prominent business historian contends that anthracite coal from eastern Pennsylvania provided the basic fuel used for power and heat in the large-scale urban factories. The availability of anthracite, advances in steam power, and increasing supplies of iron led to the extension of major enterprises in many industries. The factory system was essential to the process of industrialization, but, he queries, "Why did factories, which had become significant in British manufacturing by the end of the eighteenth century, not become a major form of production, except in the textile industry, in the Unites States until the 1840s?" The answer lay in the revolution in iron-making in the 1830s, that is, the use of coal in making wrought iron and cast iron. The availability of more and better iron through the use of coal, in combination with the increasing use of steam power, changed the very nature of manufacturing. Early textile mills, powered by water and equipped with machinery constructed of wood and leather belting, were supplanted by factories powered by steam, equipped with metal machinery, and located in major cities. The demand for anthracite, therefore, did not grow out of an energy scarcity, but rather out of a need for an improved technology to increase the supply of good quality, inexpensive iron.[18]

An alternative view is that changes in iron production, essential to the industrialization process in the United States, grew out of the labor scarcity of the era. In other words, improved methods of iron production were developed to offset the lack of adequate labor for large-scale production.[19]

Changes in iron production provide, at best, only a partial answer to the turn toward coal. In fact, the initial exploitation of American anthracite on a large scale originated with a major fuel crisis in Philadelphia. When war broke out between Great Britain and the United States in 1812, the city faced a critical fuel shortage. Although residents in the anthracite region of northeastern Pennsylvania had used local hard coal before the war, Philadelphia had depended on bituminous coal from Virginia and Great Britain. The British blockade of the East Coast in 1812 reduced supplies of trans-Atlantic coal to a trickle. As coal prices soared, Philadelphians sought another source, and were obliged to seek out merchants in northeastern Pennsylvania who saw an opportunity to exploit the high prices offered for coal. Soon coal was being carted and shipped from the anthracite region to Philadelphia. Promoters of anthracite began underwriting the cost of "anthracite canals" to bring the fuel to the major cities of the East and encouraged mechanics to devise new technologies for utilizing hard coal. Recognized as an urban-industrial fuel, anthracite came to dominate the fuel market of many Eastern cities.[20]

Both in the case of the use of coal for industrial purposes and in servicing Eastern urban markets, the depletion of wood supplies was not the single force behind the transition of the nineteenth century. At the same time, the application of coal for industrial and urban purposes did not occur overnight, nor uniformly throughout the country. Although the use of coal for industrial purposes propelled it to the front ranks among energy sources by 1885, it was only dominant in the sense that coal usage represented the highest percentage of aggregate energy consumption. In Pennsylvania and its environs, coal usage was overwhelming, with the iron industry migrating from central Pennsylvania to eastern and southeastern Pennsylvania—but on a much greater scale. In the West, however, the situation was quite different. It was out of the question to ship anthracite westward, especially because wood and bituminous coal were more plentiful. Not until after the Civil War, then, were bituminous coal and coke established as blast furnace fuels in the major pig iron districts of the West.[21]

The rise of bituminous coal as an industrial fuel followed a different path than anthracite. Like anthracite, however, it became popular because of its own special properties and because of the location of its deposits, not because of the depletion of other fuels. Central to its success was its application to steel production; the demand for soft coal evolved side-by-side with large-scale steel production in the United States. The use of the Kelly-Bessemer process in the 1860s and the later adoption of the Siemens-Martin (or Open Hearth) process after the turn of the century, made bituminous coal a necessary ingredient in both steel production and iron production.[22]

Anthracite and bituminous coal achieved dominance because they were adaptable to more than industrial needs. In the 1830s, anthracite was not only a producer of steam for factory machinery but for steamboats and locomotives as well. In fact, in the anthracite regions, a mutual dependence developed between the railroads and the anthracite industry. It was the railroads, however, which helped to make coal preeminent among fuels rather than coal making railroads preeminent among sources of transportation. Direct demand for coal by the railroads was slight before 1860 because they did not possess adequate technology for burning it. But the railroads came to dominate the anthracite industry well before they became dependent on coal as an energy source. By 1911, eleven railroads served the anthracite regions of Pennsylvania. The "anthracite railroads" not only came to dominate the transportation of hard coal but to control the mines themselves. By 1917, four railroads mined approximately 50 percent of the total coal output in Pennsylvania.[23]

The pattern of development and control in the bituminous industry was substantially different. Railroads did not control the mines; instead, coal companies with interests in Virginia and West Virginia (established by promoters or officers in railroads or their associates) bought large holdings in coal lands and entered into transit agreements with railroads. In the early twentieth century, large corporations such as U.S. Steel, Bethlehem Steel, and Ford Motor Company bought and operated their own mines, leading toward vertical integration. In other cases, several large coal companies consolidated to dominate certain coal fields and markets.[24]

Coal also invaded the domestic heating and lighting markets that wood had dominated for years. Coal had been used sporadically as a heating fuel during wood shortages on the East Coast or in the homes of the well-to-do who could afford the luxury of burning coal oil.[25] Wide acceptance of coal as a heating and lighting fuel required several preconditions, however. Predictably, anthracite became a standard home heating fuel and cooking fuel in areas bordering the anthracite regions, most notably in Pennsylvania, New York, and New Jersey. But anthracite being used for domestic purposes was no accident. Advocates produced a virtual deluge of propaganda promoting its use, and new inventions—coal-burning stoves, improved grates—flooded local retail outlets. Scientific fuel analysis added to general understanding of the fuel's properties and capabilities. Penetration in eastern markets came as early as the 1820s.[26]

Coal-oil and coal-gas challenged animal fats, tallow, and other animal byproducts in the illuminants field. Baltimore became the first city in America to build a gas works (using bituminous), followed by New York, Boston, and Philadelphia. The concentration of people in Eastern cities made the transition to coal (for heat and light) profitable. Without that concentration, coal-oil and coal-gas were likely to remain luxury items.[27]

The transition to coal was complex, especially because it came in two major waves, with anthracite emerging earliest, and then bituminous. The adoption of anthracite for industrial purposes opened the way for new technologies in utilizing coal over other sources of energy. It also set patterns in marketing and prepared consumers for further changes in energy usage. For all practical purposes, though, anthracite was a local fuel. Whereas the anthracite regions were geographically restricted, bituminous deposits could be found throughout the nation. By the mid-nineteenth century, bituminous coal was being mined in at least 22 states (although 90 percent was produced in Pennsylvania, Ohio, Illinois, Virginia, and Maryland). Accessibility was a major reason for the ultimate preference for bituminous over anthracite coal throughout much of the country. Of course, soft coal was quite versatile and possessed special heating properties not shared with anthracite. Coking of bituminous coal became popular for iron smelting; railroads found bituminous a convenient fuel for stoking boilers; and it could be converted to gas for lighting and heating with relative ease. The combination of availability, low cost, and versatility gave bituminous coal the ultimate advantage over anthracite. By World War I, sales of bituminous outpaced anthracite by about 450 percent.[28]

The transition from wood and waterpower to coal was a major turning point in the material life of the United States. While the transition itself was evolutionary, its effects were staggering, and in some cases, revolutionary. The adoption of a new energy source was intimately connected with the benefits and detriments of the industrial age in America. Coal helped to accelerate the process of large-scale manufacturing and became the essential fuel for heat and light in the major cities. Coal was indeed an urban fuel. New technologies devised to accommodate the utilization of coal produced new uses and new products for America's first "black gold."

At the same time, the industrialization and urbanization processes that coal helped to shape produced a wide array of problems, many of which the nation faced on a scale never seen before. In a more direct way, the widespread use of bituminous coal resulted in the first serious air pollution problem in the nation's history.[29] Coal mining itself led to land despoliation and some critical water pollution problems. It created a large number of jobs for Americans, but also some of the worst cases of exploitation of workers in the nation's history. On a less materialistic level, the abundance of the coal supply helped to persuade Americans that little need existed to conserve resources. It also reinforced the notion that growth and progress were strongly linked to the use and development of a single major energy source. Developing energy strategies or the wise use of resources was foreign to contemporary governments except during periods of wartime stringency; the promotion of growth and prosperity seemed to be the major calling for the political system.

The first American energy transition demonstrates the unrealized potential of the energy transition as a historical tool. The nature of the nineteenth-century American society made it impossible for a new energy source to revolutionize industry, transportation, and home heating overnight. The series of smaller, albeit significant, changes in patterns of use occurred for many reasons—consumer preference, availability, relative cost, technical innovation, geographic determinants, and so forth—which were linked to an all-encompassing transformation of the United States into an urban, industrial, mechanized culture. In a heterogeneous nation that spanned a continent, a single, convulsive energy transition was impossible. Yet while the causes of the transition produced evolutionary change, the results were indeed revolutionary.

By examining the energy transition as process, as part of the flow of history, it becomes apparent that energy development and use are intimately woven into the matrix of a society. To examine the energy transition outside of the broadest framework of the culture that produced it will provide few useful conclusions. The examination of the energy transition as process helps to restore the role of energy to its legitimate place in the sweep of history as part of the process of living.

NOTES

1. Sam H. Schurr and Bruce C. Netschert, *Energy in the American Economy, 1850-1975* (Baltimore, 1960), 45-124.

2. Ibid., 45.

3. For instance, see Lewis J. Perelman, August W. Giebelhaus, and Michael D. Yokell, eds., *Energy Transitions: Long-Term Perspectives* (Boulder, CO, 1981); Robert Stobaugh and Daniel Yergin, eds., *Energy Future: Report of the Energy Project at the Harvard Business School* (New York, 1979); Sam H. Schurr et al., eds., *Energy in America's Future: The Choices Before Us* (Baltimore, 1979); Energy Policy Project, Ford Foundation, *A Time to Choose: America's Energy Future* (Cambridge, MA, 1974); Amory B. Lovins, *Soft Energy Paths: Toward a Durable Peace* (New York, 1977); Melvin Kranzberg, Timothy A. Hall, and Jane L. Scheiber, eds., *Energy and the Way We Live* (San Francisco, 1980); Crauford D. Goodwin, ed., *Energy Policy in Perspective: Today's Problems, Yesterday's Solutions* (Washington, DC, 1981).

4. Lewis J. Perelman, "Speculations on the transition to sustainable energy," in Perelman et al., eds., *Energy Transitions,* 185-216.

5. Joseph A. Pratt, "The ascent of oil: the transition from coal to oil in early twentieth-century America," in Perelman et al., eds., *Energy Transitions,* 9-29. See also Joel A. Tarr and Bill C. Lamperes, "Changing fuel use behavior and energy transitions: the Pittsburgh smoke control movement, 1940-1950," *Journal of Social History* 14 (Summer 1981), 561-588.

6. Dolores Greenberg, "Energy flow in a changing economy, 1815-1880," in Joseph R. Frese and Jacob Judd, eds., *An Emerging Independent American Economy, 1815-1875* (Tarrytown, New York, 1980), 29-58; Thomas C. Cochran, *Frontiers of Change: Early Industrialization in America* (New York, 1981), 70-71, 92-93.

7. Hans H. Landsberg and Sam H. Schurr, *Energy in the United States: Sources, Uses and Policy Issues* (New York, 1968), 33.

8. Brooke Hindle, "Introduction: the span of the wooden age," in Brooke Hindle, ed., *America's Wooden Age: Aspects of Its Early Technology* (Tarrytown, NY, 1975), 3-5, 10-12. Albro Martin may have been overstating the case when he referred to the transition from wood to coal as "the first energy revolution." See his "James J. Hill and the first energy revolution: a study in entrepreneurship, 1865-1878," *Business History Review* 50 (Summer 1976), 179-197.

9. George Rogers Taylor, *The Transportation Revolution, 1815-1860* (New York, 1951), 56-73; Richard G. Lillard, *The Great Forest* (New York, 1947), 143-144; Arthur H. Cole, "The mystery of fuel wood marketing in the United States," *Business History Review* 44 (Autumn 1970), 355-356; Joseph M. Petulla, *American Environmental History: The Exploitation and Conservation of Natural Resources* (San Francisco, 1977), 102-103, 122-124; Curtis P. Nettels, *The Emergence of a National Economy, 1775-1815* (New York, 1962), 257-262; Roger Burlingame, *March of the Iron Men: A Social History of Union Through Inventions* (New York, 1946), 193-214. See also Louis C. Hunter, *Steamboats on the Western Rivers* (Cambridge, MA, 1949); David A. Tillman, *Wood as an Energy Source* (New York, 1978), 11.

10. Cole, "The mystery of fuel wood marketing in the United States," 352-355; Taylor, *The Transportation Revolution*, 74-103; Martin, "James J. Hill and the first energy revolution," 181.

11. W. G. Youngquist and H. D. Fleischer, *Wood in American Life, 1776-2076* (Madison, 1977), 25; Cole, "The mystery of fuel wood marketing in the United States," 354-358; Petulla, *American Environmental History*, 61-64; Tillman, *Wood as an Energy Resource*, 7-8.

12. Taylor, *The Transportation Revolution*, 226-227; Harold F. Williamson, ed., *The Growth of the American Economy* (Englewood Cliffs, NJ, 1951, 2nd ed.), 177-178.

13. Louis C. Hunter, "Waterpower in the century of the steam engine," in Hindle, *America's Wooden Age*, 161; Louis C. Hunter, *Waterpower in the Century of the Steam Engine* (Charlottesville, VA, 1979), 202.

14. Peter Temin, "Steam and waterpower in the early nineteenth century," *Journal of Economic History*, 26 (June 1966), 187-205.

15. Hunter, "Waterpower in the century of steam engine," 172. See also Hunter, *Waterpower in the Century of the Steam Engine*, 485-488.

16. Hunter, "Waterpower in the century of the steam engine," 175-183; Hunter, *Waterpower in the Century of the Steam Engine*, 159-169, 181-184, 188.

17. Tillman, *Wood as an Energy Resource*, 26-27.

18. Alfred D. Chandler, Jr., "Anthracite coal and the beginnings of the Industrial Revolution in the United States," *Business History Review* 46 (November 1972), 72-101.

19. See Thomas R. Winpenny, "Hard data on hard coal: reflections on Chandler's anthracite thesis," *Business History Review* 53 (Summer 1979), 247-255.

20. H. Benjamin Powell, *Philadelphia's First Fuel Crisis: Jacob Cist and the Developing Market for Pennsylvania Anthracite* (University Park, PA, 1978); H. Benjamin Powell, "The Pennsylvania anthracite industry, 1769-1976," in *Pennsylvania History* 47 (November 1980), 5-10. See also Frederick Moore Binder, *Coal Age Empire: Pennsylvania Coal and Its Utilization to 1860* (Harrisburg, PA, 1974), 2-6; Frederick Moore Binder, "Anthracite enters the American home," *Pennsylvania Magazine of History and Biography* 82 (January 1958), 83-84; Otis K. Rice, "Coal mining in the Kanawha Valley to 1861: a view of industrialization in the Old South," *Journal of Southern History* 31 (November 1965), 394-395; Harold W. Aurand, *From the Molly Maguires to the United Mine Workers* (Philadelphia, 1971), 9-14.

21. W. Ross Yates, "Discovery of the process for making anthracite iron," *Pennsylvania Magazine of History and Biography* 98 (April 1974), 206-223; Williamson, ed., *The Growth of the American Economy*, 177-178; Taylor, *The Transportation Revolution*, 226-227; Aurand, *From the Molly Maguires to the United Mine Workers*, 11-12.

22. Edward C. Kirkland, *A History of American Economic Life* (New York, 1969, 4th ed.), 302-304; A. C. Fieldner, "300 years of American fuels," *Industrial and Engineering Chemistry* 27 (1935), 984-985; Petulla, *American Environmental History*, 178-180. In 1856, the Englishman Henry Bessemer publicized the fact that hot pig iron could be cleansed of its carbon and silica impurities if a blast of air were forced through it. William Kelly, a Kentucky ironmaster, reached the same conclusion even before Bessemer. Litigation over the patent rights resulted in a consolidation of the two in the United States. By 1864, steel was being produced by the

Kelly-Bessemer process and was widely used by the 1870s. A competitive method, the Siemens-Martin process, ultimately surpassed the Kelly-Bessemer process in 1908. In this method, the iron was cooked by heat coming from outside the molten mass. This method was considered superior by its proponents because the processors apparently had better control over the method and produced steel with less chance of fracture. Both methods greatly vitalized the steel industry in the United States. By 1880, the United States surpassed Great Britain in the production of Kelly-Bessemer steel, and by 1900, in the production of Siemens-Martin steel.

23. Robert William Fogel, *Railroads and American Economic Growth: Essays in Econometric History* (Baltimore, 1964), 135-136; Aurand, *From the Molly Maguires to the United Mine Workers,* 13-19; Edward C. Kirkland, *Industry Comes of Age* (Chicago, 1961), 77, 82-83, 202-203; Gail Greenberg, *The Coal Industry: Where To?* (Stamford, CT, 1978), 18; Powell, "The Pennsylvania anthracite industry, 1769-1976," 14-15, 18-19.

24. Kirkland, *Industry Comes of Age,* 83, 202-203; Kirkland, *A History of American Economic Life,* 321-322.

25. See Carl Bridenbaugh, *Cities in the Wilderness: The First Century of Urban Life in America, 1625-1742* (New York, 1955; 2nd ed.), 151-152, 311-313; Carl Bridenbaugh, *Cities in Revolt: Urban Life in America, 1743-1776* (New York, 1955), 25-27, 232-235.

26. Binder, "Anthracite enters the American home," 83-92; Binder, *Coal Age Empire,* 5-6.

27. Binder, *Coal Age Empire,* 27-31; Rice, "Coal mining in the Kanawha Valley," 397-398.

28. Schurr and Netschert, *Energy in the American Economy,* 66-74; Kirkland, *Industry Comes of Age,* 139, 141.

29. See R. Dale Grinder, "The battle for clean air: the smoke problem in post-Civil War America, 1880-1917," in Martin V. Melosi, ed., *Pollution and Reform in American Cities, 1870-1930* (Austin, 1980), 83-103.

4

Railroad Smoke Control

The Regulation of a Mobile Pollution Source

JOEL A. TARR

KENNETH E. KOONS

Introduction: Railroads and Coal

The last two generations have witnessed significant progress in the improvement of air quality in the United States. Control of pollutants from mobile sources such as internal combustion engines used in automobiles and trucks, however, have shown less reduction than emissions from other sources.[1] The persistence of relatively high pollution rates from vehicles highlights the special problems encountered in reducing emissions from mobile as compared to stationary sources. The automobile and motor truck are not the first mobile sources of air pollution to affect urban air quality adversely.[2] The steam locomotive, a technology utilized to transport many millions of passengers and tons of freight for more than a century, also seriously affected the quality of urban air through its production of smoke.

The problem of controlling smoke from the steam locomotive included many of the elements present in attempts to regulate emissions from vehicles powered by the internal combustion engine. There were technical questions involving technology and fuel as well as policy questions involv-

AUTHORS' NOTE: This chapter is based on research supported by the National Science Foundation, Program in Ethics and Values and Science and Technology, Grant SS78-17308. Any opinions, findings, and conclusions or recommendations expressed herein are those of the authors and do not necessarily reflect the views of the National Science Foundation. The authors would like to thank Wesley Cohen, Edward W. Constant II, Chris Hendrickson, and Judith Powers for their perceptive comments.

ing emission standards and enforcement. Regulations, however, were primarily municipal statutes rather than national policy.

Fuel, of course, was a critical element. American railroads had originally burned wood, reflecting the cheapness and wide availability of this resource. This contrasted with the British experience, where the scarcity of wood required early reliance on mineral fuels. As wood supplies diminished, and as the railroads penetrated regions with plentiful coal deposits, fuel substitutions gradually took place. The initial mineral fuel used by the railroads was clean-burning anthracite, but as the tracks moved further west, away from the anthracite mines (northeastern Pennsylvania), they adopted the more readily available (and hence cheaper) high volatile bituminous coal. During the 1860s and 1870s, most of the technical problems associated with the burning of coal had been solved, and by 1880 coal, mostly bituminous, constituted more then 90 percent of locomotive fuel.[3]

The dominance of bituminous coal as a locomotive fuel was based on its wide distribution, its easy accessibility for mining, and its high average heat content. During the first third of the twentieth century, commercial mining of bituminous coal was carried on in 29 states, with over 90 percent of the total coming from seven states east of the Mississippi River.[4] Next to labor, fuel constituted the most expensive single material purchased and used by the railroads, ranging between a high of 11.2¢ (1920) and a low of 5.6¢ (1933) per revenue dollar between 1911 and 1950.[5] When fuel costs were high, the railroads paid special attention to factors that would help them achieve the maximum amount of transporation at a minimum fuel expense.

Coal was important to the railroads not only as their principal fuel, but also because it constituted their largest single item of revenue tonnage. In 1919, the first year for which exact figures are available, class 1 railways hauled over ten million cars of coal out of a total of 45 million cars, or 22 percent. In 1940, the ratio dropped to about 19 percent.[6] (Tonnage figures were actually larger because coal can be loaded into freight cars more heavily than any other commodity except iron ore and pig iron.) Fuel also constituted more than 50 percent of the non-revenue tonnage hauled by the railroads.[7] Some railroads, such as the Norfolk and Western, the Chesapeake and Ohio, the Pennsylvania, and the Baltimore and Ohio, specialized in coal shipping.[8] The fact that coal was the largest tonnage item carried by the railroads and, as fuel, constituted a critical item in their cost picture, gave them a vital interest in both their own efficiency of operation and factors affecting coal use in other markets.

Railroad locomotives often generated copious amounts of dense smoke and cinders, not only because they burned high volatile bituminous coal, but also because they were inefficient fuel consumers compared to stationary steam plants. The restricted space in the locomotive cab for the firebox made extremely high rates of combustion necessary, requiring a strong draft. These conditions resulted in the loss of a considerable amount of the coal heat at the stack and the emergence of cinders and gases from the stack as smoke. Furthermore, locomotive smoke, as compared to smoke produced from other industrial sources, was particularly offensive because it was discharged at relatively low levels and often dispersed over a wide area by moving trains.[9]

Railroad locomotives actually varied considerably by size and design, depending upon their function. Intercity passenger trains differed from those used for suburban runs, and both of these differed in traction requirements from freight locomotives. Switching engines, intended for use in railroad yards, created a special type of problem, with their frequent stops and starts under heavy loads. Railroad terminals, where locomotives clustered with banked fires or for firing-up, were a particular nuisance because they were often located in densely populated areas. Some authorities considered railroad terminal smoke to be the most acute smoke abatement problem in the city.[10]

Incentives for the Railroads to Control Locomotive Smoke Emissions

The primary incentives for the railroads to control locomotive smoke can be divided into internal and external factors.[11] Internal conditions involved factors that drove the railroad companies to make changes that reduced smoke in order to improve their efficiency and economy of operation and to meet special operating situations. External elements involved pressures from the outside environment—primarily municipal smoke control regulations that forced the railroads to undertake smoke control measures that they would not have voluntarily adopted because they were perceived as adding to rather than diminishing the costs of operation. Actually, the cost effectiveness of a particular innovation or action was not always clear, and in practice, there was often considerable overlap between what I have called internal and external situations.

Internal Conditions

Special Operating Situations

The most obvious special situation requiring action by the railroads to deal with the smoke problem involved the need for tunnels to secure access to city centers.[12] Steam locomotives were unacceptable in subaqueous tunnels, especially with grades, because the subterranean passages could not be adequately ventilated. Several fatalities had occurred, for instance, in subaqueous tunnels where steam was used. The solution used to deal with the problem was electrification of the lines. In 1895, in what may have been the first case where electricity supplanted steam as motive power in main-line railroad service, the Baltimore and Ohio Railroad (B & O) electrified a 3.6-mile portion of its Baltimore belt line, including the route through a 7000 foot tunnel. This gave the B & O direct access to the city and allowed it to compete with the Pennsylvania Railroad (PRR) for the Baltimore trade.[13]

Another important example of a technology substitution that occurred because of the smoke problem concerned the attempts of the PRR to secure direct access to Manhattan Island. Here, after considering construction of a bridge, the PRR management decided that the experience of the B & O in electrifying part of its Baltimore belt line, including a long tunnel, justified its construction of subaqueous tunnels. Construction of the tunnels, an electrified line, and a new station took nine years, and in 1910 the PRR began hauling passengers into its new midtown Manhattan station, using electric power.[14]

Fuel Conservation

The production of dense ("black") smoke is a sign of inefficient fuel consumption, and the railroads were sensitive to "the intimate relation between smoke abatement and fuel economy," especially when fuel costs were high.[15] The "economical utilization" of fuel, railroad managers maintained, could only be secured by continual producer supervision over coal preparation, careful coal handling in the transition from cars to locomotive tenders, the fitting of coal types to particular service requirements, the maintenance of good locomotive operating conditions, and the education of engineers and firemen in proper firing.[16]

In order to secure fuel savings, the railroad companies, who were masters of bureaucratic organization, often created central fuel bureaus that exercised supervision over all states of fuel distribution and consumption. Beginning after 1900, instructors in fuel economy were assigned to the different rail districts:

> to ride and inspect locomotives, observe the handling and firing of the locomotives, instruct the engine crews where necessary in correct methods of handling and firing, report power conditions, give attention to the methods of cleaning, banking and preparing fires in locomotives and the coaling and handling of the locomotives while in the charge of engine terminal employees, and in general to endeavor to bring about every practicable improvement in the detail conditions which effect economy in the use of locomotive fuel.[17]

The fuel consumption bureaus usually included smoke inspectors, whose duty it was to report locomotives emitting black smoke.

Industry self-regulation of smoke emissions had primarily two motivations. One motivation related to the fact that dense smoke was a sign of poor combustion and fuel waste. A second motivation involved the desire to avoid regulation and interference with operations by municipal smoke inspectors. Both motives combined to produce relatively large staffs of railroad smoke inspectors. In Pittsburgh, for instance, in the 1920s, the city's five railroads maintained a corps of twenty inspectors to observe locomotives and to correct conditions responsible for smoke. The number of railroad inspectors contrasted with only four municipal smoke inspectors. In 1943, the railroad companies employed twelve inspectors who reported to the Pittsburgh Bureau of Smoke Control on a daily basis.[18] Similar cooperation between the railroad companies and bureaus of smoke control also occurred in Chicago, Kansas City, and Hudson County, New Jersey.[19]

Railroad smoke inspectors were vulnerable in times of financial stringency. Often hired in response to public agitation over smoke pollution, they might disappear when agitation subsided and regulation was deemphasized. In addition, fuel savings became less critical when prices were low, reducing the need to maintain vigilance in the search for fuel-wasting and smoke-producing firemen and engineers. As one Pennsylvania Railroad Division Manager remarked in 1909, the cost of supervising railroad smoke "is a very serious burden on the cost of operation, and while the railways would not provide such supervision but for the belief that it will yield adequate return or from realization of the duties which the railways owe the public, there must be a limit to the amount of money which they can so expend."[20]

Protecting Passenger Comfort

Railway management wanted to reduce locomotive smoke from passenger trains in order to protect passenger comfort, as well as to conserve fuel and avoid regulation. Competition for passenger traffic was intense, and the reduction of smoke and cinders was one means to enhance travel enjoyment. As early as the 1850s, the B & O and the PRR were experimenting with smoke control devices on their passenger trains. In 1868, the Illinois Central Railroad placed special instructions in their passenger locomotive cabs concerning smoke prevention. The list concluded with the statement that "much of the annoyance from smoke and coal dust will be prevented and a large saving in fuel effected by attention to the above rules."[21] Similar concern over comfort, however, did not apply to the freight and switching trains that composed the bulk of railroad traffic.

Pressures from the External Environment

The main external pressures on the railroad corporations to reduce smoke came from the municipalities. The smoke control movement in American cities extended from approximately the late nineteenth century to the 1950s. Smoke pollution was particularly heavy in industrial cities such as Pittsburgh and St. Louis that depended on bituminous coal for their industrial and domestic fuel. In many of these cities, topographical and climatic features produced inversions that trapped the smoke and particulates and created smoke palls. As these cities grew in industry and population, air quality conditions worsened. While smoke signified economic progress to some urbanites, others became concerned with its negative affects on the quality of urban life. Smoke control advocates listed damage to buildings, higher costs of cleaning, loss of sunlight, and chronic health impairment as costs of smoke pollution. Concerned about these negative impacts and their effect on the ability of the cities to continue to attract population and business, civic associations, women's clubs, and engineering associations spearheaded a drive for smoke regulation in the early twentieth century.[22]

In 1912, the U.S. Bureau of Mines, which had conducted several studies of smoke pollution, polled a number of cities concerning their smoke control regulations. While only 29 of 300 cities with under 200,000 inhabitants had smoke ordinances, all 28 cities with over 200,000 had regulations. These laws, however, differed greatly in terms of specificity and sources regulated. No city aside from Los Angeles, for instance, mentioned private residences in their ordinance. Several ordinances prohibited the emission of "dense smoke" within the city limits as a nuisance, but did not attempt to define standards or time limits. Regulations in other cities, such as Baltimore, Chicago, and Cincinnati prohibited the emission of dense smoke for more than a specified number of minutes in an hour (usually 6-8 minutes). A few cities attempted to supply a scientific grading of smoke density utilizing the Ringlemann chart, a visual grading mechanism.[23]

The industrial cities with bad smoke conditions were also railroad centers, and urban reformers often pinpointed locomotives as especially offensive smoke generators. Estimates of the amount of the total smoke problem created by the railroads ranged between 20 and 50 percent in cities like Chicago and Pittsburgh.[24] The Committee of Investigation on Smoke Abatement and Electrification of Railway Terminals of the Chicago Association of Commerce, for instance, reported in 1915 that while steam locomotives burned 11.9 percent of the total fuel consumed within Chicago, they were responsible for 22 percent of the city's visible smoke and 7.4 percent of the solid constituents in the atmosphere. Locomotives engaged in yard freight service were the worst offenders.[25]

In the regulations reviewed by the Bureau of Mines in 1912, railroads were usually dealt with under the general smoke ordinances. In those cases where they received specific mention, they were either exempted from regulation under certain conditions or were subjected to more stringent controls than other classes of smoke producers. In Louisville and Rochester, for instance, the smoke ordinance did not apply to locomotives entering, leaving, or in transit through the city. In contrast, Jersey City, which possessed many railroad marshalling yards, had an ordinance that prohibited the emission of dense smoke from any engine or locomotive within the city limits and provided for fines in cases of injury to health or property.[26]

During the years between 1912 and 1941, the number of cities with smoke control ordinances increased, as did the severity of the standards. In 1939, the Bureau of Mines issued another survey of smoke ordinances, this time of the nation's eighty largest cities. Of the eighty, 25 followed a model ordinance prepared by a group of engineering societies in 1924, calling for the emission of dense smoke for no more than six minutes an hour. Fifty cities used the Ringlemann chart as a means to measure smoke density. Other cities had a variety of standards, with several allowing locomotive smoke for one out of every fifteen minutes. More significantly, nine cities exempted railroads from regulation, reflecting the political power of railroads within those communities.[27]

Beginning in 1940 in St. Louis, and followed by Pittsburgh in 1941, a number of cities adopted ordinances with more stringent regulations that required the use of smokeless fuels or technology and controlled domestic sources of smoke, as well as industries, commercial establishments, and railroads. The Pittsburgh Smoke Control Ordinance of 1941 was the most stringent in the nation in the 1940s and permitted railroads to produce dense smoke (defined as No. 2 on the Ringlemann chart) for no more than one minute an hour. It was adopted over railroad protests that the ordinance made it impossible for them to operate.[28]

Whatever the terms of the various ordinances, enforcement tended to be sporadic, depending on the orientation of the administration in power. Regulatory bureaus were often understaffed and underfinanced and lacked substantial powers of implementation. At times of popular outcry against the smoke nuisance, smoke inspectors would become more active and occasionally haul railroad companies into court for violations of the ordinances. The railroads, in turn, would increase the number of smoke inspectors on their staffs and make efforts to reduce locomotive smoke. Conditions generally returned to their original state, however, once the crusade had ended, although occasionally there were some permanent improvements because of retrofits.[29] Municipal smoke inspectors often tended to be sympathetic to railroad problems in reducing smoke and cooperated with them in seeking solutions rather than resorting to the sanction of legal proceedings.[30]

There are several possible explanations for the behavior of municipal smoke bureaus. One explanation derives from the common professional training and associations of municipal smoke inspectors and railroad personnel.[31] In the twentieth century, regulatory bureaus were usually headed by mechanical engineers who viewed themselves as primarily technological problem-solvers. As such, they shared a professional interest with railroad managers in seeking to improve railroad operating procedures in order to bring about efficiency and economy of operation. "Smoke abatement," they argued, "was a problem for the Engineer and not the Legislator."[32] Municipal smoke inspectors and railroad personnel also shared membership in the Smoke Control Association of America. The latter frequently delivered papers at the Association's annual meetings concerning progress in locomotive smoke control, while papers by city inspectors at these meetings often cited the railroads for their cooperative attitude.[33]

Another set of plausible explanations for the actions of these regulators derives from the various theories involving regulatory behavior. The evidence suggests, for instance, that the regulated corporations—the railroads—had actually "captured" the regulatory bureaus in regard to their normal operations.[34] Given the importance of the railroads to urban economic vitality in the 1900-1945 period, and given their political power as a major industry, municipalities were reluctant to burden them with regulatory procedures and fines that hampered their operation. On the other hand, municipal administrations were also susceptible to political pressures and agitation from various groups interested in smoke control, such as businessmen's associations and women's clubs, for more stringent law enforcement. The administrations were often forced to respond to these demands, resulting in a period of tougher law enforcement. Normally, however, given the power and importance of the railroads, it was rational for smoke control bureaus to follow a policy of cooperation and education in enforcement. At the same time, it was to the interests of the railroads to appear to be making reasonable attempts at smoke control.

Whenever possible, the railroads attempted to keep disciplinary action against the personnel responsible for smoke violations in their own hands. When city officials used legal force in enforcing ordinances, the railroads considered the action as "over-zealous" behavior on the part of the municipality. On the other hand, some railroad officials held that municipal action reflected a failure of the railroads to self-police. When discipline was required, noted the Chief Smoke Inspector of the Chicago and Northwestern Railway, the railroad itself must provide it.[35] Such discipline could take the form of reprimands, layoffs, or even discharge from the service. In 1949, for instance, there were 102 suspensions and 254 reprimands delivered by the railroads against personnel involved in violations of the Pittsburgh Smoke Control Law.[36]

The railroads were particularly concerned about laws that might take decisions regarding major capital expenditures out of their hands. This actually happened in 1903, in a case involving the New York Central Railroad. The company used a two-mile tunnel that was often filled with smoke (a partially covered cut) to reach their Manhattan terminal. It was considering the electrification of the line, but had not made a final decision by 1902. In that year, however, seventeen people died in a crash in the tunnel caused by smoke obscuring the signal lights. In 1903, in reaction to the crash, the New York legislature passed a law prohibiting the use of steam locomotives south of the Harlem River after July 1, 1908.[37] The New York Central faced the choice of either electrifying its line or abandoning its Manhattan terminal. The former had to be its choice, although the timing was not of their choosing and was forced by the legislative action. A similar situation developed in Pittsburgh and Allegheny Counties in 1946 and 1947, when the passage of strict smoke control regulations forced the Pittsburgh area railroads to convert to diesel-electric locomotives at a faster rate than had been planned.[38]

Railroad Approaches to Dealing with the Smoke Problem

There are primarily four methods by which society can deal with the problems of technology-induced air pollution besides ceasing to use that technology completely. These four approaches involve training human operators to use the technology differently than they had previously (the "human fix"); retrofitting existing equipment to reduce emissions of pollutants; switching from a dirty fuel to a cleaner fuel ("fuel switching"); and substituting a different and cleaner technology for the polluting technology. All of these approaches were tried by the railroads in their attempts to deal with the smoke problem. All involved costs, and the railroads, many of whom had financial difficulties in the early twentieth century, usually chose those options that were least costly in terms of immediate capital outlay.

The Human Fix: Educating the Engineer and Fireman

Throughout the articles and conference discussions about methods of reducing smoke, there is a consistent theme of the necessity for intelligent and well-trained firemen and enginemen. "When a railroad is in service," noted one railroad official, "no factor has so important an influence over the control of smoke as the manner in which it is fired by the fireman and operated by the engineman."[39] In order to deal with the human element, railroad managers and smoke inspectors advocated a program of education accompanied by constant supervision. Many railroads had short courses in smoke prevention for their operating personnel. Railroad smoke inspectors were expected to teach proper methods of firing as well as report bad smoke conditions. Cartoons, posters, and other literature provided regular reminders about the need to prevent smoke in order to save fuel and avoid violations of city ordinances.[40]

Even though technological innovations during the twentieth century reduced the need for human involvement in the firing process, it could not be totally eliminated. "No matter how good the design is," observed a well-known smoke control expert in 1944, "you still have to have men to operate this equipment. You are not going to do away with any of the smoke laws by the best designed locomotive and the best designed boilers of any kind, because we will still have the human element to contend with."[41] In short, the human element was responsible for smoke and, given the nature of the steam locomotive, there were limitations to the extent to which technology could replace human beings.

Technological Retrofits and Technological Forcing

Various technological retrofits to reduce locomotive smoke emissions were available during the late nineteenth and early twentieth centuries. In fact, the basic retrofitting devices remained the same for about fifty years; they improved in quality and efficiency, but not in concept. These devices were the automatic stoker, the brick arch, the pneumatic fire box door closer, and the steam-air jet.

Technological changes in regard to the steam locomotive itself were directed toward power enhancement, but within the same basic structure. Considerable improvements were made within the framework of the boiler, the frame structure, driving wheels and trucks, but no radical changes occurred. Design improvements, therefore, involved the inclusion of additional known elements. The primary changes involved the manner in which the generated steam energy was utilized in the cylinders and transmitted from the cylinders to the rails. Between 1900 and 1950, the maximum pounds of tractive effort available increased from 49,700 pounds of tractive effort to 135,375 pounds for a passenger locomotive. Simultaneously, the overall efficiency of the average high-speed locomotive increased from about 3.5 percent to 7.5 percent (1940).[42]

To a large extent, engine-horsepower output depended upon the replacement of the human element with mechanical factors. For instance, mechanical stokers were able to feed coal at a much more efficient rate than firemen. Efficient fuel feeding and consumption also meant reduced smoke. As the managing editor of *Railway Age* noted in 1946, "because . . . the human element has been unable to perform the job as effectively as the public interest demands, science is stepping in to complete the task."[43] It might be noted that this statement was made at a time when the steam locomotive was about to be replaced by the diesel-electric. Rates of adoption of innovation, therefore, were critical in smoke reduction, but there were important limitations (such as costs and technical restraints) on both the pace and extent to which human factors could be eliminated in the context of the steam locomotive.[44]

Retrofits were installed to satisfy both internal motivations of fuel efficiency and power generation and to satisfy regulatory pressures. Sometimes internal and external factors overlapped. When both motivations were involved, or when there were clear advantages in regard to fuel savings, innovations were more rapidly adopted. When retrofits were adopted parimarily to meet smoke control regulations, the pace was considerably slower.

Mechanical stokers, brick arches, and steam jets were retrofits or mechanical improvements that responded to both internal and external pressures. Mechanical stokers, for instance, both improved steam locomotive performance and reduced smoke. Railroad and locomotive manufacturers began working to develop automatic stokers in the late nineteenth century, and by 1911-12 several types had been perfected. One authority called stokers the "greatest single mechanical contribution to the coal-burning steam locomotive," because by vastly increasing fuel input they permitted large increases in power production.[45] However, firemen were still required along with mechanical stokers in order to make manual adjustments. In addition, the stokers reportedly reduced the firemen's incentive to fine-tune the fire for efficiency. Even with mechanical stokers, locomotives could produce black smoke.[46]

The brick arch was also developed in the late nineteenth century, and it both improved fuel consumption and reduced smoke production. It worked by providing a longer flame passage for burning gases, thus enhancing their ignition rather than allowing them to escape as smoke. The arches often became a source of difficulty, however, because they required constant maintenance and had short lives, needing frequent replacement. Arches enhanced the ability of the firemen to reduce smoke and improve power production but did not eliminate the necessity for intelligent firing.[47] The human element remained.

The air or steam jet was a technology that provided a uniform and constant flow of air to support the combustion process and therefore improved the efficiency of fuel consumption and prevented smoke emissions. Experiments with steam jets began in the early twentieth century and continued through the 1940s. The early jets were crude and often introduced excess air into the firebox, reducing the amount of heat and steam produced for a given amount of fuel. Most jets were operated manually, and crews often used them at the wrong time or, because they generated a large noise volume, did not use them at all. There was no consensus among railroad men as to the efficiency or utility of the steam jets, and some held that they were actually unnecessary.[48]

In the 1930s and 1940s, as the coal industry faced increased competition from competing fuels, it accelerated research efforts to retain its existing markets. In 1934, the National Coal Association formed Bituminous Coal Research (BCR) to begin exploring other coal uses. By 1946, BCR had a membership of 250 coal companies and ten railroads. It pushed the development of the relatively smokeless, coal-burning gas-turbine locomotive and advocated the adoption of a new steam-air jet as a retrofit for existing equipment. BCR leaders touted their steam-air jet as cheap, effective, and quiet. Most important, it was supposedly fully automatic and reduced the need for the human element.[49]

Under pressure from smoke control ordinances in various cities, a number of railroads installed the BCR jet. By 1949, for instance, almost all of the locomotives in the Pittsburgh area had steam-air jets.[50] The results, however, were mixed, and violations continued. The Superintendent of the Pittsburgh Bureau of Smoke Prevention reissued the old complaint that "the real problem is to control the human element. . . . It makes little difference whether the locomotive is equipped with stokers, steam-air jets or what the equipment is. So long as a valve must be turned or a firedoor cracked, we are sure to have man failures."[51]

In addition to retrofitting locomotives in order to reduce smoke, the railroads also installed smoke control devices at their terminals and roundhouses. Although there was some internal motivation to make these improvements in order to better work conditions, the pressure was primarily external. Terminals and roundhouses were especially objectionable in terms of smoke because it was more difficult to control smoke production from a sitting as compared with a moving locomotive.[52] These railroad facilities were often located in congested districts, and the companies faced pressure from citizens and smoke control bureaus to regulate the nuisance. One step the railroad companies could have taken was to relocate their facilities outside of populated areas, but this was often impracticable in regard to access. Instead, the railroad companies installed smoke collectors and washers, high chimneys, and direct steaming systems. An advantage of the latter was that they prepared locomotives quickly for runs as well as reducing smoke.[53]

Fuel Switching

Fuel switching was a method used by the railroads to control bad smoke emissions in cities. The fuel used was usually coke or low volatile coal. Ideally, the universal use of coke or low volatile fuel such as anthracite would have almost eradicated the railroad smoke problem, but the railroad corporations were unwilling to bear the higher costs of these cleaner fuels. Therefore, they were only used in regard to the worst cases—pusher locomotives working on steep grades or shifting heavy loads, on worktrains, and in locomotives without mechanical stokers.[54]

Technological Substitutions

No matter which retrofits were applied to steam locomotives burning bituminous coal, it was nearly impossible to entirely prevent smoke. The Pittsburgh Smoke Control Ordinance of 1941 was the nation's strictest, only allowing a locomotive to make one minute of dense smoke (defined as No. 2 smoke or greater on the Ringlemann Chart) an hour, but it did not eliminate the railroad smoke nuisance.[55] As the superintendent of the Pittsburgh Bureau of Smoke Prevention noted, "if dense smoke is blown from a steam locomotive stack for only 15 or 20 seconds, it makes a very objectionable black cloud that may hang in the atmosphere for some time."[56] Such a condition, however, did not violate the ordinance. In addition, a group of locomotives could legally produce No. 1 smoke that formed a heavy cloud without breaking the law. Harsher standards, the superintendent noted, would have placed a heavy burden on the railroads and made it exceedingly expensive to operate.

If making the steam locomotive smokeless was almost impossible, there existed the option of replacing it with a smokeless alternative. The electric locomotive, which was technologically superior to the steam engine in terms of traction, reliability, safety, riding quality, cleanliness, and ease of operation, was first used on American railroads in 1895. Its technological advantages, plus its smokeless operation, made electrification a favorite cause of civic and business associations concerned with railroad smoke.[57] Yet electrification also required large amounts of capital, and financially pressed railroads hesitated to make the expenditures. In Chicago, for instance, which was one of the world's great railroad centers, electrification was advocated as an alternative by various reform and business organizations. In 1915, a committee of experts was assembled by the Chicago Association of Commerce to examine its practicality. The committee concluded that improvements in the steam locomotive were still possible and that complete electrification of Chicago's railroad terminals was "financially impracticable." The high capital costs of electrification, combined with railroad financial difficulties, prevented all but a few companies from adopting the system in spite of its attractive technological and environmental qualities.[58] Aside from New York in 1903, no governmental body enacted and enforced regulations so strict that a railroad was forced to electrify a portion of its system in order to comply with the law.

A second technological substitution for the steam locomotive became available in the 1920s and 1930s. This was the diesel-electric which, while involving initial large capital costs, did not require the central power sources and extensive building of catenary necessitated by electrification. Railroads substituted diesels for steam locomotives on some long-distance passenger runs in the 1930s, and also used them for switching engines in a number of cities. Railroad adoption of the diesel-electric was relatively slow, however, considering its technological advantages, and massive changes did not come until after World War II.[59]

Railroad adoption of the diesel locomotive was inhibited in some areas not only by conservative management but also by the role of the railroad companies as heavy coal haulers. In the Pittsburgh region, for instance, the railroads hesitated to adopt the diesel because of coal industry pressure for continuation of the steam locomotive. The coal industry also applied pressure to the railroads to help them oppose a strong Allegheny County Smoke Control law that threatened to drive coal users to alternative fuels and force the railroads to retrofit their steam engines or shift to diesel locomotives. When the law was finally passed in 1949, the railroads rapidly converted to diesel, with an 88 percent dieselization rate by 1954.[60]

Throughout the nation during the post-war years, the diesel-electric finally displaced the steam locomotive as the chief form of railroad motive power, especially as its operating efficiencies became clear. In 1946 there were 39,592 steam locomotives in service, 867 electric, and 5,008 diesels. By 1951, there were almost as many diesel locomotives (19,014) in service as steam (22,590), while electrics had begun a slow decline (817). In 1960, there were 30,240 diesels, 498 electrics and only 374 steam locomotives (see Figure 4.1).[61] The substitution of an environmentally and technically superior and cost effective technology for the steam locomotive had finally solved the railroad smoke problem.

Conclusions

The problem of railroad smoke pollution must be put in the context of environmental pollution in general. The free market pricing system has

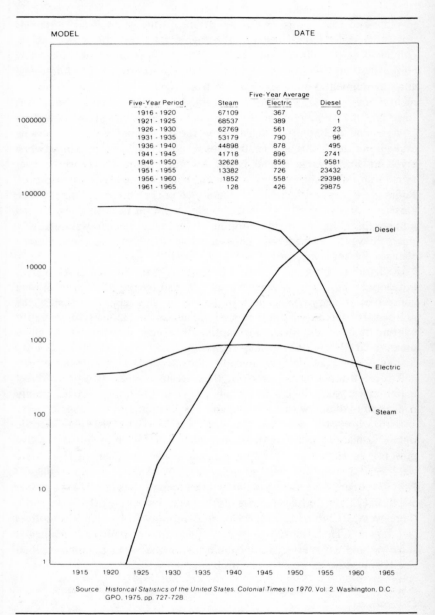

MODEL   DATE

Five-Year Period	Steam	Five-Year Average Electric	Diesel
1916 - 1920	67109	367	0
1921 - 1925	68537	389	1
1926 - 1930	62769	561	23
1931 - 1935	53179	790	96
1936 - 1940	44898	878	495
1941 - 1945	41718	896	2741
1946 - 1950	32628	856	9581
1951 - 1955	13382	726	23432
1956 - 1960	1852	558	29398
1961 - 1965	128	426	29875

Source   Historical Statistics of the United States. Colonial Times to 1970. Vol. 2. Washington, D.C.
GPO, 1975. pp. 727-728.

Figure 4.1 Number of Steam Electric and Diesel Locomotives in Service in the United States, 1916-1960 (5-year averages plotted on semi-logarithmic scale)

historically failed to provide incentives to protect the environment—that is, to guard the society's common property in clean air, water, and undegraded land resources.[62] With air pollution by smoke from the burning of bituminous coal, the true social costs were not adequately valued. The incentive structure for reducing smoke came either from the internal cost savings available to the railroads that might be generated by fuel conservation measures, management concern over public response to the smoke nuisance that might decrease passenger revenues, or public policy that threatened legal sanctions. Ultimately, none of these approaches brought results that satisfied public demands for the reduction of smoke pollution and the improvement of air quality.

Not surprisingly, the railroads themselves undertook few initiatives to reduce smoke without the expectation of improving performance. From the point of view of maximizing profits, their action was rational; environmental considerations did not enter into their considerations. Retrofits such as brick arches or mechanical stokers, whose installation management could justify as cost-reducing and power-enhancing, were more readily adopted than other retrofits such as the steam-air jet that threatened to reduce power supply. Steam-air jets were not widely installed until the 1940s, when the steam railroads were faced with intense competition from other, cleaner modes of transport, such as the automobile and the motor bus, or when municipal regulations and regulators became tougher.

In addition to the retrofits, the railroads attempted to educate their personnel (the "human fix") to reduce smoke, especially when such training promised fuel savings or was needed to meet municipal standards and avoid penalties. (It can be argued that the "human fix" was cheaper and more flexible for the railroads than retrofits or technological substitutions.) Without such incentives, however, the railroads generally ignored the problem. In 1948, for instance, when the city of Cumberland, Maryland enacted its first smoke control ordinance, the representatives of the Baltimore & Ohio Railroad hastened to promise their cooperation. In apologizing for delays in inculcating their personnel with "a sense of smoke consciousness," they observed that Cumberland's ordinance was new. The implication was clear that before the passage of the ordinance, the railroad had made little or no attempt to train its men to prevent smoke.[63]

The function of public policy from the perspective of the public interest was to persuade or force the railroads to reduce their smoke emissions to conform to municipal smoke standards. The political power of the railroads and their economic primacy in the cities, however, often resulted in limited implementation by the smoke control bureaus. Smoke control inspectors shared professional interests with railroad personnel and were often sympathetic to the technological difficulties of controlling railroad smoke. They therefore preferred to follow a policy of cooperation and education rather than one of strong sanctions. Often, they allowed the railroads themselves to undertake disciplinary action against firemen and engineers responsible for breaking the law.

Thus, public policy toward locomotive smoke followed a path of what James E. Krier and Edmund Ursin call "least steps along the path of least resistance,"[64] except in cases of crisis, such as New York City in 1905, or of strong public concern, such as in Pittsburgh in 1941 and 1947. "Policy-by-least steps" permitted the railroads to make gradual adjustments at their own pace and according to the industry's own rate of technological progress. Municipal smoke control policy did develop tougher standards over time, but cooperation with the railroads usually avoided a resort to using the courts to compel technological retrofit or technological substitutions to meet new standards.

Most engineers involved in locomotive smoke regulation realized that the ultimate answer to the railroad smoke problem was to replace the steam engine. Both the electric and diesel locomotives were options, but conservative management and concern over high capital costs, as well as pressure from coal producers, prevented all but a few lines from electrifying and retarded the rate of adoption of the diesel engine. Eventually, in the post-World War II period, the diesel replaced the steam locomotive and cities no longer faced a railroad smoke problem.

The issue of railroad smoke abatement presented a difficult problem of environmental regulation. The problem lay in the nature of the technology itself, the principal fuel consumed, and the political power and economic importance of the regulated industry. Complicating the situation were the pressures applied to the coal carrier railroads by the coal industry to continue using the steam locomotive. The railroad smoke problem finally disappeared due to the substitution of a new and superior technology, but environmental considerations played a very small role in the change. Economic factors were eventually dominant, but Thomas G. Marx has shown that railroad managers were motivated by considerations aside from pure profit maximazation in their attachment to the steam engine and resisted adoption of the diesel-electric long after its many advantages over the steam locomotive were obvious.[65]

Given this conservatism on the part of the private sector managers, the ideal public policy posture for the purpose of controlling railroad smoke would have been to force the railroads to speed up their rate of substituting a smokeless technology for the steam locomotive.[66] But, given the political and economic power configurations in American cities, and the limited strength of environmental values, such an approach never received serious consideration.

NOTES

1. U.S. Environmental Protection Agency, *Trends in the Quality of the Nation's Air—A Report to the People* (Washington, 1980).

2. The horse was also a mobile pollution source. It was eliminated as a pollution problem by the automobile. See Joel A. Tarr, "Urban pollution—many long years ago," *American Heritage* 22 (October 1971), 65-69, 106.

3. John H. White, Jr., *American Locomotives: An Engineering History, 1830-1880* (Baltimore, 1968), 83-90; Frederick Moore Binder, *Coal Age Empire: Pennsylvania Coal and its Utilization to 1860* (Harrisburg, 1974), 111-132.

4. W. L. Robinson, "Locomotive fuel," *Proceedings of the Second International Conference on Bituminous Coal* (Pittsburgh, 1928), 366.

5. Association of American Railroads, Bureau of Railway Economics, *Railroad Transportation: A Statistical Record 1911-1951* (Washington, 1953), 37.

6. Ibid., 23.

7. Robinson, "Locomotive fuel," 367.

8. For a discussion of the coal shipping railroads, see Joseph T. Lambie, *From Mine to Market: The History of Coal Transportation on the Norfolk and Western Railway* (New York, 1954).

9. John O'Connor, *Some Engineering Phases of Pittsburgh's Smoke Problem*, Bulletin No. 8, Smoke Investigation, Mellon Institute of Industrial Research and School of Specific Industries (Pittsburgh, 1914), 71-81; Benjamin Linsky, ed., *A Different Air: The Chicago Report on Smoke Abatement* (Elmsford, NY, 1971), 175-178.

10. J. B. Irwin, "Railway smoke abatement," *Transactions of the American Society of Mechanical Engineers* (1927-1928) Vols. 49-50, Pt. 156; and I. A. Deutch and S. Radner, "Abating locomotive smoke in Chicago," in Smoke Prevention Association of America (hereafter referred to as SPAA), *Manual of Ordinances and Requirements* (1941).

11. The question can also be viewed from the perspective of technology forcing. For instance, in regard to the internal combustion engine, technological advances were improving engine efficiency, but not necessarily fast enough to meet the clean air standards desired by policy makers. The 1970 Amendments to the Clean Air Act attempted to speed up the development of a cleaner and more efficient engine through various sanctions (fines). For a discussion of technology forcing, see Eugene P. Seskin, "Automobile air pollution policy," in Paul R. Portney, ed., *Current Issues in U.S. Environmental Policy* (Baltimore, 1978), 83-90.

12. In the early stages of railroad development, steam locomotives had actually been banned from some city centers because of the hazard and nuisance they presented and because they frightened horses. For New York see George Rogers Taylor, "The beginnings of mass transportation in urban America: Part 1," *Smithsonian Journal of History* (Fall 1962), 31-38; for Pittsburgh, see Joel A. Tarr, *Transportation Innovation and Changing Spatial Patterns in Pittsburgh, 1850-1934* (Chicago, 1978), 56, note 23.

13. Carl W. Condit, *The Pioneer Stage of Railroad Electrification—Transactions of the American Philosophical Society* (Philadelphia, 1977), Vol. 67, Pt. 7, 10-17.

14. Michael Bezilla, *Electric Traction on the Pennsylvania Railroad 1895-1968* (University Park, PA, 1980), 9-55.

15. D. F. Crawford, "The abatement of locomotive smoke," *Railway Age Gazette* 53 (Dec. 24, 1913), 762-765.

16. Ibid.; Robinson, "Locomotive fuel," 372-377.

17. Robinson, "Locomotive fuel," 373-374; A. W. Gibbs, "The smoke nuisance in cities," *Railroad Age Gazette* 5 (Feb. 26, 1909), 415. For railroad organization, see Alfred D. Chandler, Jr., ed., *The Railroads: The Nation's First Big Business* (New York, 1965).

18. H. B. Meller, "Smoke abatement, its effects and its limitations," *Mechanical Engineering* 48 (November 1926), 1279; Sumner B. Ely, "Steam-air jet application to locomotives," *Proceedings,* SPAA 38th Annual Meetings, June 6-9, 1944, 81.

19. Roy V. Wright, "Railroad smoke abatement," *Proceedings,* SPAA, 1946, 27; Linsky, ed., *A Different Air,* 52.

20. Gibbs, "The smoke nuisance in cities," 415.

21. White, *American Locomotives,* 89-90; Binder, *Coal Age Empire,* 127-130.

22. R. Dale Grinder, "The battle for clean air: the smoke problem in post-Civil War America," in Martin V. Melosi, ed., *Pollution & Reform in American Cities, 1870-1930* (Austin, 1980), 83-104; and Joel A. Tarr, "Changing fuel use behavior and energy transitions: the Pittsburgh smoke control movement, 1940-1950," *Journal of Social History* 14 (Summer 1981), 561-588.

23. Samuel B. Flagg, *City Smoke Ordinances and Smoke Abatement,* Bull. 49, Bureau of Mines (Washington, DC, 1912).

24. O'Connor, *Some Engineering Phases of Pittsburgh's Smoke Problem,* 71-81; Linsky, ed., *A Different Air,* 175-178.

25. Ibid., 175-178.

26. Flagg, *City Smoke Ordinances,* 10-25, gives a review of the terms of smoke control ordinances in cities of over 200,000 residents.

27. J. S. Barkley, "Some fundamentals of smoke abatement," Information Circular 7090, *Bureau of the Mines,* 1939.

28. "Hearings before the Pittsburgh City Council on the smoke control ordinance," June 25, 1941, Pittsburgh City Council Records.

29. For a discussion of the debate over strict and nominal enforcement in municipal smoke control, see Grinder, "The battle for clean air," 95-99. For policy shifts in regard to railroads, see Irwin, "Railway smoke abatement," 153-154. Descriptions of alterations in railroad smoke conditions can be found in the *Annual Reports* of most municipal smoke control bureaus.

30. For examples of papers by municipal smoke inspectors discussing the necessity of cooperation rather than legal sanctions, see Meller, "Smoke abatement," 1279; and W. H. Kimberly, "Railroad smoke control in Pittsburgh," *Proceedings,* SPAA, 1943, 113.

31. For a discussion of how professional training can influence positions taken on public questions involving environmental regulations, see Joel A. Tarr, Terry Yosie, and James McCurley III, "Disputes over water quality policy: professional cultures in conflict, 1900-1917," *American Journal of Public Health* 70 (April 1980), 427-435. Also see Edward T. Layton, Jr., *The Revolt of the Engineers: Social Responsibility and the American Engineering Profession,* especially 53-79.

32. Quoted in Grinder, "The battle for clean air," 99.

33. See *Annual Reports,* SPAA.

34. For a discussion of the various regulatory models, see R. A. Posner, "Theories of economic regulation," *The Bell Journal of Economics and Management Science* 5 (Autumn, 1974), 335-358.

35. Irwin, "Railway smoke abatement," 153.

36. Pittsburgh Department of Public Health, Bureau of Smoke Prevention, *Report on Railroad Smoke Conditions* (Pittsburgh, 1949), 4.

37. Bezilla, *Electric Traction,* 28.

38. The railroads opposed the emission standards in the Pittsburgh Smoke Control Ordinance in 1941 and fought passage of county enabling legislation in 1947. When the county law was passed, the railroads began dieselization on a significant scale (Pittsburgh Press, Aug. 26, 1949).

39. Irwin, "Railway smoke abatement," 153.

40. Wright, "Railroad smoke abatement," 27; R. E. Howe, "Fuel conservation and smoke abatement," *Proceedings, SPAA,* 1947, discussion after p. 16; S. E. Back, "Action taken by the Pennsylvania Railroad to eliminate smoke through educational activities and the application of smoke eliminating appurtenances to locomotives," *Proceedings, SPAA,* 1947, 105-110.

41. William Christy, commenting in discussion after paper by Sumner B. Ely, "Steam-air jet application to locomotives," *Proceedings, SPAA,* 1944, 87. See also William G. Christy, "The human side of smoke abatement," *Mechanical Engineering* (June, 1933), 350.

42. Alfred W. Bruce, *The Steam Locomotive in America: Its Development in the Twentieth Century* (New York, 1952), 387-393; Harold Barger, *The Transportation Industries, 1889-1946: A Study of Output, Employment, and Productivity* (New York, 1951), 104-105.

43. Wright, "Railroad smoke abatement," 28; Bruce, *The Steam Locomotive,* 387-388.

44. For discussions of the rate of innovation in the railroad industry, see Edwin Mansfield, "Innovation and technical change in the railroad industry," National Bureau of Economic Research, *Transportation Economics* (New York, 1965), 171-197; and Jacob Schmookler, *Invention and Economic Growth* (Cambridge, 1966), 104-130.

45. Bruce, *The Steam Locomotive in America,* 159-163.

46. W. S. Bartholomew, "Locomotive stokers and smoke prevention," *Railway Age Gazette* 65 (Sept. 6, 1918), 451-453.

47. "Pennsylvania locomotive brick arch tests," *Railway Age Gazette* 62 (May 4, 1917), 926, 933-935; Bruce, *The Steam Locomotive,* 149-150.

48. For early development of the jets, see D. F. Crawford, "The abatement of locomotive smoke," *Railway Age Gazette* 55 (Dec. 24, 1913), 763. For criticisms of their performance, see Ely, "Steam-air jet application," 78-82, 85.

49. Harold J. Rose, "BCR developments to prevent smoke," *Proceedings, SPAA,* 1946, 56.

50. Back, "Action taken by the Pennsylvania Railroad," 105; Pittsburgh Department of Public Health, Bureau of Smoke Prevention, *Report on Railroad Smoke Conditions,* 1947, 4.

51. Ibid.

52. Linsky, ed., *A Different Air,* 175-178.

53. M. D. Franey, "Washing locomotive smoke," *Railway Age Gazette* 59 (Sept. 24, 1915), 538-540; Irwin, "Railway smoke abatement," 156; Meller, "Smoke abatement," 1279; Deutch and Radner, "Abating locomotive smoke in Chicago."

54. Irwin, "Smoke abatement," 155-156; O'Connor, *Some Engineering Phases of Pittsburgh's Smoke Problem,* 75.

55. For a discussion of the Pittsburgh law, see J. C. Kuhn and David Stahl, eds., *Public Health Laws of the City of Pittsburgh* (Pittsburgh, 1950), 302-344.

56. Pittsburgh Department of Public Health, Bureau of Smoke Prevention, *Report on Railroad Smoke Conditions* (Pittsburgh, 1949), 1.

57. For the electric locomotive, see Bezilla, *Electric Traction on the Pennsylvania Railroad*; and Condit, *The Pioneer Stage of Railroad Electrification.*

58. Linsky, ed., *A Different Air*, 1046-1050.

59. For the diesel-electric, see Charles F. Foell and M. E. Thompson, *Diesel-Electric Locomotive* (New York, 1946); and Thomas G. Marx, "Technological change and the theory of the firm: the American locomotive industry, 1920-1955," *Business History Review* 50 (Spring, 1976), 4-6.

60. Pittsburgh Department of Public Health, Bureau of Smoke Prevention, *Report* (Pittsburgh, 1954), 20. Dr. Edward Weidlein, the first director of the Allegheny County Air Pollution Control Bureau, told the author that the presidents of the Pittsburgh area railroads had confided to him that they opposed the county law because of pressure from the coal companies. Interview with Dr. Edward Weidlein, Nov. 14, 1978.

61. U.S. Bureau of the Census, *Historical Statistics of the U.S.* (Washington, DC, 1975) Vol. 11, 727-728.

62. See, for instance, Gerald Garvey, *Energy, Ecology, Economy: A Framework for Environmental Policy* (New York, 1972), 33-35.

63. See George M. Hitchcock, Department of Smoke Abatement, Cumberland, Maryland, "Annual Report" (1948), n.p. The B & O had a Department of Fuel Conservation with trained inspectors in fuel economy and smoke abatement. The railroad cooperated to a certain extent with the city's regulations, but there were still violations. In 1951, the city hired Raymond R. Tucker, a noted mechanical engineer and the man responsible for controlling smoke in St. Louis, as a consultant. Tucker reported that "the railroads appeared to be flagrant violators as far as the emission of dense smoke." See Raymond R. Tucker, "Report to the Mayor and City Council of the City of Cumberland on the results of the survey made for the elimination of smoke and dust," (unpublished manuscript in *Raymond R. Tucker Papers*, Washington University Library, St. Louis). See also Charles Z. Heskett to The Honorable Thomas S. Post (Mayor, City of Cumberland), July 24, 1951, ibid. Heskett noted that although the railroads had had three years in which to install over-fire jets, many engines operating in and through Cumberland were not equipped with them.

64. The concept of "Policy-by-least-steps" is that of James E. Krier and Edmund Ursin, in *Pollution & Policy: A Case Essay on California and Federal Experience on Motor Vehicle Air Pollution, 1940-1975* (Berkeley, 1977), 11-12.

65. Marx notes that World War II had a great impact on the development and rate of diffusion of the diesel freight locomotive because it caused high utilization and generated public policy that favored General Motors as a producer over steam locomotive manufacturers. See Marx, "Technological change and the theory of the firm," 6-7.

66. Eugene P. Seskin observes that present policy in regard to automobile emissions has generated a series of modifications and additions to the standard internal combustion engine rather than experiments with different and riskier substitute technologies. See Seskin, "Automobile air pollution policy," 86-87; Lester B. Lave, "Conflicting objectives in regulating the automobile," *Science* 212 (May 22, 1981), 893-899.

PART II

Organizations and Politics

5

Petroleum Refining and Transportation
Oil Companies and Economic Development

AUGUST W. GIEBELHAUS

One of the important issues that has remained from the energy crisis of the mid-1970s is a questioning of the relationship between American citizens and their automobiles.[1] Not only has this marvelous machine stood as a major symbol of Yankee ingenuity and achievement, but social scientists have long commented upon its profound effect on our society and culture. Within the history of technology, "Fordism" represents the chief example of modern mass production, and among students of American business "Sloanism" is consonant with both systematic managerial methods and twentieth-century strategies of mass marketing.[2] Moreover, without the proliferation of the automobile at a price available to middle America, the suburbia of the post-World War II epoch would not have been possible. The economist Robert L. Heilbroner has argued that "to an extraordinary extent our entire economy has become 'mobilized'—which is to say, dependent on the existence of wheeled, self-propelled transportation."[3]

As the automobile has attained this lofty status, its handmaiden has been the modern, vertically integrated petroleum industry. Without the gasoline to fuel its internal combustion engine, the motor car could never have developed the way it has. To be sure, oil shortages related to the cyclical pattern of glut and scarcity in the world's petroleum resources have engendered concern in the past about the industry's ability to meet the insatiable demands of the automobile, but at least until recently these crises have proved to be shortlived. The OPEC embargo of October 1973, combined with major price increases for gasoline and continuing pessimistic estimates of proven petroleum reserves, have now convinced many Americans that our society is on the brink of a major change in our lifestyle. Many now believe that the "auto-industrial age"[4] is about to end.

Yet long before the gasoline lines of the 1970s, several writers had begun to raise doubts about the "car culture" that the automobile and petroleum industries had helped to create. In his irreverent and entertaining book, *The Insolent Chariots* (1958), John Keats explores the marriage metaphor by analyzing Americans and their cars and finds disturbing grounds for divorce. In the following passage, for example, Keats describes a typical family of four on a glorious motoring trip through New England:

> Fred is carsick. Donna and Ralph are fighting and dripping fried clams onto the new seat covers. Edgar and the radiator are approaching the boiling points, Sue Ella's hair is uncoiling on the nape of her neck and her face is livid with fatigue and the radio is blaring away. The announcer is telling them that for that extra go, for that power the jet jockeys know, for the gasoline that keeps your motor clean, see your POWERBLAST dealer today.[5]

Although Keats here casts a plague on both houses—the petroleum as well as the automobile industry—he directs most of his criticism at what he views as Detroit's unethical business practices and the bland, homogeneous culture that they have promoted. From a more scholarly podium in that same year, Lewis Mumford argued that "the American has sacrificed his life as a whole to the motor car, like someone who, demented with passion, wrecks his home in order to lavish his income on a capricious mistress who promises delights he can only occasionally enjoy."[6]

In the economy of petroleum abundance that preceded the crisis of the 1970s, the top twenty oil companies had promoted the car culture through a classic pattern of oligopolistic competition that, with the exception of the occasional local gas war, saw little real comparative price advertising. Rather, companies boasted of their special gasoline additives, friendly service, or clean restrooms, and lured the customer with marketing gimmickry ranging from Green Stamps to free glassware.[7] Although there were periods of relative petroleum scarcity, such as during World War II, the supply of petroleum remained high and the price of gasoline low as new domestic exploration and innovative refinery technology succeeded in keeping pace with demand. The thrust of public policy in the oil industry was to promote conservation and the elimination of waste during periods of excess crude capacity, not the contemporary concern of conserving resources in a time of dangerously depleted national reserves. This chapter will explore the symbiotic relationship that has historically arisen between the petroleum and automobile industries, focusing on ways in which their corporate decisions have encouraged the expansive growth of the modern American automobile culture.

The Birth of the Gasoline Age

In the formative years of the American petroleum industry in the latter nineteenth century, the chief product refined and marketed both here and abroad was not gasoline but "illuminating oil," or kerosene. Except for a limited use in air-gas illuminating machines, gasoline had very little utility, and refiners frequently flared this lighter distillate or allowed it to run off onto the ground or into streams.[8] It was not until the simultaneous invention of the gasoline-powered automobile in 1885 by two Germans, Karl Benz and Gottlieb Daimler, that a viable market would develop for this petroleum product.[9] Indeed, contracting markets for kerosene following the introduction of the Edison incandescent light in 1879 had caused alarm in some quarters of the oil industry. By the turn of the century, the increased electrification of urban areas had caused a significant decline in the demand for kerosene as electric lights began to supplant both oil lamps and manufactured illuminating gas or "town gas" in many homes.[10]

Europeans would continue to pioneer in automotive development for the next several years, but American inventors soon began to play a growing role. The Duryea brothers of Springfield, Massachusetts (Charles E. and J. Frank) are usually credited with inaugurating the automobile age in the United States when their one-cyclinder car appeared in 1893. Successful vehicles developed by Elwood Haynes (1894), Ransom E. Olds (1896), and Henry Ford (1896) soon followed. By the eve of World War I, the oil industry no longer sought a market for gasoline, but worried instead about how it could boost production to meet the demands of the automobile.[11] The revolutionary impact of the mass-produced and relatively inexpensive Ford Model T in 1908 also had a dramatic effect on petroleum marketing. In that year, the total output of the American automobile industry was 65,000 units; but in less than ten years, Ford alone would be manufacturing more than half a million cars annually.[12] During this same decade, gasoline passed kerosene in both volume of production and total value of refined product for the first time.[13]

It was fortuitous when the Spindletop gusher of 1901 on the Texas Gulf Coast inaugurated a new era in the domestic petroleum business.

Supplies of Western crude oil, first from Texas and soon from California and the Midcontinent fields, provided the raw material for the burgeoning gasoline market. But as had been the case since the earliest days of the oil age in Pennsylvania, the flow of crude was uneven, and periodic shortages worried those who had projected a glorious future for the motor car.[14] It was exactly this uncertainty over oil reserves which had led to the creation of the Standard Oil Trust and John D. Rockefeller's attempt to rationalize the industry through a strategy of consolidation decades earlier. The opening of the new Western fields now effected a second major change in the organizational structure of the petroleum industry. The emergence of new, vertically integrated firms such as Texaco, Gulf, and Cities Service— all engaged in the four major functions of producing, refining, transporting, and marketing—and the expansion of older independent firms, such as Pure and Sun, brought about a market erosion of Standard Oil's near-monopoly by the time that the United States Supreme Court ordered its dissolution in 1911.[15] The speed by which non-Standard firms responded to and stimulated further demand for new products, including fuel oil, gasoline, and lubricants, was also a significant factor in their competitive struggles with the Rockefeller empire.[16]

In order to meet increased gasoline demand, oil companies adopted innovative marketing practices. Initially, refiners had sold gasoline, like kerosene before it, to distributors, including grocery stores and hardware dealers. By 1911, however, pumps to dispense gasoline at these retailers were generally available, and by 1914 the drive-in station had appeared in most major marketing areas. It was not long before the industry began to expand into sales of automotive accessories and to provide repair services at wholly-owned or franchised full-service stations, thus heralding the birth of what has become a prominent feature on the American landscape.[17]

The greatest concentration of refineries needed to process the flow of Western crude was on the East Coast, close to large population centers. Tank ships brought crude oil from Gulf ports to refineries which the established Pennsylvania and Ohio-Indiana fields had previously supplied by pipeline.[18] Post-Spindletop companies, led by Texaco and Gulf, had constructed refining capacity in the Beaumont-Houston area, but these plants primarily refined heavy Texas crude into fuel oil. Increased gasoline demand after 1910, however, soon found both large and small Texas refineries manufacturing more gasoline for regional markets. Because profit margins on gasoline were higher than on fuel oil, it was now to the refiner's advantage to process as much of his crude as possible into motor fuel.[19]

Changes in Refining Technology

Firms soon discovered that expanded crude oil supplies were insufficient to meet increased gasoline demand, and they sought ways to stretch the relatively small percentage of gasoline (1.5 to 15 percent, depending on the crude) obtained through straight fractional distillation. Initially, they increased production through incremental improvements in refining equipment, principally the replacement of batch processes with continuous operations. Refiners also broadened the "cut" of gasoline by including in the final product the lighter ends of the kerosene fraction, since the roles had reversed the kerosene now enjoyed a much smaller market. Another new technology that helped was the extraction of "natural" or casinghead gasoline obtained from natural gas. The refiner could blend this light, highly aromatic product to enrich gasoline of poorer quality.[20] By far, however, the most important innovation in petroleum refining developed specifically to meet the need for gasoline was the introduction of thermal pressure cracking by Dr. William Burton of Standard Oil (Indiana) in 1913. Cracking, the literal rearrangement and transformation of hydrocarbon molecules by heat, had been used by refiners for some time in the production of kerosene. By dramatically increasing both the temperature and pressure in his distillation units, Burton found that he could double the amount of gasoline obtained from a given barrel of crude oil.[21]

The success of the patented Burton process stimulated a great competitive race by competing companies to develop their own cracking technologies. Standard Oil (New Jersey), the main lineal descendent of the Rockefeller Trust, specifically established a subsidiary, The Standard Oil Development Company, to develop cracking processes outside the Burton patents, succeeding with Jersey's patented tube and tank process. This research arm was an early example of the institutionalized research and development operations that are so commonplace in corporations today.[22] A number of companies who, like Standard of New Jersey, had patented their own competitive processes, initiated a series of patent infringement suits that threatened chaos in the industry until peace was achieved through the formation of a cooperative pool in 1922, which the press appropriately termed the "patent club."[23] This intraindustry cooperation among the major integrated oil firms was only one of a number of developments indicating that the Standard Oil near-monopoly that had existed prior to 1911 was being replaced by a new oligopoly of major integrated firms. Through its new trade association, the American Petroleum Institute, the industry fostered extensive cooperation on such matters as basic research, standardization, and business-government relations, and it was clear that the top twenty companies played a commanding role in the industry by the end of the 1920s (see Table 5.1).[24]

This oligopolistic trend was also readily apparent in the sister automobile industry in the 1920s. In the new mass market for cars, only the larger firms seemed able to survive. Between 1923 and 1927, the number of firms manufacturing motor vehicles shrunk from 108 to 44 and the "Big Two" of Ford and General Motors clearly dominated the industry, producing more units than all others combined. The consolidation of Dodge into Chrysler in 1928 established the third member of the present-day "Big Three" of General Motors, Ford, and Chrysler.[25] Decisions made by these giant automobile and petroleum companies over the past fifty years have represented on one level a series of rational market responses to the legitimate demands of the public. Through their advertising and promotions, these firms have also consciously shaped the face of the modern automobile culture and the American landscape. The annual model change, with the emphasis on styling rather than safety or economy, and the need for increasingly higher octane fuels have often not been decided with an eye to consumer preference but on the basis of the "bottom line" of short-run profitability.

In discussing the automobile industry's slowness to produce small cars and adopt safety devices and pollution controls in the 1950s, economist Lawrence J. White argued that "it is important to see this lack of response by the Big Three not as a conspiracy 'to do the public in' among a handful of men, but rather as a result of a tight oligopoly that is constantly looking for the joint profit-maximization solution in the auto market."[26] It is in this sense that the present chapter seeks to explain in part how the automobile culture has come to be. Before we can intelligently analyze the present and make future recommendations, it is essential to first clarify the past.

The Problem of Fuel Quality

As automobile registrations multiplied during the 1920s, it became increasingly apparent that gasoline quality as well as quantity was an important concern for both engine designers and the marketing departments of the oil companies. The problem of engine knock had arisen in the years immediately before World War I when refinery increases in the "cut" of the gasoline fraction had resulted in a less volatile, what would later be termed lower octane, gasoline. The problem became greater as engines

TABLE 5.1   Total Assets of Twenty Major Oil Companies, 1924-1938
(In millions of dollars)

Name of Company	1924	1929	1932	1935	1938
1. Standard Oil Co. (New Jersey)	$1,244.9	1,767.4	1,888.0	1,894.9	2,044.6
2. Socony-Vacuum Oil Co., Inc.	406.2	708.4	1,000.5	784.9	919.1
3. Standard Oil Co. (Indiana)	361.5	697.0	693.2	693.5	724.7
4. The Texas Corporation	288.3	609.9	513.8	473.8	605.4
5. Standard Oil Co. of California	352.8	604.7	578.0	575.8	601.1
6. Gulf Oil Corp.	252.0	430.8	435.9	430.2	546.9
7. Shell Union Oil Corp.	257.0	486.5	393.0	357.6	397.5
8. Consolidated Oil Corp.	346.2	400.6	368.0	328.2	357.1
9. Empire Gas & Fuel Co.	301.4	327.1	405.2	398.9	337.1
10. Phillips Petroleum Co.	78.7	145.4	178.4	174.5	226.7
11. Tide Water Associated Oil Co.	211.4	251.4	192.0	182.8	202.8
12. The Atlantic Refining Co.	131.0	166.2	156.6	163.0	199.1
13. The Pure Oil Co.	181.6	195.5	144.6	157.2	180.4
14. Union Oil Co. of California	184.2	211.2	197.7	151.7	166.0
15. Sun Oil Co.	51.1	85.3	96.7	107.1	139.1
16. The Ohio Oil Co.	97.7	110.7	177.3	139.7	138.7
17. Continental Oil Co.	93.9	198.0	87.5	91.7	125.1
18. Standart Oil Co. (Ohio)	42.9	48.7	60.4	56.9	70.5
19. Mid-Continent Petroleum Corp.	79.7	85.9	73.2	60.6	63.7
20. Skelly Oil Co.	39.9	62.8	45.2	46.1	62.0
Total	$5,002.5	7,593.6	7,685.0	7,269.2	8,107.5

Source: *TNEC Hearings,* Part 14-A, p. 7842 (adapted from annual reports to stock-holders and Moody's Manual of Industrials).

with a higher compression-stroke ratio appeared in the early 1920s; they demanded superior fuels in order to perform efficiently. The "technological fix" for knocking (a loud "ping" and subsequent loss of power) was the introduction of tetraethyl lead as a fuel additive. In 1922, a DELCO (General Motors subsidiary) research team headed by the legendary Charles Kettering announced the commercial availability of this successful anti-knock ingredient. To solve the problem of lead oxides fouling valves and other working engine parts, Kettering's researchers blended tetraethyl lead with ethylene dibromide in the patented Ethyl Fluid. This compound combined with lead residue following combustion and was funneled out the exhaust system into the atmosphere.[27]

Yesterday's solution has once again become today's problem, as lead exhaust emissions are currently of acute environmental concern. In light of the present, it is interesting that the only health and safety questions raised at the time related to the risk of lead absorption through the skin in both the manufacturing and distribution processes. After a shaky beginning, in which lead poisoning had caused several deaths at Jersey Standard's Bayway refinery and a Dupont plant, tighter governmental controls and improved safety measures, including the mandatory dyeing of Ethyl fuels red, opened the way for resumed leaded gasoline sales in 1926.[28]

Initially wary of the public's concern for safety in handling Ethyl Fluid, several refiners either ignored the product or sought alternative ways to improve octane while at the same time marketing some leaded product. They could achieve this through blending selected distilled gasoline from high-grade crudes or natural gasoline, but most significantly through raising the pressure and temperature of thermal cracking chambers still further to yield gasolines of higher octane.[29] The Ethyl Corporation, a firm jointly owned by Standard Oil (New Jersey) and General Motors, had introduced an octane scale in 1926 to serve as a standard anti-knock index. The octane number ascribed to a given gasoline was the percentage of 100 octane pure anti-knock iso-octane in a mixture of iso-octane and normal heptane.[30] With modifications over the years, this basic way of labeling gasolines has endured. The fact that Ethyl was a firm controlled by the single biggest gasoline marketer and the nation's largest automobile manufacturer prompted some old-line "independent" oil companies to upgrade their octane through refining rather than "paying tribute" to Ethyl by purchasing their patented anti-knock fluid.[31]

Many companies also marketed a third grade unleaded gasoline advertised as having adequate anti-knock qualities. Among these were the Atlantic Refining Company's "White Flash" brand ("white" gasoline was undyed and lead-free) and Standard of Ohio's "X-70" product. The Sun Oil Company, A Standard Oil (New Jersey) competitor since the 1880s, introduced its "Blue Sunoco" brand in 1927, the "high-powered knockless fuel at no extra price." Dyeing its product blue to differentiate it from the red-dyed "poison" Ethyl fuels, Sun exclusively sold this one brand at a price above that of regular gasolines but below that of "premium" Ethyl fuels. Widespread acceptance of this product encouraged Sun to expand its Eastern marketing territory and to incur the wrath of the Ethyl group of companies with this unusual strategy of price competition.[32]

Under Ethyl leadership, a pricing structure of an unleaded "regular" gasoline and a more expensive "premium" (leaded) fuel had become the dominant market mode. The consumer acceptance of unleaded third grade fuels challenged this situation. In 1931, E. W. Webb, Ethyl Corporation president, wrote to fellow Board member, Irénée duPont (the duPonts were at this time the controlling interest in General Motors) that

> the competition of the standard brands of Sun Oil Company, Atlantic Refining, and Standard of Ohio, during the period they have been marketing 65-75 octane gasoline has been most distressing to Ethyl. The Ethyl sales have decreased very substantially in such areas. Sun is not a customer of ours and does not sell a premium gasoline, but because of the good antiknock quality of their Blue Sunoco they have made it very difficult for their competitors' brands of regular gasoline as well as Ethyl.[33]

Webb recommended that Ethyl use its unique position of connections with General Motors and Standard Oil (New Jersey)—each owned 50 percent of Ethyl—to urge a new strategy. Arguing that "Ethyl sales are going to be hurt unless higher compression engines are brought out," he called for General Motors to manufacture engines with at least a 78 octane requirement.[34]

From a systems engineering perspective, it is obvious that neither engine compression advances nor fuel technology could proceed independently of one another, and Ethyl's intimate relationship with the nation's largest automobile manufacturer and its biggest oil company placed it in the center of the innovation process. The availability of higher octane, anti-knock fuels had made possible the introduction of high compression engines in the mid-1920s, and these advances translated into gains in both mileage and power. Furthermore, consumers demonstrated their appreciation of these new models by their purchases. Yet, was the dramatic increase in automobile performance that resulted really necessary?

TABLE 5.2   Engine Compression Ratios and Gasoline Octane Ratings: 1930-1941

| Year | Engine compression ratios | Gasoline octane ratings* | |
		Regular	Premium
1930		63.0	74.0
1931	5.23	63.0	75.0
1932	5.29	64.0	77.0
1933	5.57	68.0	77.0
1934	5.72	72.0	78.0
1935	5.98	72.0	78.0
1936	6.14	72.0	79.0
1937	6.25	73.3	81.0
1938	6.32	74.5	83.0
1939	6.32	74.5	83.0
1940	6.41	77.9	83.0
1941	6.60	80.4	85.3

*Research method.

Source: John Lawrence Enos, *Petroleum Progress* (Cambridge, MA, 1962), 289. Used by permission of the MIT Press.

The octane rating of regular gasolines sold in 1938 was higher than that of premium brands sold in 1930 (see Table 5.2). It was during this period that Ethyl had changed its marketing so that lead was available to upgrade both regular and premium grades, but the firm continued to be a major force in the establishment of price differentials between the two fuels. Here as elsewhere, it is difficult to differentiate between the chicken and the egg (consumer desire and corporate strategy), but the Ethyl story is an interesting case of where giant oil and giant auto came together to promote larger and more powerful cars. Between 1921 and 1941, the Chevrolet grew from 2500 to 3000 pounds, while its horsepower increased from 46 to 90, and by the mid-1950s the average car weighed 4000 pounds and several Big Three models boasted 200-plus horsepower.[35]

As the great American "gas guzzler" evolved through the 1950s, leaded gasoline was universally sold throughout the United States. Refinery practice had shown clearly that it was far cheaper to raise octane with tetraethyl lead than to achieve necessary standards through advanced cracking. The passage of the Clean Air Act of 1970 and the mandated phasing out of lead for environmental reasons altered this situation dramatically. All automobiles manufactured since 1975 in the United States are equipped with a catalytic converter that is effectively ruined by leaded gasoline.[36] Thus, although a large percentage of automobiles on the road can still burn leaded-regular gasoline, an increasing number cannot. Because there is a decrease in the total gasoline obtained when you raise octane through refining technology, there is a very real economic cost in the EPA ruling on lead. In 1980, the Ethyl Corporation (not tied to either General Motors or Jersey Standard since 1965) petitioned the EPA to loosen the phasedown on leaded gasoline, arguing that some 400,000 barrels of crude could be saved a day by continuing the allowance of 0.8 gram per gallon of lead rather than reducing the maximum to 0.5 gram per gallon.[37] Ethyl failed in its bid, and a glut of world oil in 1980-81 quickly dampened general enthusiasm for the proposal, but it is very likely that the issue will reappear in the face of new shortages.

The Continuing Appetite for Gasoline

Although the economy in general faced serious dislocation during the Great Depression of the 1930s, automobile and gasoline demand remained high, and the large oil companies performed relatively well.[38] When Robert and Helen Lynd returned to "Middletown" to continue their community stratification study in 1935, they were struck by the fact that despite the Depression, "filling stations have become in ten years one of the most prominent physical landmarks."[39] The oil industry did have anxious moments, especially in the early 1930s, when the output from the giant East Texas field caused badly depressed prices for crude. It was the independent Texas producers rather than the large integrated firms who suffered most, however, as the majors were able to balance production losses with continuing profits from the other ends of the business. Moreover, it was in response to the problem of crude overproduction that the industry first demonstrated its considerable political clout. Initially through the Petroleum Code of the National Recovery Administration (NRA), and later through the Connolly Hot Oil Act, Interstate Compact Commission, and state regulatory agencies, the industry effected a cooperative regulatory relationship with government to control production, and thus indirectly the price structure for both crude and refined products.[40]

To supply gasoline from the refinery to bulk storage centers and regional distributors more efficiently, the major firms also introduced product pipeline systems in the 1930s. Jersey Standard had taken the first step when it began to pipe gasoline from its Bayway refinery into Pennsylvania in 1929 by reversing the flow of its old Tuscarora crude oil pipeline. Other firms soon followed suit. Sun Oil's Susquehanna pipeline, completed in 1931, carried Blue Sunoco from its Marcus Hook, Pennsylvania refinery north to Syracuse and west to Cleveland. The Atlantic Refining Company constructed a similar system, and soon the product pipeline became a regular feature of gasoline marketing.[41]

The broad acceptance of tetraethyl lead discussed above had for the most part solved the problem of octane for the industry by the 1930s. For a number of reasons, however, Sun Oil remained the only major integrated firm to persist in marketing only a lead-free product, and some companies continued to sell an unleaded third grade or "white gasoline." Convinced of the superiority of unleaded gasoline, and further prompted by a desire to remain independent of the Ethyl-Jersey Standard group of companies, Sun Oil's managers, members of the Pew family, refused to purchase Ethyl fluid. The continuing octane squeeze brought about by higher compression engines soon forced the Sun to turn to a new technology, the Houdry process of catalytic cracking, to obtain sufficiently high quality fuel without lead.[42]

Invented by a Frenchman, Eugene Houdry, in the 1920s, this process coupled a catalyst phase with conventional thermal cracking units to produce a gasoline of superior octane rating. In an environment of oil glut in the 1930s, Sun was the only firm with sufficient reason to pursue the commercialization of this process. By the end of the decade, Sun and a partner added to the venture later on, Standard Oil of New York (SOCONY), had perfected a successful fixed-bed catalytic process. On the eve of World War II, a Houdry group of companies, led by Sun and SOCONY, were in a position to supply the large quantities of high octane gasoline demanded by motorists and the growing aircraft industry.[43] The intervention of the war, however, found both the Houdry process and its new competitor, the Jersey Standard fluid catalytic cracking process, used primarily for the refining of high octane aviation fuel for the military rather than for the domestic market.[44] If the Allies had floated to victory in World War I on American fuel oil, they flew to victory by 1945 on the wings of American-produced aviation gasoline.

At the war's end, the major petroleum companies were gearing up for what they correctly predicted would be a tremendous automobile boom.[45] The pent-up demand for the family car (the production of models for the home market had ceased in February 1942) launched the

American automobile industry into a period of unprecedented growth that extended well into the 1950s. Coupled with a major expansion of highway construction programs underscored by the Federal Aid [Interstate] Highway Act of 1956, the apogee of the auto-industrial age was achieved.[46] By the mid to late 1950s, automobile sales records reached an all-time high, and for the first time in history there were more cars on the road than there were households in America.[47]

The total demand for petroleum products, the major share of which was gasoline, increased by approximately 80 percent during the period 1945-1959. This demand stimulated a large rush for foreign crude and thus brought about the single biggest change in the petroleum industry structure in the postwar era—its increasingly multinational character.[48] Today, Americans frequently bemoan the high cost of OPEC crude upon which we depend for domestic needs, but in the 1950s, independent American producers fought long and hard to place restrictions on the importation of cheap Middle Eastern oil. In retrospect, it made a great deal of sense in the long run to burn as much foreign oil as possible while conserving our limited domestic reserves, an argument which still holds some validity.

The Automobile and Suburbia

The initial acceleration of suburban growth associated with the automobile had occurred in the 1920s, continuing a process begun during the 1890s by the electric streetcar. There was a slight decline in the rate of movement from the cities during the Depression, and the war held suburbia further in check. But after 1945, America had resumed its march to the suburbs with a vengeance. Metropolitan areas with increasingly spread-out housing tracts and automobile-accessed shopping centers became the norm.[49] For good or ill, none of this would have been possible without the increased availability of automobiles and the fuel to power them. To many social critics of the latter 1970s, the energy crisis seemed to have at least one hidden benefit—the demise of an automobile-based suburban America of mediocre tastes and materialistic values. The collapse of suburbia, it was argued, would result in a widespread return to central cities and urban mass transit accompanied by radical changes in the American lifestyle.

Among the many criticisms of society voiced in the turbulent 1960s was a growing disenchantment with the automobile culture, punctuated by consumerist Ralph Nader's *Unsafe at Any Speed* (1965).[50] Two years after the appearance of Nader's book, Chevrolet sales of its Corvair (the prime target of Nader's attack) dropped from a respectable 209,000 units in 1965 to under 25,000 in 1967.[51] General Motors' displeasure with Nader surfaced in a much-publicized program of personal harassment that has done more to further the career of this consumer advocate than has any of his published work.

Emma Rothchild's *Paradise Lost: The Decline of the Auto-Industrial Age* (1973), investigated a growing list of industry problems including consumer consciousness, environmental awareness, the foreign car invasion, and Detroit's increasingly obsolescent technology, to question the survival of the industry as a continuing leading sector in the economy.[52] In his wide-ranging work, *The Car Culture* (1975), historian James J. Flink penetrated many of the legends that underlie the development of the automobile industry to present a critical view of America on wheels. Concluding that the automobile has had a more profound effect on American culture in the twentieth century than did the frontier of Frederick Jackson Turner's nineteenth century, Flink portrayed this culture as "the age of the superstate serving the supercorporation, with self-interest, greed, and waste being its cardinal and ultimately self-destructive values."[53]

Not all scholars were willing to forsake the positive achievements of the American automobile. A more sympathetic historian of the automobile, John B. Rae, has argued that "unless there is a radical change in our social and economic structure, people will continue to want and use transportation that will give them maximum freedom to move about and to choose where they live, work, or locate their business."[54] In this more optimistic view of technological progress, the automobile continues to represent personal freedom, democratic values, and the mobility historically cherished by Americans.

Students of suburbia, foremost among them urban geographers, have recently suggested a similar interpretation. Americans will take and have already taken steps to become more fuel-efficient with their cars, but there is no hard evidence that they will surrender them.[55] The publicity given to neighborhood revitalization programs in recent years masks the reality that most new residents have moved from other parts of the central cities rather than in from suburbia. New mass transit systems in Washington, Atlanta, Denver, Miami, Baltimore, and Buffalo, designed in the 1970s on an obsolete city-as-hub pattern, have ignored the fact that there remains a trend toward the expanding multinodal suburban metropolis, even in an era of expensive gasoline.[56] Of the urban passenger-miles covered in the United States, 98 percent are still by private automobile. Both the

National Academy of Sciences' study, *Energy in Transition, 1985-2010,* and Resources for the Future, Inc.'s *Energy in America's Future* support the continued use of buses, van pools, and car pools over capital-intensive, fixed-rail transit systems that in reality save little energy over automobiles.[57] Despite the aesthetic and emotional arguments that have been mustered against suburbia, there is every indication that it will continue to exist in somewhat modified form, with people increasingly working as well as living outside the center city. The automobile will also have to adapt, but it too appears able to survive through the coming decades.

Automobiles and Oil: Adjustment and Survival

Just as the Big Three automobile manufacturers have belatedly responded to the most recent German and Japanese import challenge with smaller and more fuel-efficient cars, so have the major oil companies attempted to adjust to changing conditions and improve their tainted image. Advocacy advertising led by Mobil Corporation and its aggressive Vice President for Public Affairs, Herbert Schmertz, has tried to minimize the poor image of the huge profits made by the industry in recent years.[58] Arguing the high costs of exploration and the need for investment capital, the majors apparently found a sympathetic ear in the political administration of President Ronald Reagan. Deregulation of domestic crude oil in 1981 rapidly brought about price increases for gasoline that stayed at high levels, even though a relative glut of oil remained on world markets. Traditional patterns of oligopolistic competition—competition in everything but price—continue to characterize the advertising programs of large oil.

The major integrated oil firms have also abandoned much of their traditional opposition to alternative liquid fuels with the realization that continued profits and future longevity may rest on their ability to obtain an interest in these alternative technologies. A bitter opponent of the farm lobby's attempts to promote alcohol fuels in the 1930s, the American Petroleum Institute expressed cautious interest in gasohol in December 1978.[59] In the midst of the phase-out of leaded gasoline discussed above, the oil companies have taken a look at ethanol blended with gasoline as an octane booster as well as gasoline extender. Indeed, the most visible spokesman for gasohol for a time was not a radical farm lobbyist nor a solar-eyed advocate of decentralized renewable energy, but Bob Hope, the television salesman for the Texaco Company. At this writing, however, a temporary glut of world oil and an inability to develop cost-competitive ethanol production technologies have dampened national interest in gasohol.

There has been a similar turnabout by the oil industry in the case of coal liquefaction technology. The oil oligopoly played a major, if not decisive, role in pressuring the Eisenhower administration to dismember the U.S. Bureau of Mines coal hydrogenation project in 1953. Working from captured German technology obtained at the end of World War II, the Bureau had come up with some impressive results at its pilot project in Louisiana, Missouri.[60] Almost all of the majors are presently experimenting with synthetic fuels derived from coal, in many instances with federal government tax dollars.[61] Allen Murry, president of Mobil's marketing and refining division, which has been Department of Energy-funded for its experimental ZSM-5 catalyst synthetic fuel program, summed it up this way: "What's going to happen is if I have a good idea, I'm going to do it myself; if I have a lousy idea, I'm going to get the government to finance it so I don't lose any money."[62] Although it is difficult not to be critical of the cynicism represented here, the oil companies do have a problem with the conflicting political signals emanating from Washington. Why invest millions in the synthetic liquid fuels programs that had been pushed by the Carter administration, when the Reagan administration's lower priority for them and an apparent oversupply of world oil later make the entire project economically unattractive?

Further evidence of the major oil companies' sense of survival is found in the recent diversification strategies that they have followed. Much of this activity has centered in energy-related fields, and the top firms now portray themselves as "energy" rather than oil companies. CONOCO's huge holdings in coal that made its 1981 acquisition by Dupont so crucial, and EXXON's role as a major uranium fuel processor, are only two examples. The oil companies have also moved to cover their options and insure their futures by expanding into numerous non-energy areas, ranging from retail marketing to real estate.[63] The strategies developed by these firms represent rational responses to changing market conditions. These adjustments, formulated by the career managers now at the helm of these corporate giants, are consistent with the policies identified by Alfred Chandler in his Pulitzer Prize-winning study, *The Visible Hand.* The career managers, he found, "favor the long-term stability and growth of these enterprises to those that maximize current profits."[64] In this sense, there is evidence of a fundamental change in corporate philosophy.

Conclusion

Two of the most powerful industries in America, automobiles and oil, have risen to prominence in the twentieth century as the nation embraced the convenience, mobility, and personal freedom represented by the motor car. The evolution of fuel technology has necessarily had to keep pace with innovations in automobile design, as fuel quality as well as fuel quantity threatened to place limits on the automobile's growth at different stages of its history. But aside from short-term cyclical fluctuations in petroleum resources, most of this history has seen an overall abundance of gasoline that has allowed free reign to growth in both industries. Contrary to contemporary concern with high gasoline prices, much of the history of the automobile epoch has been characterized by oil industry struggles to bolster falling prices in the face of new domestic discoveries of crude. Inexpensive gasoline has fueled far more than the automobile itself; it became the lifeblood of a new American culture whose work and recreational habits increasingly gravitated around this independent and flexible mode of transportation.

By the late 1970s, however, predicted oil shortages and higher prices had more than ever convinced Americans that their long association with the automobile might be ending. Most agree that the world's petroleum reserves will eventually become depleted; the only question is when. It is clear that there will be a great deal of oil around for many years to come, at least long enough to forestall the demise of the automobile in the near future, but the days of abundant, cheap gasoline are now over.

Consumers have not radically altered their lifestyles in the face of these economic pressures, but have sought to purchase more fuel-efficient models and to modify their own driving habits. No longer enjoying the economic prosperity of the 1950s, the Big Three auto makers have absorbed dramatic profit losses in recent years, but there is no reason why they cannot rebound with better designed, economical cars able to fight back a second major import invasion. The oil companies have shown a different profit picture. They have accumulated enormous profits, but because of the high cost of doing business, their investment-to-profits ratio is not that impressive. Their diversification strategies and overall economic health have nevertheless assured that they will play a continuing role in patterns of energy use well into the next century. The replacement of the conventional internal combustion engine with electric cars or vehicles powered with fuel cells may see the automobile changed, but not its essential form.[65] If history is any guide to the future, and barring any fundamental change in the political and economic structure of the country, the modern, major integrated oil companies and their partners, the Big Three auto makers, will continue to have a major voice in determining the parameters of the future automobile culture.

NOTES

1. For example, see Lester R. Brown, Christopher Flavin, and Colin Norman, *Running on Empty: The Future of the Automobile in an Oil-Short World* (New York, 1979).

2. Henry Ford's moving assembly line is well known. "Sloanism" here refers to the series of managerial innovations introduced at General Motors in the 1920s by Alfred P. Sloan, Jr. and other professional managers. On Henry Ford and mass production, see John B. Rae, *The American Automobile: A Brief History* (Chicago, 1965), 53-68; and Rae, "The rationalization of production," in Melvin Kranzberg and Carroll W. Pursell, Jr., eds., *Technology in Western Civilization,* Vol. II (New York, 1967), 37-52. On Sloan and modern scientific management at GM, see Alfred D. Chandler, Jr., *Strategy and Structure: Chapters in the History of the American Industrial Enterprise* (Cambridge, MA, 1962), 114-162.

3. Heilbroner, *The Making of Economic Society: Revised for the 1980s* (Englewood Cliffs, NJ, 1980), p. 98.

4. See Emma Rothschild, *Paradise Lost: The Decline of the Auto-Industrial Age* (New York, 1973).

5. Keats, *The Insolent Chariots* (New York, 1958), 18.

6. Mumford, "The highway and the city," in *The Urban Prospect* (New York, 1968), 93. Orginally published in *Architectural Record* (April 1958).

7. For a marketing analysis of this subject, see Fred C. Allvine and James M. Patterson, *Highway Robbery: An Analysis of the Gasoline Crisis* (Bloomington, 1974), especially ch. 1, "Where have all the Green Stamps gone?" and ch. 2, "Competition, conflict, and cooperation in the marketing of gasoline," 1-35.

8. Harold F. Williamson, Ralph L. Andreano, Arnold R. Daum, and Gilbert C. Klose, *The American Petroleum Industry: The Age of Energy, 1899-1959* (Evanston, IL, 1963), 192-195.

9. Rae, *American Automobile,* 7; James J. Flink, *America Adopts the Automobile, 1895-1910* (Cambridge, MA, 1970), 12-15.

10. Williamson et al., *The American Petroleum Industry,* 170-171.

11. Rae, *The America Automobile,* 9; Williamson et al., *The American Petroleum Industry,* 188, 192-195; Flink, *America Adopts the Automobile,* 19.

12. Rae, *The American Automobile,* 62.

13. Williamson et al., *The American Petroleum Industry,* 110-112.

14. Ibid., 19-29; Joseph A Pratt, *The Growth of a Refining Region* (Greenwich, CT, 1980), 33-36.

15. Harold F. Williamson and Ralph L. Andreano, "Competitive structure of the American petroleum industry, 1880-1911," in Editors of *Business History Review, Oil's First Century* (Cambridge, MA, 1960), 71-84; Pratt, *The Growth of a Refining Region*, 33-34; Gerald D. Nash, *United States Oil Policy, 1890-1964* (Pittsburgh, 1968), 8.

16. Williamson et al., *The American Petroleum Industry*, 217.

17. Ibid., 223.

18. Ibid., 180.

19. Pratt, *The Growth of a Refining Region*, 42-50; Henrietta M. Larson and Kenneth Wiggins Porter, *History of Humble Oil & Refining Company* (New York, 1959), 47-50.

20. Williamson et al., *The American Petroleum Industry*, 132-136.

21. Ibid., 136-142; John T. Enos, *Petroleum Progress and Profits* (Cambridge, MA, 1962), 1-59.

22. Chandler, *Strategy and Structure*, 179.

23. Williamson et al., *The American Petroleum Industry*, 150-163, 375-389; see also August W. Giebelhaus, *Business and Government in the Oil Industry: A Case Study of Sun Oil, 1876-1945* (Greenwich, CT, 1980), 69-72.

24. In 1938, the Roosevelt administration launched a major investigation of business consolidation under the auspices of the Temporary National Economic Committee (TNEC). The oil industry was one of those that demonstrated a high degree of consolidation in the form of a "top twenty" group of major, vertically integrated firms. See Roy C. Cook, *Control of the Petroleum Industry by Major Oil Companies*, TNEC Monograph No. 30 (Washington, DC, 1941).

25. Rae, *The American Automobile*, 99-104.

26. Lawrence J. White, *The Automobile Industry since 1945* (Cambridge, MA, 1971), 260.

27. T. A. Boyd, "Pathfinding in fuels and engines," *Society of Automotive Engineering (SAE) Quarterly Transactions* 4 (April 1950), 182-183; Lynwood Bryant, "The problem of knock in gasoline engines," (unpublished manuscript, 1972); Williamson et al., *The American Petroleum Industry*, 409-414; "That day in Dayton," *Ethyl News* (May/June 1959), 37-40.

28. Boyd, "Pathfinding in fuels and engines," 184-189.

29. Paul H. Giddens, *Standard Oil Company (Indiana): Oil Pioneer of the Middle West* (New York, 1955), 292; Rae, *The American Automobile*, 90; Giebelhaus, *Business and Government in the Oil Industry*, 74-75; "Widening sale of ethyl gasoline carries challenge to refiners," *National Petroleum News* 18 (September 22, 1926), 21-23; Gustav Egloff and Jacque C. Morrell, "Cracking Spindletop crude yields gasoline of 45-50 per cent benzol equivalent," *National Petroleum News* 19 (April 17, 1927), 87-90.

30. Rae, *The American Automobile*, 90; Williamson et al., *The American Petroleum Industry*, 414-415.

31. "Sun Oil," *Fortune* (February 1941), 52.

32. Giddens, *Oil Pioneer*, 292; Giebelhaus, *Business and Government in the Oil Industry*, 75-79.

33. E. W. Webb to Irénée duPont, October 19, 1931 and enclosed memo of October 7, 1931, *Papers of Irénée duPont*, Eleutherian Mills Historical Library, Greenville, Wilmington Delaware, File VC 25.

34. Ibid.

35. Eugene Jaderquist, "The horsepower race," *The Atlantic Monthly* (June 1954), 56-58; George R. Leighton and Joseph L. Nicholson, "Has the automobile a future?" *Harper's Magazine* (June 1942), 68, 72.

36. "Catalytic converters and sulfur emission: the dangers of legislating technology," *Motor Trend* (June 1975), 13.

37. George H. Unzelman, "Conservation via antiknocks–lowest cost crude." Presented at the fall meeting of the Pacific Energy Association, October 4-5, 1979; "Fuels and fuel additives: petition to revise lead phasedown regulations," *Federal Register* 45 (October 7, 1980).

38. Robert Sobel, *The Age of Giant Corporations: A Microeconomic History of American Business, 1914-1970* (Westport, CT, 1972), 122-128; *Annual Report of the Sun Oil Company* (Philadelphia, 1930, 1931, 1936, 1938).

39. Robert S. Lynd and Helen M. Lynd, *Middletown in Transition: A Study in Cultural Conflicts* (New York, 1937), 265-266.

40. The most concise discussion of these developments in business government relations in the oil industry in the 1930s is found in Nash, *United States Policy*, 128-156.

41. Arthur M. Johnson, *Petroleum Pipelines and Public Policy, 1906-1959* (Cambridge, MA, 1967), 255; Henrietta M. Larson, Evelyn H. Knowlton, and Charles S. Popple, *History of Standard Oil (New Jersey): New Horizons, 1927-1950* (New York, 1971), 233; "History and growth of pipelines," *Our Sun* (Sun Oil Company Magazine) 3 (1936), 17.

42. Giebelhaus, *Business and Government in the Oil Industry*, 170-178.

43. Ibid., 178-191.

44. Ibid., 190-192, 249-250; Enos, *Petroleum Progress and Profits*, 148-154.

45. *Board Minutes of the Sun Oil Company (New Jersey)*, Office of the Assistant Secretary, Sun Company, Radnor, Pennsylvania, May 23, 1944, Minute Book #7, 268; September 5, 1945, Minute Book #8, 54; "Blue Sunoco dynafuel," *Our Sun* 11 (November 1945), 1-2.

46. James J. Flink, *The Car Culture* (Cambridge, MA, 1975), 189-190; John B. Rae, *The Road and The Car in American Life* (Cambridge, MA 1971), 187-194. For a more detailed study of the Federal Aid [Interstate] Highway Act of 1956, see Mark H. Rose, *Interstate: Express Highway Politics, 1941-1956* (Lawrence, KS, 1979), especially 69-94.

47. "Detroit enters new competitive year with its 1960 models," *Business Week* (August 8, 1959), 62, 71-72.

48. Williamson et al., *The American Petroleum Industry*, 805, 815-821. For a more critical examination of these international developments, see Benjamin Schwadran, *The Middle East, Oil and the Great Powers* (New York, 1955); Michael Tanzer, *The Political Economy of International Oil and the Underdeveloped Countries* (Boston, 1969); and Anthony Sampson, *The Seven Sisters* (New York, 1975).

49. Rae, *The Road and the Car*, 225-228.

50. Nader, *Unsafe at Any Speed: The Designed-in Dangers of the American Automobile* (New York, 1965).

51. White, *The Automobile Industry Since 1945*, 45.

52. Rothschild, *Paradise Lost*, 3-25.

53. Flink, *The Car Culture*, 233.

54. Rae, *The Road and the Car,* 372.

55. Peter O. Muller, "Suburbs geared for higher gas prices," *Philadelphia Bulletin* (December 23, 1979), 5; "Scholars take optimistic view of energy crisis," New York Times (July 5, 1979), B7.

56. Peter O. Muller, *Contemporary Suburban America* (New York, 1981), 1-17, 175-179.

57. National Academy of Sciences, *Energy in Transition, 1985-2010,* Final Report of the Committee on Nuclear and Alternative Energy Systems, National Research Council (San Francisco, 1980), 89-90; Sam H. Schurr, Joel Darmstadter, Harry Perry, William Ramsay, and Milton Russell, *Energy in America's Future: The Choices Before Us* (Baltimore, 1979), 150-152.

58. "Industry fights back: the debate over advocacy advertising," *Saturday Review* (January 1, 1978), 20-24.

59. See August W. Giebelhaus, "Farming for fuel: the alcohol motor fuel movement of the 1930s," *Agricultural History* 54 (January 1980), 173-184; and Giebelhaus, "Resistance to long-term energy transition: the case of power alcohol in the 1930s," in Lewis J. Perelman, August W. Giebelhaus, and Michael D. Yokell, eds., *Energy Transitions: Long-Term Perspectives* (Boulder, CO, 1981), 35-63. The change in posture by the API is reported in *Energy Resources & Technology* 6 (December 8, 1978), 483-484.

60. See Arnold Krammer, "An attempt at transition: the Bureau of Mines synthetic fuel project at Louisiana, Missouri," in Perelman et al., eds., *Energy Transitions,* 65-107; Krammer, "Technology transfer as war booty: the U.S. technical oil mission to Europe, 1945," *Technology and Culture* 22 (January 1981), 68-103; and Richard H. K. Vietor, "The synthetic liquid fuels program: energy politics in the Truman era," *Business History Review* 54 (Spring 1980), 1-34.

61. "A desperate search for synthetic fuels," *Business Week* (July 30, 1979), 53-54: *Solvent Refined Coal-II: Turning Coal into Clean Energy* (Pittsburgh, 1980).

62. Berkeley Bedell, "Mobil—put up or shut up," *Common Cause* (April 1981), 6.

63. For a critical discussion of developments in the oil industry during the 1970s, see Norman Medvin, *The Energy Cartel: Who Runs the American Oil Industry?* (New York, 1974). Although an increasing amount of oil industry profits has been reinvested in exploration and drilling, there is still much criticism of the fact that these companies have used much of their financial clout to acquire new properties, many of them outside of the energy field (see "Where oil firms are putting their profits," *U.S. News and World Report* [February 11, 1980], 67).

64. Chandler, *The Visible Hand: The Managerial Revolution in American Business* (Cambridge, MA, 1977), 10.

65. See David Gordon Wilson, "Alternative automobile engines," *Scientific American* (July 1978), 39-49.

6

Oil and Public Opinion

The American Petroleum Institute in the 1920s

JOSEPH A. PRATT

In the years between World War I and the onset of the Great Depression, leaders of the American petroleum industry developed several important new methods for influencing the public standing and political influence of their industry. The American Petroleum Institute (API), the major trade association of the oil industry,[1] took a leading role in coordinating industry-wide efforts to understand and shape the "external environment" of oil.[2] The API pioneered in collecting statistics on the overall operations of the industry, lobbying for the industry as a whole before various government officials, and organizing national public relations campaigns to improve the image of the industry. Its efforts dramatically altered the position of the industry in public policy debates by establishing channels of influence through which oil men could exert systematic and sustained pressure—at least on those issues about which there was general agreement within the industry. In the 1920s, the API helped alter the basic stance of its industry in business-government relations. Instead of waiting for political attacks and then responding as had been the case before World War I, the industry learned to anticipate its political needs and to pursue them with a variety of new techniques.

For most of its history before World War I, the petroleum industry followed the lead of Standard Oil of New Jersey, which largely ignored the functions now generally organized under the headings of public and governmental affairs.[3] In the new era after the war, however, the industry recognized its need to understand and, if possible, control the impact of changes in its external environment. In an uncertain and at times threatening political climate, many oil men sought to improve the public and political standing of their industry in a systematic manner unprecedented before the war. The API became the primary vehicle for these efforts to manage the industry's external environment, and it sponsored broad, industry-wide initiatives to explain the industry's views to the government and to the general public in the 1920s.

Robert Welch originally organized the primary external affairs functions undertaken by the API in its Department of Publicity and Statistics, which was created in September 1920. By collecting data about the oil industry and presenting it to the government in easily understood and readily available form, this department laid the foundation on which the API subsequently built its reputation as the central source of information about petroleum. Amid the rapid expansion of such activities in the mid-1920s, the API created a Public Relations Department separate from the Department of Statistics. Through these two departments and a Washington-based Governmental Affairs office, the API worked with its members and with other oil and gas trade associations to contain political challenges to the industry's welfare and to foster a more favorable image for an industry long hampered by public mistrust.[4]

The heart of the API's external affairs work was the collecting and disseminating of statistics about the operations of the petroleum industry. Such statistical services were a standard activity for most trade associations in the 1920s, but the API's efforts went beyond those of most other associations. By making the collection of statistics one of its major tasks, the API filled important gaps in the information about oil available to business and to government. The near void of systematic information about petroleum before the creation of the API reflected fundamental changes that had transformed the industry after the turn of the twentieth century. Until 1911, only eight years before the creation of the API, the industry had been sharply divided between Standard Oil and the "independent" companies, with little exchange of information between the two factions. The dissolution of Standard by the Supreme Court in 1911 further fragmented the industry, breaking up the one institution previously capable of collecting statistics about a large percentage of the oil business. At the same time, dramatic changes in the volume and type of petroleum products heightened the need for better information about the supply and demand for petroleum.[5]

The mobilization effort in World War I clearly revealed the inadequacies of existing information about the oil industry. At the beginning of the war, the United States Bureau of Mines and the Geological Survey conducted a joint study on the oil industry's ability to meet the growing demands generated by the Allied dependence on American oil. In completing this survey, the government agencies relied primarily on their own previous, less than comprehensive efforts to collect data on oil production and refining. The Geological Survey had long published annual statistics of oil production as part of a series entitled "Mineral Resources of the United States." The Bureau of Mines was just beginning to collect and publish a monthly summary of refinery statistics. Both sets of figures were compiled from regular reports required by law of individual companies. Although comprehensive in their coverage of refiners and producers, these reports did not cover other important aspects of the oil industry's operations, and they were seldom available soon enough to be of much use in coordinating the operations of the oil industry.[6]

To meet its need for quicker access to more detailed information, the fuel administration appointed as Chief Statistician Frank Silsbee, who had worked for Union Oil of California before the war. In soliciting Silsbee's assistance, the director of the oil division urged him to "develop a system that would meet all needs" because "since [the] dissolution of Standard these figures have not been kept."[7] On his arrival at his new job, Silsbee quickly encountered what he later called "the non-existence in Washington of competent and coordinated petroleum statistics," and he turned for assistance to his colleagues in the industry, as organized through the National Petroleum War Service Committee. After overcoming the resistance of several companies, Silsbee succeeded in compiling national figures on petroleum production, refining, and distribution that were vital to the smooth supply of oil to the battlefields of Europe. Silsbee set an important precedent that continued throughout the war by "recognizing the point of the ownership of the statistics . . . as resting in the hands of the National Petroleum War Service Committee" and "taking no action that would have the effect of attaching this work as a permanent feature to any government agency."[8] While helping the oil division coordinate the war effort, he thus began teaching oil men the utility of detailed statistics about their industry.

After the war, Robert Welch, who had collected statistics for several regional trade associations in the oil industry before taking over the direction of the API, aggressively pushed the newly organized API into the void created by the dismantling of the federal fuel administration's statistical services. Several prominent directors of the API pushed back. Even amid the enforced cooperation of war, Silsbee had encountered problems in collecting information about the refining and pipeline operations of

several companies.[9] The end of hostilities further weakened the cooperative spirit of many company executives. Some feared that the collection of
detailed information about the industry would open the API to anti-trust
prosecution; others feared that such statistics would inevitably affect the
sale of their stock. But the most common objection was that information
supplied to the API might somehow find its way into the hands of
competitors. Welch quieted the first concern by proclaiming at every
opportunity that the API would have absolutely nothing to do with data
on prices. Experience quickly dissipated the second fear. However, concern about the possible competitive uses of statistics remained strong
enough to hamper Welch's efforts to increase the quality and quantity of
statistics published by the API. The dispute over the institute's proper role
in this area climaxed in a public confrontation between Welch and Robert
Stewart, the president of Standard of Indiana, with the two men almost
coming to blows during a meeting of the API.[10]

Despite such determined opposition from powerful individuals within
the American Petroleum Institute, Welch did not back away from his
commitment to collecting statistics. Indeed, when the directors named him
General Secretary, they assured that this function would be a major
undertaking of the API. Welch's passion for statistical information had
been evident before World War I in his work for two organizations of
independent oil men, the Western Oil Jobbers' Association and the Western Petroleum Refiners' Association, and during the war in his work on the
Statistical Committee of the National Petroleum War Service Committee.
He reaffirmed this passion in his first major address to the API, asserting
that "the collection, study, and dissemination of oil statistics and facts
ought to be one of the great objectives of the American Petroleum
Institute."[11] Welch felt that accurate information about the oil industry
would dispel a legacy of misunderstanding inherited from the era of
Standard Oil's dominance. In addition, he hoped that good data on
fundamental conditions of supply and demand would help to break the
traditional cycle of boom and bust that had plagued the oil industry.
Finally, Welch strongly believed that the API could use statistics to
respond to assaults on the oil industry by misguided and misinformed
critics:

> I state it as a fundamental principle that no Industry should permit
> any other agency to give out information concerning the industry
> itself without the Industry being in a position to check up on the

accuracy of the statements, no matter by whom they are made. If a Statistical Department is established by the Institute it should be its purpose to gain a reputation of being so deathly accurate in its work that it would command universal respect and confidence.[12]

Welch's personal quest to gain acceptance for the statistics services of the API ended with his death in 1929, but by that time the API had established its reputation as the most important source of up-to-date information about the American oil industry.

Welch's most persuasive argument in converting skeptics in the industry to join his crusade to develop the API's statistical capacities was his personal pledge that the information submitted to the API would be treated as strictly confidential. Publishing only aggregate figures, the API staff scrupulously avoided disclosing statistics from individual companies. Welch even used a coding system so that his staff could compile composite data without knowing the name of the company whose figures they were adding into the total. No officer of the API, including the president, had access to the submittals of individual companies. Extreme care in handling this proprietary information paid quick dividends. As experience proved the trustworthiness of the procedures and of the staff the API employed to collect statistics, industry cooperation steadily increased.

Welch wanted timely information above all else, and he sought to capitalize on the API's close connections to the oil industry to avoid delays. In collecting figures on production, for example, he made use of a long-standing informal network of information in the oil fields: the "scouts" traditionally employed at an estimated annual cost of one million dollars by producers in large fields to collect confidential information on the activities of rivals. Gaining the cooperation of the scouts was not difficult, since they generally provided data about competing firms, not about their own employers. Their weekly telegraphic reports gave the API a dependable and detailed source from which to compile weekly estimates of production in each major oil field that were published in an API *Bulletin* and sent to all members within three or four days of the original reports. The accuracy of these figures was checked by comparing the estimates of various scouts active in the same fields, and further tested when the Geological Survey published its official figures several months later. As it gained experience in using the scouts' estimates, the API established a reputation for publishing the nation's most current and most accurate estimates of production.[13]

Refinery statistics proved more difficult to collect. In February 1922, the API's *Bulletin* offered the following plea:

> In the near future it is hoped that the refiners of the country will offer to cooperate in such a manner as to enable us to give a reasonably full statistical table showing the condition of the industry from week to week. Do you want this service?[14]

Despite the repetition of such appeals in subsequent *Bulletins,* in Welch's personal correspondence with oil executives, and in several presidential addresses at the API's annual conventions, weekly refining statistics did not appear until 1929. Throughout the 1920s, the API released the most complete information available to it on refining. Monthly statistics on changes in refinery stocks—published only two weeks after the end of the month—appeared regularly in the *Bulletin* after 1922. These figures initially included approximately 55 percent of the national refining capacity. But during the next five years, the monthly refinery statistics edged up to approximately 82 percent of the total capacity east of California. Because these figures revealed much about the production and movement of the basic refined products, they could be used by the individual refiner to better understand his position in the market. Indeed, so useful were up-to-date refining statistics that the president of the API hailed the advent of the weekly series in 1929 as "the most valuable thing statistically the Institute has ever done."[15]

Such a statement covered a lot of ground, for by 1929 the API had become involved in the publication of a wide array of information on many aspects of the industry other than production and refining. Drawing from its own sources as well as from statistics gathered by various government agencies, the API regularly published information on oil consumption by railroads, vessels, and public utilities, imports and exports of petroleum products, the consumption of gasoline and kerosene by state, drilling activities, and receipts of California oil at Atlantic and Gulf ports. As both a tabulator of some statistics and a clearing-house for others, the API fostered a revolution in the availability of information about the petroleum industry. The regular publication of its statistics in tabular form in the API's *Bulletin* and in the oil trade journals fulfilled Welch's desire to "show the fundamental facts relative to the petroleum industry in such a manner as to make it easy to interpret the relationship of the supply and the demand."[16]

Of course, the interpretation of the facts was just as important as their collection, since even the most comprehensive statistics often support different and even contradictory arguments. The API's statistics on conditions within the industry proved useful to individual oil companies because they allowed each to place its own operations in the context of industry-wide trends. They also proved invaluable to the industry as a whole in testifying on fundamental facts about oil before government agencies and Congress. Indeed, by the end of the 1920s, the API's investment in collecting information about the industry had already paid handsome dividends in the form of greatly increased input into the political decision-making process.

In sharp contrast to the decades before the creation of the API, public officials learned to expect expert presentations from oil industry spokesmen in the 1920s. When, for example, the Federal Trade Commission launched an investigation of oil prices and profits after World War I, Welch immediately offered the fledgling institute's services. Welch testified at great length about the "fundamental conditions" in the industry. His fact-filled presentation sought to prove that postwar price hikes were reasonable in light of changing conditions in the industry, and this opinion found support in the testimony of several other leading oil men. Welch again gave detailed statistical testimony two years later before the Senate Committee on Manufactures, which Senator Robert LaFollette used to present his case for a renewed anti-trust campaign in the oil industry. Subsequent FTC investigations and congressional hearings on water pollution throughout the 1920s also heard well-documented presentations by API spokesmen.[17]

Probably the API's most controversial effort to use statistics drawn from its member companies to influence public policy involved the Federal Oil Conservation Board (FOCB), an interdepartmental agency created in 1924 in response to fears of an impending oil shortage. This board was an advisory body with a mandate to investigate conditions in the oil industry, and the API became one of its major sources of information. The Institute's initial response to the creation of the Federal Oil Conservation Board was to appoint a committee of eleven of its directors to report on the reserves of oil available to the nation. The committee's conclusions that reserves were sufficient to supply America's needs and that the lack of significant waste in the industry made government conservation efforts unnecessary raised a chorus of protests from within the industry, from outside critics, and even from dissenters within the API. To present its conclusions, the API went outside the industry to secure the service of the renowned Charles Evans Hughes, former candidate for president and retired Chief Justice of the Supreme Court. Despite the protests encouraged by its initial report to the Federal Oil Conservation Board, the API continued to present forceful and detailed information to the board until its dissolution in 1933. As with its testimony before other agencies, the overall impact of the API submittals to the Federal Oil Conservation Board is impossible to determine. But the quality of the information available to the API through its members, the institute's growing reputation for "deathly accuracy," and the array of authoritative expert witnesses available to the institute made it a formidable advocate of the oil industry's position on matters of public policy.[18]

The API also undertook sophisticated lobbying through its Washington office. The original charter of the API had called for the establishment of its headquarters in Washington, but New York was subsequently chosen, in part because "if located in Washington, the Institute would be misrepresented as an organization intended primarily to influence legislation to exert pressure on government."[19] Instead, the institute created a governmental affairs office in Washington and retained as its head Fayette Dow, a former attorney for the Interstate Commerce Commission, who also represented several other oil trade associations in Washington. Much of Dow's original work was on petroleum freight rate and pipeline rate cases before the Interstate Commerce Commission and testimony on tax legislation before the House Ways and Means Committee and the Senate Finance Committee. But the steady increase in regulatory activity affecting the oil industry in the 1920s and 1930s expaned the responsibilities of the Washington office, which became, in Dow's words, "sort of an industry clearing house" where government agencies could call for information. Dow saw his function as exposing government officials to the oil industry's perspective on specific issues. He worked hard to establish a reputation for honesty and accuracy so that government agencies would usually accept his information "without question," whether it was presented in the form of written testimony or off-the-record conferences with officials. In short, Dow acted as a modern lobbyist, seeking to influence legislation and regulatory policy through organized and documented presentations of his industry's position to the key officials who determined policy.[20]

The API's ability to present the best available information about the oil industry guaranteed its spokesmen ready access to public officials. Although API officials lobbied effectively during the 1920s, their direct access to government policy makers probably peaked between 1933 through 1935, when the API transferred much of its statistical division from New York to Washington to help administer the National Recovery Administration oil code.[21] Welch's judgment of the importance of statistics thus proved accurate. As the API organized previously fragmentary information about oil into a systematic, accurate, and comprehensive portrait of conditions in the industry, it greatly enhanced its authority and ultimately its influence over public policy. The API's stated policy from the beginning of its statistical activity was to discontinue the collection of any information that became available in timely and accurate form from other sources. In the 1920s, however, the government's underdeveloped capabilities in this area made such a policy largely irrelevant, and a tradition of public sector reliance on the API for many petroleum statistics thus began in this era.

In the early 1920s, public relations was the neglected other half of the API's Publicity and Statistical Department. Robert Welch felt strongly that good statistical work made public relations unnecessary; straightforward facts, not "P.R.," would educate the public about the oil industry. Others, notably J. Howard Pew of Sun Oil, disagreed, voicing "no enthusiasm" for statistical work and urging instead the organization of "a Publicity Committee, whose duties it will be to educate the public, first as to the great benefits to be derived from each of the products manufactured from mineral oils, and second, that the prices at which these products are sold are exceedingly low as compared with other commodities."[22] Such arguments gained increasing favor among the API's directors, who created a temporary Public Relations Committee in 1924 before establishing a permanent Division of the institute four years later. The early history of this division is an important part of the history of the coming of age of public relations in the oil industry, for the API brought many of the techniques associated with modern public relations to the industry.

The American Petroleum Institute did not, of course, introduce public relations to the industry. That role is generally accorded to Ivy Lee, who worked for John D. Rockefeller and Standard Oil of New Jersey before World War I. During the war, Lee's firm handled several minor publicity matters for the fuel administration and the National Petroleum War Service Committee, and A. C. Bedford sought to "transfer" Lee to the API in its early years. After addressing the board "on the subject of publicity as related to the American Petroleum Institute and then the petroleum industry," Lee worked briefly for the API, but Welch proved uncooperative. In an extraordinary demonstration of his strong opposition to public relations, Welch first ignored Lee and then finally fired him, risking the anger of Bedford, who was at once a patron to Lee, to Welch, and to the API itself. After Lee's departure, Welch continued to focus the attentions of the Publicity and Statistics Committee away from public relations, which he considered pap, and toward what he considered essential—the collection of statistics.[23]

There the matter rested until the mid-1920s, when a series of events left the industry reeling. In the first four years of the API's existence, the Federal Trade Commission and Senator LaFollette conducted highly publicized and highly critical investigations of the oil industry. Then the Teapot Dome scandals broke, dragging the industry's public standing to new depths—and implicating several prominent directors of the API in criminal activities. Against this backdrop of unfavorable publicity, many within the industry saw the need for a vigorous "education campaign" to improve the public's understanding of the oil industry and to shore up its sagging public—and political—image. A leading trade publication, the *Oil and Gas Journal*, took the lead in defending the industry with the publication in March 1924 of an entire issue presenting "The Oil Industry's Answer" to its critics. Stressing the economic and social benefits generated by the oil industry, the *Journal*'s approach foreshadowed that subsequently taken by the API.[24]

Others in the industry followed the lead of the *Oil and Gas Journal*. In the summer of 1924, Standard of New Jersey began a series of "directly educative" advertisements in newspapers throughout its primary marketing regions in the East. These ads drew from "The Oil Industry's Answer" to attempt to explain the functioning of the industry.[25] At the same time, several of the largest regional oil trade associations began to explore two ways of conducting a national publicity campaign of a sort never before attempted by the industry. J. Howard Pew and his cousin, J. Edgar Pew, who was an active member of both the Mid-Continental Oil and Gas Association and the API, took the lead in deflecting such sentiment toward the API. In pressing the case for API leadership on Robert Welch and A. C. Bedford, J. Edgar Pew argued that "this is not a matter for the Standard Oil to handle."[26] Bedford soon agreed that although "individual companies could do effective work in reaching their own customers," general publicity work had to be done by the industry as a whole.[27] Pew had no doubt that "if the Institute does not take some action, something will be done by one or more of these various organizations (the smaller, regionally based oil trade associations) along these lines, that will not be as advisedly carried out as it should be if the Institute took hold of it."[28] In short, Pew felt that public relations was exactly the kind of industry-wide endeavor the API could best coordinate.

While pushing their arguments in meetings with other directors of the institute, the Pews also used their influence to help convince the smaller associations that only a national organization active in all phases of the industry—that is, only the API—could successfully coordinate an effective national publicity campaign. The Pews' arguments prevailed, and in early 1924 the API adopted a resolution calling for the creation of a committee to study this issue. W. N. Davis, who was both a director of the institute and the president of the Mid-Continent Oil and Gas Association, took charge of this joint committee of nine API members and eight representatives of the smaller associations. This "Committee on Education" was given thirty days to prepare a public relations plan, complete with budget, for the approval of the API's board.[29]

During this time, a three-day meeting educated the Committee on Education by exposing them to prominent practitioners of public relations. Speakers included public relations men from the Eastern and Southern Railroad, American Telephone and Telegraph, the Motion Picture Producers' Association, and the National City Bank of New York, representatives of the consulting firms of Ivy Lee and Bruce Barton, and the director of publicity for Herbert Hoover's relief organizations. The committee seemed especially impressed with the public relations programs of the railroads, and they left the conference eager to sell these modern techniques to the API's board. In exploring the world of public relations for the industry as a whole, the Committee on Education fulfilled an important general function of a trade association; it introduced members of the API to new concepts and developments in related industries and professions.[30]

The board of directors agreed with the committee's recommendations, and in December 1924 it created a Public Relations Committee composed of members from both the API and the smaller associations. The board authorized an annual $100,000-per-year budget for three years, with the money to be raised through appeals to the industry. Thus, in order to begin its work, the Public Relations Committee had to pass the litmus test for most new activities sponsored by the API: It had to demonstrate its acceptance within the industry by attracting financing. This proved difficult. Despite strong pleas for support from W. N. Davis and J. Edgar Pew, the regional trade associations that had originally petitioned the API to direct a public relations campaign did not back their call for action with dollars. Instead, the committee came to be supported primarily by the contributions of the large companies that were the backbone of the API.[31]

After a reasonable start in securing pledges of financial support, the committee sought a suitable person to direct its efforts. They found no strong candidates within the industry, since most of the advertising men in the individual companies who had been "brought up with the organization" were considered "ineffectual" in planning a broad publicity campaign.[32] The committee chose instead to "employ some outside talent" to guide the industry's attempt to shed its traditional ineptitude in dealing with the public. After considering several of the men who had addressed the three-day meeting, the committee settled on Judson Welliver, an experienced newspaperman who had served on Warren Harding's White House staff. Welliver proved an excellent choice. He had good connections within the newspaper business, a working knowledge of reporting, and a national reputation from his White House years that gave him a measure of independence from the leadership of the API.

During 1926, Welliver guided the API's Public Relations Committee into several "more or less experimental" ventures in reaching the public with information about oil. Welliver specialized in preparing and widely distributing general information about the oil industry's role in the economic life of the nation. He did this in subtle and persuasive ways. An excellent example of his work was a newspaper article with the headline "A Billion Dollars in Tolls Yearly Provide Modern Highways," which appeared in an estimated 300 daily papers and 3000 weeklies, with a total circulation of approximately 15 million. This attractive feature story had been prepared by Welliver's staff, who contacted state highway departments throughout the nation to compile statistics on gasoline taxes and on road improvements. They then organized this information as if it had originated in an interview with the Chief of the United States Bureau of Public Roads. After being sent to the chief for his approval, the article was made available to newspapers in a finished form that could be published as received. The end product was an engaging story that summarized for the reader the central role of petroleum in the dawning age of the automobile, reminded him of the mobility and freedom provided by the gasoline-powered car, and gently warned of the growing burden on drivers caused by steadily rising gasoline taxes. All this reached the reader from the lips of a government official, with no clear indication of the API's role in preparing the "interview."[33] Similar API releases featured interviews with an official from the Bureau of Mines about the nation's oil supply and a discussion by a retired admiral of the strategic importance of oil for modern naval warfare. These articles embodied Welliver's conception of public relations as a long-run effort to build a more favorable public attitude toward the oil industry.

Welliver's outpouring of publicity for the oil industry did not generate enthusiastic support within the API. Welch remained unshaken in his lack of regard for such work. It seems likely that others in the industry also remained skeptical of Welliver's indirect approach. Pew summed up the frustrations of Welliver and those who supported his work with the bitter comment that "apparently there are a lot of narrow-minded men in the Institute who are either opposed to or jealous of Welliver and his achievements."[34] As was to be expected in the early years of a new organization, disagreements about proper goals and methods hampered the API's efforts to define its role in this new area. Disputes among strong-willed oil executives accustomed to imposing their views within their own organizations were especially difficult to resolve. One victim of such disputes was Judson Welliver, who resigned his job when the $100,000-per-year budget he had been promised could not be raised from the industry.

In his place, the API appointed Leonard Fanning, an insider with broad experience. Fanning had worked for the *Oil Trade Journal* as financial editor, for the Publicity and Statistics Department of the API, and for the *Oil and Gas Journal* before joining the API's Public Relations Division in 1928. Under Fanning's direction, the division made a subtle turn from the path marked out by Welliver. Fanning continued to release general information about the industry, but he emphasized enhancing the value of the API's public relations work to its member companies. He began to coordinate his division's work with that of the individual companies by having one man in each supporting company designated as the contact person for the API's work. These individuals, who were often high-level advertising men, served as Fanning's consultants while facilitating the distribution of the API's work within their companies. The establishment of a speakers' bureau, the publication of a handbook to aid speakers from the companies and the API in presenting the oil industry's case, the production of special information pamphlets aimed at filling station customers and at stockholders, the making of a film in the oil industry, the development of materials specifically designed for publication in the house organs of the companies, and the publication in 1928 of the first edition of *Petroleum Facts and Figures,* a comprehensive collection of facts and statistics on the oil industry, all moved the Public Relations Division into more direct contact with the companies. Fanning's work sought to reach more specific "publics"—customers, stockholders, and workers—than had the broader efforts of Welliver to reach and educate "the" public.[35]

As was the case with some of the statistical work of the API, another public, the voter, was also targeted for special appeals. In the late 1920s, steadily rising gasoline taxes became the dominant political concern of the API's Public Relations Division. In 1929, the API and the American Automobile Association combined to develop a major publicity campaign against rising taxes on gasoline and against the diversion of these taxes to uses other than road building. The campaign featured widely distributed pamphlets pointing out the magnitude of gas taxes and reminding the public of their rapid rise in the 1920s. One such pamphlet, captioned "Where does my mileage go?," showed a cartoon character labeled "legislature" punching holes in a gas tank to siphon off dollars as another character ran toward him with a bucket labeled "for other uses."[36] As the gas tax and other legislative concerns mounted in the early 1930s, the API created a well-financed, semi-autonomous new organization—The American Petroleum Industries Committee—"to give persistent and active impetus to the efforts of the industry to reduce taxes, to prevent the diversion of the gasoline tax, to stop evasion (of gasoline taxes by "bootleg" dealers), and to correlate the activities of the industry on all legislative matters, national and state."[37] Using state committees under the direction of a central committee, the APIC sought to "permit pooling of the common resources and strengths of the petroleum industry and permit united action on well-coordinated fronts."[38]

Such activities inevitably raised questions among critics of the oil industry about the fine line between "education" and "lobbying" or "propaganda."[39] The most strenuous objections to the API's efforts to present "the facts as the industry sees them" to the public generally came from those who held a different version of the facts and who did not have the same access to public or political opinion as did the well-organized and well-financed API. Indeed, the institute's numerous organizational advantages over its political opponents gave it one of the most powerful voices in the nation on oil-related matters. This marked a sharp reversal from the situation that had existed before the creation of the API, when critics of the industry enjoyed a near monopoly on the supply of publicity and information about oil to the public. The API's public relations work in the 1920s helped place the petroleum industry's perspective forcefully and systematically before the public for the first time.

Its growing prominence as a spokesman for the industry led some critics to charge that the API was simply a public relations instrument for the large oil companies.[40] In fact, it was that and much more. Welch had misjudged the coming role of public relations, but he had correctly recognized the difference between the two functions originally placed together in the Publicity and Statistics Department. Statistics were useful in a variety of activities, from coordinating the economic decisions of the individual oil companies, to presenting the industry's point of view in governmental arenas, to more general efforts to alter the climate of public opinion toward the industry. World War I taught leaders of the institute that information about the fundamental conditions in the oil industry was essential in a political economy becoming increasingly dependent on petroleum for energy and national defense. On the other hand, public relations seemed essential to many oil men who feared that unfavorable public opinion might encourage greater government involvement in their industry. The collection and presentation of information about oil in the form of detailed statistics, testimony to government agencies and to Congress, and public relations campaigns all became permanent functions of the API as it sought to respond to changes in the external environment of the oil industry.

In confronting and managing such changes for the industry as a whole, the API served as a bridge between private and public interests in the post-World War I era, when important departures in oil policy occurred. As the only organization then capable of coordinating the activities of much of the oil industry, the API became a vital link between the individual oil companies and federal government officials concerned with defining petroleum policy. Of course, it should not be forgotten that the API was not a "neutral" institutional conduit of information and ideas; it was an appendage of the major oil companies. As such, one of its overriding functions was to "educate" government officials and the voting public as to the correctness of the oil industry's views on a range of issues affecting petroleum policy. In the 1920s, its most difficult problem was defining "the oil industry's view" amid diverse pressures from its membership. In subsequent decades, the API would face increasing problems outside the industry as competing sources of information and ideas about petroleum gradually became available.

NOTES

1. The American Petroleum Institute (API) is the major trade association of the American petroleum industry. Founded in 1919, it has attracted a diverse membership which includes small and large oil companies active in all phases of the industry. These large, vertically integrated companies have generally played the leading role in governing and financing the API. For a history of the API from 1919 through the 1950s, see Leonard Fanning, *The Story of the American Petroleum Institute* (New York, 1959).

2. Here, as throughout the chapter, I am using the phrase "the external environment" to include that set of concerns which includes the relationship of the industry to government and the general standing of the industry with the public. Most major oil companies now have specialized organizations to manage "governmental affairs,"

"regulatory affairs," "public relations," "public affairs," or "community affairs." Indeed, many have specialists with separate authority in several of these closely linked areas. In the 1920s, however, the American Petroleum Institute performed many of these functions for the industry as a whole. The early efforts of the API in these areas laid the groundwork for the evolution of more sophisticated programs to shape political and public opinion by the oil industry in subsequent decades.

3. For an account of Standard's belated entry into public relations in the years before its dissolution in 1911, see Ralph and Muriel Hidy, *Pioneering and Big Business* (New York, 1955), 698-708.

4. The real and imagined abuses of the Standard Oil Trust had created a great deal of uneasiness about the power of "Big Oil," and the API encountered this sentiment in its formative years, when critics called it a tool of the Standard Oil interests.

5. These changes are described in detail in Harold Williamson et al., *The Age of Energy* (Evanston, 1963).

6. An unpublished history of the Bureau of Mines is contained in the Records of the Bureau of Mines, Record Group 70, National Archives, Suitland, Maryland.

7. Mark Requa to L. P. St. Clair, February 21, 1918, File 2664 (F. J. Silsbee—personnel), Oil Division-General Files.

8. F. J. Silsbee to Mark Requa, July 8, 1918, File 2664 (Silsbee, F. J.), Oil Division-General Files.

9. For example, see F. J. Silsbee to George S. Davidson, May 13, 1918, File 694 (Davidson, George), Oil Division—General Files.

10. Leonard Fanning, *The Story of the API*, 49.

11. Report of R. L. Welch to the Board of Directors of the API, August 28, 1919. API Board Minutes, API Library, Washington, DC, 36.

12. Ibid., 37.

13. Welch described his methods for assuring the secrecy of information from the member companies to representatives of the Federal Trade Commission in 1927. See, "Minutes of meeting of API, FTC," January 24, 1927, "API, Federal Trade Commission" folder, Box 39, J. Edgar Pew, Vice President files, Sun Oil Collection, Eleutherian Mills Historical Library, Wilmington, Delaware. (This collection will be cited hereafter as Sun Oil Collection.)

14. API *Bulletin* (February 16, 1922), 2. A complete set of these bulletins is available at the API Library, Washington, DC.

15. "What does the Institute do?" an address by E. B. Reeser, December 3, 1929, "American Petroleum Institute—1930" folder, Box 52, Administrative File, General Correspondence, Series 21-A, Sun Oil Collection.

16. API *Bulletin* (March 29, 1922), 1.

17. The preparation and presentation of such testimony became a time-consuming job for Welch. Much of his testimony was published in the *Bulletin,* and it is characterized by a tendency toward overkill; Welch's love of statistics expressed itself in a detailed and even repetitious use of numbers.

18. For an account of the activities of the Federal Oil Conservation Board, see Gerald Nash, *United States Oil Policy, 1890-1964* (Pittsburgh, 1968), 84-95.

19. *API and Its Activities,* Vol. 5, ch. 10, 5 and 6. This study of the API's various activities was made to aid in the reorganizing of the institute in 1930. The Sun Oil Collection contains only a portion of the study. See Box 2, J. Howard Pew, Presidential-Private, Sun Oil Collection.

20. Ibid., 6.

21. *API and Its Activities*, Vol. 4, ch. 7, 6. While in Washington in 1933-1935, the API's statisticians worked with the Planning and Coordination Committee, a committee of oil men that advised the Petroleum Administrative Board on the enforcement of the NRA code in oil. See, for example, Minutes of the Planning and Coordination Committee, October 5, 1933, 10 a.m., Planning and Coordinating Committee Meetings, Records of the National Recovery Administration, Record Group 9, National Archives, Washington, DC.

22. J. Howard Pew to R. L. Welch, August 21, 1919, "API ... Admin. & Organiz ... Organization, Organization Policies, and Activities, Circulars & Correspondence, July-Dec. 1919," File 5995, shelf 9A, API Historical Records, API Library, Washington, DC. For a general history of public relations, see Richard Tedlow, *Keeping the Corporate Image: Public Relations and Business, 1900-1950* (Greenwich, CT: 1979).

23. Leonard Fanning, *The Story of the API*, 60.

24. *Oil and Gas Journal* (March 20, 1924).

25. L. M. Fanning, "How one company is presenting facts about oil to the public," *Oil and Gas Journal* (August 7, 1924), 104.

26. J. Edgar Pew to R. L. Welch, letter dated May 19, 1924, in "Public Relations Committee, API" folder, Box 16, Administrative File-General Correspondence, Series 21-A, Sun Oil Collection.

27. A. C. Bedford to J. Edgar Pew, May 24, 1924, ibid.

28. J. Edgar Pew to J. Howard Pew, May 20, 1924, ibid.

29. For the operations of this committee in greater detail, see ibid.

30. The speeches of each expert and the question and answer sessions after each speech were printed in a booklet prepared for the committee and contained in the folder cited in note 26.

31. J. Edgar Pew to C. C. Herndon, April 30, 1925, "API, 1925" folder in Box 20, Administrative File-General Correspondence, Series 21-A, Sun Oil Collection.

32. J. Edgar Pew to J. Howard Pew, June 3, 1924, in folder cited in footnote 26.

33. Judson Welliver to J. Howard Pew, July 28, 1926, "1926 Public Relations Comm." folder in Box 25, Administrative File-General Correspondence, Series 21-A, Sun Oil Collection. Copies of all of the articles discussed in the text can be found in this folder and the one cited in note 26.

34. J. Howard Pew to J. Edgar Pew, September 7, 1927, "Adm. Gen. API, 1927" folder in Box 25, Administrative File-General Correspondence, Series 21-A, Sun Oil Collection.

35. Leonard Fanning, "Proposed activities for division of public relations for 1928," undated memorandum, "Adm. Gen., 1928, PR Committee, API" folder in Box 35, Administrative File-General Correspondence, Series 21-A, Sun Oil Collection.

36. "Where does my mileage go?" "API Public Relations" folder in Box 42, J. Edgar Pew-Vice Presidential File, Sun Oil Collection.

37. C. B. Ames (president of the API) to J. Howard Pew, December 16, 1932, "Adm. Gen. API, 1932" folder, Box 65, Administrative File-General Correspondence, A-1932, Series 21-A, Sun Oil Collection.

38. B. H. Markham (director, APIC) to J. Howard Pew, January 25, 1933, "Adm. General-API, 1933, APIC, 21-A-37" folder, Box 73, Administrative File-General Correspondence, API-1933, Series 21-A, Sun Oil Collection. See also August Giebel-

haus, *Business and Government in the Oil Industry: A Case Study of Sun Oil, 1876-1945* (Greenwich, CT, 1980), 119-120.

39. The use of this phrase by the public relations staff at the API can be found in *API and Its Activities,* ch. 9. This bound notebook is contained in Box 2, J. Howard Pew-Presidential-Private, Sun Oil Collection.

40. Writing in 1938, for example, one critic asserted that "the American Petroleum Institute early embarked on its practical function as a public relations or propaganda organization." See William Kimnitzer, *Rebirth of Monopoly* (New York, 1938).

7

Federal Management of Fuel Crisis

Between the World Wars

JOHN G. CLARK

Beginning in August 1917 with the passage by Congress of the Food and Fuel Control Act (Lever Act), the role of the federal government in fuel policy formulation has been continuous and, in the long run, expansionist. In the short run, between the two World Wars, for instance, the pervasiveness of the federal presence in fuel management waxed and waned as the government responded to or ignored the discrete needs of particular fuel industries and reacted jerkily to this or that economic crisis. Not surprising, yet requiring some explanation, was the absence of anything remotely resembling a concept of the public interest inherent in fuel resource use. Equally lacking were policy discussions and policy-making decisions which subsumed individual fuels under the broader rubric of energy, and any concrete recognition that even a fuel-by-fuel approach demanded planning on a national, if not an international, scale.

The failure of more holistic strategies toward fuel resources to emerge during the interwar years stemmed from several interwoven factors. While it might be tempting to explain the failure in terms of the relatively undeveloped state of national planning, or of ideologies hostile to federal intervention, neither of these explanations survives careful scrutiny. Important precedents for a comprehensive approach and an impressive body of knowledge about fuel resources had developed since 1917. Ideologies proved mutable, particularly those articulated by such strong industry organizations as the National Coal Association (NCA) and the American Petroleum Institute (API), both of which World War I gave birth to. The NCA and the API represented but two (albeit the most influential) of

135

dozens of fuel associations, each competing for influence over federal policy, and each seeking to exert some leverage over the administration of that policy. The substance of this chapter will revolve around specific fuel crises which developed between the wars and on the interaction between fuel industry interest groups and those public agencies upon which the crises impinged most directly.

World War I demonstrated several truths about fuel resource management: that the voluntaristic mobilization attempted by the Council of National Defense could not work; that a coordinated approach by a central federal agency endowed with sufficient coercive authority could work; that many Americans readily accepted federal intervention when the private sector proved incapable of meeting fuel needs equitably; that many Americans were quite willing to extend the regulatory controls into the post-war period; and, of course, that national security demanded an adequate supply of efficiently distributed fuels.

The United States Fuel Administration (USFA), created by President Wilson to implement the Lever Act, bore the essential responsibilities. Its mission encompassed the fixing of mine-mouth coal prices and dealer margins, readjusting the geographic distribution of coal, and reordering allocation among consumers. Assisting, and in certain cases superseding, the fuel agency in fulfilling its responsibilities were several other federal agencies, most notably the War Industries Board, the United States Railroad Administration (USRA), and the Capital Issues Committee.[1]

Fuel distribution was perhaps the most essential of the USFA's tasks. Until Wilson nationalized the railroads on December 26, 1917, placing them under the jurisdiction of the USRA, the fuel situation in the nation had steadily deteriorated. Price-fixing and other USFA strategies to assure fuel supplies meant nothing if fuels failed to move from mine to user. The railroads, under private management, were not moving goods expeditiously, and the transportation system slid inexorably toward paralysis during the last months of 1917.[2]

Between January 1, 1918 and April 1, 1918, the USFA and the USRA formulated a national fuel distribution policy, dramatically prefaced on January 17, 1918 by a USFA-USRA order that closed virtually all industries and businesses for five consecutive days in order to clear up railroad congestion.[3] Then, on April 1, 1918, the USFA implemented a nationwide distribution and allocation scheme based on a zone system and designed to prohibit unnecessary traffic and to divert rolling stock and coal eastward toward the major war industries, ports, and population centers on the Atlantic coast.[4] Allocation policies established in March and April functioned in tandem with the zoning and affected oil as well as coal.

The zone system, roundly criticized by various interests and parts of the country, nevertheless produced the desired results. Zoning assured eastern residents a monopoly of available anthracite supplies, and in mandating permissible shipping patterns siphoned transportation, coal, and oil from the Trans-Mississippi West into the eastern industrial area. The distribution pattern achieved by zoning represented a more serious invasion of the private enterprise system than did price controls. Zoning erected impassable barriers between groups of states.

Still, if credibility is granted to innumerable letters received by local and national USFA officials, many Americans would have accepted even more severe restrictions on fuel use and did support the continuance of restrictions after the Armistice. But business and industry successfully urged immediate disengagement, even though the National Retail Coal Merchants Association urged the retention of regulations until April 1919, the beginning of the new coal year.[5] Peace, however, did not bring immediate relief from either real or threatened shortages of fuel.

In 1919 and 1922, coal strikes closed over 70 percent of the nation's bituminous coal-producing capacity and 100 percent of anthracite at a time when coal supplied almost 75 percent of the nation's total energy needs.[6] The strikes combined with inadequate transportation to cause severe hardship in many parts of the country months after their conclusion. The federal government responded to both crises in three ways: by conducting hearings on numerous bills which dealt with various aspects of the coal industry; by authorizing investigations of the coal industry; and by empowering several agencies to deal directly with the problems of coal scarcity.

To manage the coal shortages of 1919-1920, the federal government resurrected the U.S. Fuel Administration and reimposed some of the wartime fuel controls. But the USFA had no authorized personnel, so it delegated authority to the USRA to administer all regulations concerning price, allocation, and distribution. The USRA itself was in the process of liquidation, and powers granted to the Interstate Commerce Commission (ICC) by the Transportation Act of 1920 infringed on areas of USRA responsibility. By 1920, only the ICC possessed authority to manipulate the distribution system. With its new powers, the ICC could declare a fuel emergency (which it did in May 1920), assign priorities in the movement of fuel, relocate empty equipment, delay the loading of unnecessary goods, and act in other ways. It did some of these things, with reluctance, and so inefficiently that massive amounts of coal ended up in the stock-piles of utilities and other large consumers, particularly the railroads, while other consumers barely scraped together sufficient coal for use on a day-to-day basis. Price controls had failed to prevent retail increases of from 50 to 75 percent in many urban markets. Dealers, unafraid of punishment for non-compliance, charged what the market would bear.[7]

Similar ineptness in applying essentially adequate powers attended the even more severe coal shortage crisis of 1922-23. In meeting that emergency, Congress established a new agency, the Federal Fuel Distributor (FFD), granted additional powers to the ICC, and created the United States Coal Commission to study the industry. The FFD had no powers other than moral suasion and was designed to function as a liaison between the ICC, the coal operators and distributors, and state fuel organizations. Congress believed, probably correctly, that in granting the ICC almost blanket powers to order embargoes against carriers and other parties, that the Commission possessed sufficient authority both to moderate coal price increases and to assure equitable and efficient distribution of available fuel supplies. Congress obviously intended that the ICC deny transportation to parties who charged unreasonable prices.[8]

The ICC, however, proved reluctant to use its muscle. Neither it nor the FFD invoked the embargo or price powers. Instead, both agencies relied upon importuning coalmen to act reasonably, a method quite acceptable to coal operators and dealers. Coal distribution rested in the hands of the railroads and states with fuel agencies.[9] Neither the FFD nor the ICC wished to institute a zone system which matched regional productive capacity with regional demand, partly because of an unwillingness to disturb existing competitive relationships, and partly because neither agency possessed the expertise to adapt the wartime system to peacetime needs. Coal price-fixing was similarly beyond the range of the specialized competence of the ICC.

Several reasons may be suggested to explain the ambivalent, inconsistent, and partial responses of the federal government to these severe coal shortages. While Congress did authorize the ICC to exercise broad price and distribution powers, ideological beliefs may have precluded the adoption of World War I strategies to resolve or control peacetime problems. The ICC erroneously believed that the railroads could somehow manage coal distribution and assumed (also erroneously) that coal dealers would exercise restraint in advancing prices. Lacking experience in fuel management, both the ICC and the FFD relied too heavily on the action of individual states. But only one state, Pennsylvania, because of the location of anthracite mines, could actually influence national distribution as well as take care of its own needs. All other states operated in region-wide coal markets over which individual states could exert little influence. Federal intervention in coal also aroused the immediate hostility of the organized coal industry, particularly the National Coal Association. But the coal industry itself suffered from serious internal divisions, a condition exacerbated by coal's deteriorating competitive position relative to other fuels. Coal did not have a single spokesperson, nor were the largest producers nearly so influential as, for instance, the largest oil companies. Leadership at the federal level was lacking. Oil concerns, which I will shortly turn to, preoccupied the Interior. The Federal Trade Commission had been purposefully bypassed by President Wilson when he created the USFA. The ICC could barely handle its freight rate dockets, and most commissioners did not want the authority over fuel which Congress gave them.

As for Congress, it did grant authority. But it was not—and is not—an efficient policy-generating body. Neither did it possess effective oversight mechanisms to exercise some control over semi-autonomous federal agencies. Congress did authorize a comprehensive study of the coal industry, debated several of the dozens of coal industry bills submitted, and held frequent hearings on coal bills and coal industry problems. Although the NCA invariably opposed most of the bills as destructive to the free market economy, congressional inaction might best be attributed to the short-lived nature of particular crises, none of which were caused by a lack of resources in the ground.[10]

While coal crises commanded federal attention between 1919 and 1924, federal concern with oil languished. It was, however, during those years that many individuals within the oil industry and in such agencies as the U.S. Geological Survey and the Bureau of Mines published and publicized gloomy estimates of the nation's oil supply. Beginning in 1915 and continuing through the mid-1920s, domestic crude consumption exceeded domestic crude production by a steadily widening margin. Imports made up the difference. Knowledgeable engineers, geologists, and oil industry executives were speaking in terms of fewer than twenty years of reserve. In 1922, J. E. O'Neal, President of Prairie Oil & Gas Company, foresaw shortages within ten years unless abundant new sources were discovered.[11] Responding to the shortage thesis, in 1924 President Coolidge appointed the Federal Oil Conservation Board (FOCB) and instructed it to formulate methods of safeguarding national security through the conservation of oil. Through the next several years, the FOCB existed at the center of debate over conservation policy and the role of the federal government.

The industrial and political milieu of coal and oil differed substantially. Various factors—spatial location, technology, transportation, organizational structure—explain this divergence. Coal was located in many states, while oil was confined to a few. Markets for coal were essentially local or regional, while national and international markets and sources of supply dominated planning and policy in the oil industry. Thus, such issues as tariffs and import quotas, controversial within oil, were basically irrelevant in coal. The location of the resource created within the oil industry two potentially hostile forces, the oil-producing states and the oil-consuming states, a distinction which was not germane to the rhetoric and practice of coal politics. During the 1920s and 1930s, a score of major integrated firms came to dominate all phases of the industry. A sizable public of independent operators bitterly resented the dominance of the major integrated firms, and from time to time demanded divorcement (breaking up the majors into their constituent parts), tariffs or quotas on imported crude and fuel oil, and equal access to national markets through the use of trunk pipelines or greatly reduced freight rates. The FOCB became the filter through which mutually contradictory notions of self-interest passed.[12]

Initially, the FOCB sought to create a consensus within the oil industry around the idea of conservation. The board sought to define the most efficient end-uses of oil and to investigate the feasibility of substituting other sources of energy for fuel oil. This was a hopeful beginning, for it provided an opportunity to discuss all of the fuels and fuel-generated electricity as well as hydroelectric power. But these initiatives met with resistance. Too many interests were involved in one or another end-use of oil to permit the identification of any single use as superior. An official of the American Oil Burner Association denied the concept of essential uses of fuel oil, maintaining that consumer preferences and price mechanisms determined the use of oil. Others questioned the social benefits of substituting coal for oil given the polluting effects of coal. Hearings held by the FOCB demonstrated conclusively that conservation could not be achieved through more efficient resource use, not because of the inability to scientifically distinguish between more and less efficient uses of a particular fuel, but because of the accumulated economic investment of both fuel producers and fuel equipment manufacturers. FOCB officials, aware that segments of the oil industry viewed their agency with suspicion, refused to further pursue this discussion, preferring to shift the nature of the Board's mission from protecting the public interest to serving the interests of oil.[13]

Production controls remained as an option for the FOCB, although this raised the bugaboo of federal intervention. The American Petroleum Institute sent Charles Evans Hughes, its general counsel, to the hearings to squelch any notions that diminishing oil reserves warranted federal action. Some oil men, such as Cities Service President Henry L. Doherty, favored controls based on the unitization or unit management of oil fields, prorationing of the daily flow among producers, and the negotiation of an agreement among the producing states to implement unitization and prorationing. The FOCB endorsed these techniques, but had it not been for the great discoveries of 1925-1930, particularly the East Texas field in 1930, it is unlikely that they would have been implemented in any significant way. Both large and small oil, before the great discoveries, perceived few benefits in production limitations.[14]

The great flush fields coupled with the Depression changed the views of the major oil companies toward production controls. From 1927 until its demise, the FOCB vigorously promoted such policies with the vocal support of the API. Strong opposition from the so-called independents confronted the FOCB-major alliance.

In each of the newer fields, clashing interests pitted the small producers, who endorsed unlimited pumping, against the larger producers, who favored prorated pumping. Major producers in Oklahoma's Seminole Field, led by Standard of Indiana, Standard of New Jersey, and Gulf, had imposed prorationing over the protest of a minority of small producers, an action soon overturned by the courts. The independents, including small refiners, asserted that production controls further strengthened the already dangerous preeminence of the majors, a position amply substantiated by the FTC investigation of the petroleum industry conducted in 1928.

The Okmulgee (Oklahoma) District Oil and Gas Association blamed the majors for overproduction and charged that they now wished the federal government to bail them out. According to the independents, prorationing increased the costs of production per barrel, which majors, but not independents, could readily absorb. Independents did not possess adequate storage facilities and were compelled to sell their crude as quickly as possible regardless of price, mostly to refineries owned by the majors. Moreover, the majors controlling the crude pipelines denied the independents access to them, thus forcing independents to ship via more expensive railroads. Prorationing limited the oil supply available to independent refiners while the majors could draw on stored crudes, bring in oil from states without effective prorationing, or import it from abroad. The

Okmulgee Association and the National Association of Independent Oil Producers criticized the majors and the FOCB for flooding the nation with propaganda designed to weaken anti-trust legislation.[15]

Depression compounded the problems of both the oil and the coal industries, but few new ideas germinated. Instead, New Dealers adopted the production control proposals of the FOCB, which then formed the basis of the petroleum code of fair competition, the Interstate Oil Compact, and the Connally Act of 1935 (the hot oil act). Somewhat ironic were late New Deal assessments of the FOCB as a tool of the majors from its inception.[16] These criticisms conveniently ignored the fact that the production control proposals of the Board represented a response to scarcity. New Deal oil legislation sought price stabilization by means of production controls administered by producing states and supplemented by federal action to prevent hot oil from entering interstate commerce. The New Deal did not revive the original conservationist impulse of the FOCB. The rhetoric of conservation employed by the New Deal masked objectives that only incidentally related to the protection of the nation's oil resources from wasteful exploitation and rapid depletion.

Moreover, the oil code and the oil compact, informally initiated in 1931 and 1932 and given congressional sanction in 1935, met the unswerving opposition of the independents. Throughout the life of the National Recovery Administration (NRA) codes of fair competition, the Petroleum Administrative Board (PAB) under Harold L. Ickes—oil was the only commodity not administered by the NRA—was the target of strident criticism from independent producers, refiners, wholesalers, and retailers. The PAB, like the FOCB, was labeled a tool of the majors and of the consuming states. Independent political power in Oklahoma, Texas, Kansas, and Illinois served to obstruct the operation of production controls into 1937. Independents persistently resisted domestic production restrictions, legally if possible, but surreptitiously if necessary.[17]

If federal oil policy had reached a dead end by 1935, so too had coal policy. The Bituminous Coal Conservation Act of 1935, which the Supreme Court held unconstitutional, and the Bituminous Coal Act of 1937—the so-called Guffey acts—as well as the earlier coal codes, all ran afoul of court decisions and the antagonism of shifting coalitions of producers, distributors, carriers, and consumers. By the onset of the Depression, an impressive body of knowledge existed which documented in detail the illness of the coal industry and the dreary insecurity of thousands of underemployed and unemployed miners. It was well known that coal capacity exceeded demand, and that this caused cutthroat competition and competitive waste of the resource. Thus, coal producers constantly shaved prices, attempting to maintain a margin of profit by pressing wages lower and by reducing the labor force. Suggested remedies centered upon an improved competitive stance with other fuels and the limitation of intraindustry competition. To achieve this required the simultaneous introduction of controls over production, capacity, stocks, and price.[18]

Price controls were a familiar device in coal and, moreover, dovetailed with New Deal strategies to stop deflation by establishing minimum prices for hundreds of commodities. The United Mine Workers of America opposed production controls, believing that they would further reduce employment. Many coal operators and coal carriers also viewed production controls suspiciously. Thus the production control provisions of the original Guffey-Snyder bill were eliminated, and the entire New Deal strategy to stabilize the coal industry rested upon the establishment of minimum prices. This approach did not work. The price-fixing procedures adopted by the two National Bituminous Coal Commissions (NBCC) were so incredibly complicated that only on the eve of World War II were they established with some finality. By early 1940, the production of coal and other goods was on the rise, stimulated by Allied orders for war materials. At the very time the NBCC applied its minimum prices to the coal market, price increases occurred which nullified the relevance of the entire minimum-price exercise. The New Deal response to the perplexing difficulties of the coal industry produced some gains for labor but failed to address the most critical dilemma, that of the role of coal in the rapidly changing fuel-mix which powered the nation.[19]

A full exposition of federal involvement in fuel resource management would, of course, benefit immeasurably by highlighting the fascinating behind-the-scenes maneuvering of innumerable interested parties, the cumulative effects of which produced the mish-mash that was federal fuel policy. Throughout the interwar years, a host of antagonistic interests, including federal agencies, sought to protect vital concerns and, if possible, to weaken competitors by influencing policy and manipulating its application. A commitment to inflexible ideologies moved few of the principals. The leadership of the NCA, the API, or other industry associations accepted federal intervention if their particular domains benefited. Interested parties such as railroads, utilities, and municipalities rationally adopted positions based on the costs of fuel. Thus, in 1937, the city of Atlanta and other communities successfully challenged in court the legality of the NBCC's price-fixing procedures at the same time that the agency went to court to prevent the extension of natural gas pipelines into the urban markets of Appalachian coal producers. The Department of Interior blossomed into the citadel of the major integrated oil companies, despite Secretary Ickes's protests to the contrary, and became the dominant federal authority in fuels, a role persisting through World War II and into the postwar years.

By 1939, no advance had been made in outlining a manageable federal fuel policy. Each crisis provoked federal responses based in part on the precedents of World War I. Each response defined new operational parameters and established additional precedents which influenced future federal activity in the energy field. Policy discussions during the 1920s, particularly regarding coal and petroleum, anticipated all of the strategies which the New Deal applied to fuels during the Depression.

A workable concept of the public interest in energy had not emerged. It was not that the strong evidence amassed by the U.S. Coal Commission, which demonstrated the public interest in coal, had been forgotten. Nor was it that the knowledge contributed by the FOCB or FTC investigations of the oil industry had been purged from the records. Indeed, coal and oil remembered all too clearly the implicit dangers of those findings. Many private interests used this knowledge and their political power to deflect any real threats to their autonomy. Federal fuel resource managers from Harry A. Garfield of the USFA to Harold L. Ickes constantly invoked the proposition that the state could and should intervene in economic life to reconcile conflicting interests, and they believed that the state was capable of defining the general interest without succumbing to the pressures of special pleaders. Unhappily, they were mistaken.[20]

NOTES

1. This brief discussion of the USFA is drawn from USFA Records, RG67, Washington National Records Center (WNRC). For the Lever Act and all other USFA orders and regulations, see *General Orders, Regulations and Rulings of the United States Fuel Administration,* compiled by the Legal Division of the Administration (Washington, DC 1920). See also Robert Cuff, *The War Industries Board: Business-Government Relations during World War I* (Baltimore, 1973); Woodbury Willoughby, *The Capital Issues Committee and War Finance Corporation,* The Johns Hopkins University *Studies* in Historical and Political Science, Series LII, No. 2 (Baltimore, 1934).

2. Figures compiled by USFA for October 1917 through March 1918 demonstrated that bituminous coal mines worked on the average less than 80 percent

capacity and that the primary constraint was the shortage of coal cars. USFA, *Report of the Distribution Division, 1918-1919, Part I: Distribution of Coal and Coke,* by C. E. Lesher (Washington, DC, 1919), 21-28.

3. For the closing order, *General Orders, USFA,* 433-435; for representative letters of protest, see USFA, RG67, Bureau of Conservation, Box 1064, Essential and Non-Essential Industries.

4. For the zone system, *General Orders, USFA,* 213-362; USFA, *Final Report, 1917-1919; Report of the Administrative Division, 1917-1919, Part II; Reports of Bureaus with Headquarters at Washington, D.C.; Report of the Oil Division, 1917-1919* (Washington, DC, 1921), 255.

5. See, for example, USFA, RG67, Records of the Bureau of State Organizations, Missouri, Kansas, Colorado folders; National Retail Coal Merchants Association, *Meeting of the Executive Committee* (Washington, DC, November 11, 1918), 4-7; and *Meeting of the Executive Committee* (Cincinnati, January 27-28, 1919, 9-11.

6. Sam H. Schurr, Bruce C. Netschert, et al., *Energy in the American Economy, 1850-1975: An Economic Study of Its History and Prospects* (Baltimore, 1960), 35.

7. USFA, *Final Report, 1917-1919,* 15-16; Walker D. Hines, Director-General of Railroads to the President of the Senate, "Distribution of coal and coke," *Senate Document* No. 235, 66 Cong., 2 Sess., February 26, 1920 (Washington, DC, 1920); Interstate Commerce Commission, *34th Annual Report,* December 1, 1920 (Washington, 1920), 6-7, 14-22; Council of National Defense Memorandum regarding support of the ICC, May 18, 1920; Department of the Interior Records, RG48, Office of the Secretary, 1-53 (Part 8), National Archives (NA); American Coal Wholesaler *Bulletin,* 107 (October 25, 1919), 7-8; 110 (November 8, 1919), 8-9; *The Coal Mercant,* 2 (January, 1920), 1; 3 (February, 1921), 5.

8. U.S. House of Representatives, 67 Cong., 2 Sess., Committee on Interstate and Foreign Commerce, *Hearings on Coal: Federal Fuel Distributor* (Washington, DC, 1922), passim; U.S. Coal Commission, *Report . . . in Five Parts, Part 1: Principal Findings and Recommendations,* 1923 (Washington, DC, 1925), vii; Federal Fuel Distributor, *Final Report . . . to the President of the United States, September 21, 1923* (Washington, DC, 1923), 1.

9. In 1922, 28 states organized fuel commissions by executive or legislative action. Some of these held considerably more authority than did the FFD. For comments on state commissions, see Federal Trade Commission Records, RG122, Coal Investigation, REP3 HO5, Part 1; and Federal Fuel Distribution Records, RG89, Boxes 5 and 28, NA.

10. For representative reports and hearings on coal, in addition to those already cited, see FTC, *Report on Anthracite and Bituminous Coal Situation and The Relation of Rail and Water Transportation to the Present Fuel Problem,* June 20, 1917, House Document 193, 65 Cong., 1 Sess., Vol. 35, serial 7300 (Washington, DC, 1917); U.S. Senate, 65 Cong., 1 Sess., Subcommittee of the Committee on Interstate Commerce, *Hearings on the Increased Price of Coal, Part I* (Washington, DC, 1919); U.S. House of Representatives, 69 Cong., 1 Sess., Committee on Interstate and Foreign Commerce, *Hearings on Coal Legislation, Part I* (Washington, DC, 1926). See also *Proceedings of the Fourth Annual Convention of the National Coal Association* (New York, 1921), 8-9, for a review of hostile legislation.

11. O'Neal, in *Oil & Gas Journal,* 21 (December 28, 1922), 70. See F. G. Cottrell, "Relations of Bureau of Mines to the oil industry," Bureau of Mines, *Reports of*

Investigations, Serial No. 2166 (Washington, DC, 1920); Joseph E. Pogue, *The Economics of Petroleum* (New York, 1921), 289-290.

12. See FOCB, *Complete Record of Public Hearings, February 10 and 11, 1926* (Washington, DC, 1926); and FTC, *Report on Petroleum Industry: Prices, Profits, and Competition* (Washington, DC, 1928). A full analysis of FOCB might divide its history into two periods: the first, 1924-1927, corresponding to the years in which perceptions of threatened oil scarcity dominated, and the second, 1928-1934, encompassing a period in which new fields were discovered and flush production flooded markets with oil. The second period could be subdivided into the pre-Depression and Depression years. In this chapter, however, the details will be more or less ignored and attention will focus on the policy actually formulated by the FOCB.

13. FOCB *Hearings, 1926; Report of the Federal Oil Conservation Board to the President of the United States, January, 1928* (Washington, DC, 1928), 1, 5, 9; statement of L. D. Becker, American Oil Burner Association, May 27, 1926, Petroleum Administrative Board Records (PAB), RG232, Federal Oil Conservation Board (FOCB), WNRC, Box 10.B.

14. Henry L. Doherty to the President, August 11, 1924, ibid., Box 12, Board file; and Doherty to FOCB, May 18, 1926, ibid., Box 9; Digest of API report (mid-1920s), ibid. Box 26; "Those who would regulate coal industry may drag in oil also," *National Petroleum News,* December 7, 1927; FOCB, *Hearings, 1926,* 25-28.

15. FTC, *Petroleum Industry;* "Relation of 20 major oil companies to entire industry in the United States," *The Independent Petroleum Association of America Monthly,* 1 (March, 1931), 16-17, PAB, RG232, FOCB, Box 12; W. H. Gray, president, National Association of Independent Oil Producers, Tulsa, to Hubert Work, Secretary of the Interior, December 14, 1926, ibid., Box 10.G; A. L. Derby, president, The Derby Oil & Refining Corporation, Wichita to E. S. Rochester, Secretary, FOCB, February 24, 1932, ibid., Box 14, Letters from Oil Industry; E. F. Jones, president, E. F. Jones Oil & Gas Co., Wichita to Harold L. Ickes, Federal Oil Administrator, February 23, 1935, Department of the Interior Records, RG48, Office of the Secretary, 1-289 (Part 1).

16. U.S. Temporary National Economic Committee, *Control of the Petroleum Industry by Major Oil Companies,* by Roy C. Cook, Investigation of Concentration of Economic Power, *Monograph No. 39* (Washington, DC, 1941), 15; National Resources Committee, *Energy Resources and National Policy, Report of the Energy Resources Committee to the U.S. National Resources Committee* (Washington, DC, 1939), 210, 387. For a more objective view of FOCB, see Myron Watkins, *Oil: Stabilization or Conservation? A Case Study in the Organization of Industrial Control* (New York, 1937), 40-45.

17. Charles Fahy, chairman of PAB, addressed the criticisms of the independents in a speech to the Independent Petroleum Association of America, "Independence within sound public policy," December 7, 1941. Printed Archives of the United States, RG149, Interior Department, I32.2:Ad2, NA. For a representative attack on the NRA oil code, see The Automotive Maintenance and Gasoline Dealers of Cambria and Somerset Counties, PA to Hugh S. Johnson, NRA, August 6, 1933, PAB, RG232, Box 40.A.

18. For a full discussion, see National Resources Board, *A Report on National Planning and Public Works in Relation to Natural Resources and Including Land Use and Water Resources with Findings and Recommendations* (Washington, DC, 1934),

400-403. All of the points made by the National Resources Board had surfaced earlier. See especially U.S. House of Representatives, 69 Cong., 1 Sess. Committee on Interstate and Foreign Commerce, *Hearings on Coal Legislation,* Part 1, March . . . and April . . . 1926; Part 2, April . . . and May . . . 1926; Part 3, May . . . 1926 (Washington, DC, 1926) and U.S. Senate, 70 Cong., 2 Sess., Committee on Interstate Commerce, *Hearings on S.4490, A Bill to Regulate Interstate and Foreign Commerce in Bituminous Coal . . . and to Create a Bituminous Coal Commission,* Part 1, December 14 and 17, 1928 (Washington, DC, 1929).

19. The basic documents for a study of New Deal coal policies are located in: National Bituminous Coal Commission Records, RG150, WNRC; and Bituminous Coal Division (of the Department of Interior) Records, RG222, the latter including the records of the Second National Bituminous Coal Commission. See also Eugene Rostow, "Bituminous coal and the public interest," *The Yale Law Journal* 50 (February, 1941), 543-594; and Glen Lawhon Parker, *The Coal Industry: A Study in Social Control* (Washington, 1940), 131, 135-147 passim.

20. In this very brief discussion, originally presented orally, I have failed to acknowledge intellectual debts to the important work of several scholars, among whom are: August W. Giebelhaus, *Business and Government in the Oil Industry: A Case Study of Sun Oil Company, 1876-1945* (Greenwich, CT, 1980); James P. Johnson, *The Politics of Soft Coal: The Bituminous Industry from World War I Through the New Deal* (Urbana, IL, 1979); Albro Martin, *Enterprise Denied: Origins of the Decline of American Railroads, 1897-1917* (New York, 1971); and Gerald D. Nash, *United States Oil Policy 1890-1964: Business and Government in Twentieth Century America* (Pittsburgh, 1968). I am now writing a book on federal fuel policies, 1900-1948, which will identify the areas of agreement and disagreement between myself and the above authors.

8

The Nixon Administration and the 1973 Energy Crisis
A New Departure in Federal Energy Policy

JACK M. HOLL

In response to the Arab oil embargo of 1973, the administration of President Richard M. Nixon initiated a historically innovative federal energy policy. Although the federal government had been involved in various energy programs for decades, the numerous agencies responsible for energy policy, regulation, research, development, and production usually did not coordinate their activities or programs. In short, prior to 1973 the federal government did not have a comprehensive energy policy. Rather, the government pursued several energy policies reflected in goals and priorities previously set by various presidents and congresses. The Nixon administration took the first steps toward consolidating federal energy policy in the Executive Branch.

U.S. "Energy" Policy Prior to 1973

In the half-century of relatively cheap and abundant energy before the energy crisis of 1973, the federal government's role in formulating national energy policy was severely limited. For the most part, Americans expected private industry to establish production, distribution, marketing, and pricing policies where "natural monopolies" could not guarantee fair prices, as in the interstate transmission of gas and electricity. On occasion, the federal government financed major energy research and development projects, particularly in the areas of nuclear and hydroelectric power, when national emergencies or the public interest was deemed to require national action. Yet even when the government's involvement was extensive and vigorous, as in the hydroelectric development of the Tennessee and Columbia River valleys, federal energy management was restricted both by region and technology.

Historically, the federal government has been a reluctant manager and guardian of America's energy resources.[1] Always mindful of national security, the federal government has generally confined its role to monitoring energy data and responding to national emergencies. When the government imposed strict regulations and controls, including rationing, during World Wars I and II, Americans regarded such actions as emergency measures. More typically in peacetime, as in dam building, power marketing, or rural electrification, federal programs sought to promote growth in energy industries to ensure consumers plentiful and inexpensive energy. Although the government played a small role in allocating limited resources among energy uses and users, federal regulations were established to control pricing where free market conditions were absent,[2] as for instance in the case of the interstate transmission of gas.

From the 1920s to the 1970s, energy programs scattered throughout the federal departments and agencies reflected the government's benign approach to energy management as a whole. Indeed, government officials generally thought in terms of particular fuels, technologies, and resources rather than "energy." Each fuel presented special characteristics and problems. The Departments of State and Defense, for example, sought to secure reliable sources of both foreign and domestic oil to increase national security. In some agencies, energy or fuel technologies were handled almost independently from one another, as in the Office of Oil and Gas and the Office of Coal Research in the Interior Department.

The Bureau of Mines' relationship to the coal industry, which was highly decentralized and labor intensive, contrasted sharply with the Atomic Energy Commission's monopoly of nuclear technology prior to 1954. The Federal Power Commission sought to establish "fair prices" for the transmission of gas and electricity in interstate commerce, while the Department of Justice and the Federal Trade Commission attempted to promote competition within energy technologies. Energy research was conducted at energy research centers, stations, and laboratories scattered throughout the country.[3]

Often "energy policy" became intertwined with other federal policies and programs. During the Great Depression, the Army Corps of Engineers and the Bureau of Reclamation built multipurpose dams that not only generated power but also promoted conservation, reclamation, and recreation. For example, the Bonneville Dam, which the Corps built in the 1930s on the Columbia River about 35 miles east of Portland, Oregon, epitomized federal energy policy. Bonneville Dam was constructed to stimulate the regional economy and to produce inexpensive electrical energy. At the same time, Bonneville contributed to national security by providing reliable power to the aluminum, aircraft, and other defense industries located in the Pacific Northwest. The project was also important for flood control, irrigation, and navigation. Nevertheless, large concrete dams significantly altered the environment, particularly by blocking upstream migration of spawning fish. At Bonneville, the Corps built ingenious fish ladders and channels to assist migratory fish around the 70-foot high dam. Thus, federal energy policy, as expressed in the building of the Bonneville Dam, was regionally and technologically limited, promoted low energy prices and national security, and evidenced concern for Bonneville's impact on the surrounding wildlife habitat.[4]

The Federal Government: A Cautious Energy Broker

Thus, prior to 1973, the federal government moved cautiously in energy policy, acting more as a broker among diverse interests than as a master planner. Even when energy allocation became a public issue, as in the case of petroleum during World War II or atomic energy for peaceful purposes after 1945, the government primarily and naturally limited itself to the immediate problems at hand, leaving the task of long-range planning and energy utilization to private industry or state, local, and regional authorities.[5] Energy as a public issue cut across all sectors of national life, including political, economic, social, and regional interests. In its role as a cautious energy broker, the federal government had to coordinate research, development, implementation, and regulation of energy systems with public and private, local, state, regional, national, and international constituencies and institutions.

In an era when energy resources seemed boundless, the American people did not call upon the federal government to make difficult decisions about the nation's energy future. To be sure, conflicts between energy systems and the environment forecast the bitter choices that lay ahead. Furthermore, the nation experienced some minor energy shortages, especially in the great blackout of 1965 and the "brownout" of 1971. On June 4, 1971, President Richard M. Nixon, in his first energy message to Congress, warned that the United States could no longer take its energy supply for granted. Since 1967, Nixon observed, America's rate of energy consumption had outpaced the nation's production of goods and services. In order to assist private enterprise in developing an adequate supply of clean energy for the future, the President asked Congress to establish a Department of Natural Resources that would unify all important energy resource development programs in one government agency. Largely in response to Nixon's energy message, on August 11, 1971, Congress authorized the Atomic Energy Commission to pursue research and development projects in areas of superconducting power transmission systems, energy storage, solar energy, geothermal resources, and coal gasification.[6]

Nixon's larger plans, however, made little headway. Political considerations were partly responsible, but most importantly, the public just did not believe energy shortages were more than temporary or regional. Americans could perceive of no "energy crisis" as long as there was an ample supply of cheap gas for their cars, electricity and fuel for their homes, and power for their industries and businesses.[7]

The Energy Crisis of 1973

For the Nixon administration, the energy crisis of 1973 underscored the need to develop a comprehensive national energy policy, as well as to focus the government's various energy programs into one agency. On April 18, 1973, six months before renewed conflict in the Middle East, President Nixon noted that the United States, with 6 percent of the world's population, consumed one-third of the world's energy. In the immediate future, the President predicted, the United States might face energy shortages and increased prices. Again, as in 1971, Nixon cautioned that America's energy "challenge" could become an energy crisis if current trends continued unchecked. As the energy situation worsened, the President amended his proposal of 1971 for a cabinet department, requesting Congress to establish a Department of Energy and Natural Resources with responsibility for energy policy and management as well as research and development. In the interim, Nixon established a Special Energy Committee of senior White House advisors, including special assistants for domestic, foreign, and economic affairs, and a National Energy Office to identify issues and coordinate energy analysis among federal offices and agencies.[8]

Nixon Energy Policies—1973

Although President Nixon's proposal for a Department of Energy and Natural Resources stalled in Congress, he did not abandon hope for an energy department. At the urging of Roy L. Ash, Director of the Office of Management and Budget, Nixon established the Energy Policy Office, which combined and expanded the responsibilities of the Special Energy Committee and the National Energy Office. The new Energy Policy Office, established June 20, 1973, became responsible for the formulation and coordination of energy policies at the presidential level.

At the same time, Nixon proposed the creation of an Energy Research and Development Administration that would be given central responsibility for the government's energy research programs and for working with industry to develop and foster new energy technologies. This new agency would combine the energy research and development activities of the Atomic Energy Commission and the Department of the Interior. The Atomic Energy Commission's licensing and regulatory responsibilities were to be continued in a five-member Nuclear Regulatory Commission.[9] In the interim, Nixon directed the Chairman of the Atomic Energy Commission, Dixy Lee Ray, to conduct an immediate review of federal and private energy research and development activities and to recommend an integrated program for the nation.

By September 1973, the President, while still not seeing an energy "crisis," continued to stress America's energy "problem." Nixon especially encouraged congressional enactment of four bills that would provide for the construction of the Alaskan pipeline, construction of deepwater ports, deregulation of natural gas, and new standards for surface mining. He also expressed hope that Congress would quickly authorize the creation of the Department of Energy and Natural Resources and the Energy Research and Development Administration.[10] Unfortunately, on October 6, 1973, war broke out again in the Middle East. America's energy challenge and problem would soon become a bona fide crisis.

The consequences of the Israeli victory in the "Yom Kippur" war quickly spread to North America when the Organization of Arab Petroleum Exporting Countries (OAPEC) placed an embargo on crude oil shipped to the United States. By November 1973, oil supplies were critically low, creating "the most acute shortages of energy since World War II."[11] The Arab oil embargo, subsequent long gas lines, and complex but fragmented energy projects and regulations demanded bolder action by the President. No longer regional, in 1973 the energy shortages became nation-wide and threatened virtually every sector of the economy.

In a televised address on the energy emergency on November 7, 1973, President Nixon urged Americans to lower their thermostats, drive slower, and eliminate unnecessary lighting. Recalling the Manhattan Project that had built the atomic bomb, and the Apollo Project that had landed two

Americans on the moon, the President expressed his faith that American science, technology, and industry could free the United States from dependence on foreign oil. Pledging increased funding for energy research and development, Nixon launched "Project Independence" to achieve energy self-sufficiency by 1980. In addition, as winter cold began to grip the Northeast, the President announced plans to increase the production of home heating oils while reducing gasoline supplies and closing gasoline stations on Sundays. Across the nation, communities reduced holiday lighting and implemented various schemes for distributing short supplies of gasoline. As motorists scrambled for a place in line, in some states matching their license plates to the date on an odd-or-even system, the 50-year era of energy affluence ended.[12]

White House Energy Initiatives, 1973-1974

On December 4, 1973, President Nixon created the Federal Energy Office in the Executive Office of the White House. Although presidential concern over petroleum supply and pricing extended back to the 1950s and earlier, Nixon's executive order for the first time institutionalized the federal government's response to post-World War II energy shortages. Nixon assigned to the Federal Energy Office the tasks of allocating reduced petroleum supplies to refiners and consumers and of controlling the price of oil and gasoline. By January 1974, the Federal Energy Office had established a comprehensive allocation program including gasoline, aviation fuel, propane, butane, residual oil, crude oil and refinery yield, lubricants, petrochemical feedstocks, and middle distillates. In addition, under the leadership of William Simon, former Deputy Secretary of the Treasury, the Office became the center for energy policy and planning at the White House. In this role, the Federal Energy Office replaced the Energy Policy Office in gathering data, coordinating policy, and implementing "Project Independence."[13] Simon picked John Sawhill, formerly at the Office of Management and Budget, to be his deputy. Together, they recruited personnel from energy offices located in the Treasury Department, the Department of the Interior, the Cost of Living Council, and the Internal Revenue Service.[14]

Nevertheless, a Gallup public opinion poll released in January 1974 indicated that the administration's energy planners would have a difficult time convincing Americans that energy shortages were not artificial.

Although only 7 percent of Americans blamed the Arab nations for energy shortages, 25 percent blamed the oil companies, 23 percent criticized the federal government, another 19 percent specifically held Nixon or his administration responsible, and 16 percent thought American consumers were at fault. Virtually no one believed that depletion of national or world-wide petroleum reserves had contributed to the winter's crisis. Thus, as they fashioned energy plans for the Nixon administration, Simon and Sawhill faced great public skepticism that identified the government itself as a major cause of the energy problem.[15]

Because of the energy crisis resulting from the October Arab oil embargo, Nixon decided to break tradition in January 1974 and present his energy request to the Congress before delivering his State of the Union address. Basing his message on Chairman Ray's December report, "The Nation's Energy Future," Nixon proposed a five-year, $10 billion energy research and development program. Among several actions, Nixon called for the establishment of the Federal Energy Administration which, replacing the Federal Energy Office, would carry out new federal programs in energy resource development, energy information, and energy conservation. Nixon also renewed his commitment to "Project Independence" and the establishment of the Energy Research and Development Administration. Conceding that the political climate made the creation of the Department of Energy and Natural Resources unlikely, Nixon nevertheless encouraged Congress to expand the federal government's responsibility for meeting the nation's energy crisis.[16]

Not surprisingly, federal energy policy, programs, and reorganization languished through the Watergate crisis of 1974. The establishment of the Energy Research and Development Administration and the consolidation of federal energy programs and activities into a single cabinet-level agency, two goals long sought by the Nixon administration, were not accomplished until after Nixon's resignation as President. In the rhetoric that followed, the Nixon administration's contributions to federal energy policies and programs were either forgotten or ignored. During the presidential campaign of 1976, Jimmy Carter promised to be the first president to fashion a "comprehensive" federal energy policy. What was overlooked in the campaign was the fact that Richard Nixon had taken the first steps toward such a goal as early as 1971, and had fully committed his administration to the development of a comprehensive federal policy during the energy crisis of 1973.

NOTES

1. Harold Sharlin, John DeNovo, Richard G. Hewlett, and Jack M. Holl, "The federal government as manager and guardian of energy resources," American Historical Association, Dallas, Texas, December 1977.

2. John G. Clark, "The energy crises of 1919-1924 and 1973-1975: a comparative analysis of federal energy policies," in S. William Gouse, ed., *Energy Systems and Policy*, (Crane Russak, 1980), 239-271.

3. Neil De Marchi, "Energy policy under Nixon: mainly putting out fires," in Craufurd D. Goodwin, ed., *Energy Policy in Perspective: Today's Problems, Yesterday's Solutions* (Washington, DC, 1980), 395-473 (hereafter cited as Goodwin, ed., *Energy Policy in Perspective*).

4. Gus Norwood, *Columbia River Power for the People: A History of Policies of the Bonneville Power Administration* (Washington, DC, 1981); American Public Works Association, *History of Public Works in the United States* Washington, DC, 1976), 357-358.

5. Elliot L. Richardson and Frank G. Zarb, "Perspective on energy policy," Energy Resources Council, December 1976.

6. Alice L. Buck, "A history of the Atomic Energy Commission," in Jack M. Holl, ed., *Institutional Origins of the Department of Energy* (Washington, DC, 1982).

7. Rodney P. Carlisle and Jack M. Holl, "The significance of energy abundance in recent American history," DOE Historian's Office, April 1980; De Marchi, "Energy policy under Nixon," in Goodwin, ed., *Energy Policy in Perspective*, 447-452.

8. Richard M. Nixon, "Message to Congress," April 18, 1973, as reprinted in *Executive Energy Documents*, published by the Senate Committee on Energy and Natural Resources, July 1978, 13-47 (hereafter cited as SCEN, *Energy Documents*).

9. De Marchi, "Energy policy under Nixon," in Goodwin, ed., *Energy Policy in Perspective*, 434-435; Nixon, "Statement," June 29, 1973, SCEN, *Energy Documents*, 49-67.

10. Nixon, "Remarks on the nation's energy policy," Sept. 8, 1973, 69-72, and "Meeting the energy challenge: excerpt from message to Congress," Sept. 10, 1973, 73-76, both in SCEN, *Energy Documents*.

11. Roger M. Anders, "The federal energy administration," in Holl, ed., *Institutional Origins of the Department of Energy*.

12. Nixon, "Address on the energy emergency," in SCEN, *Energy Documents*, 81-93.

13. Anders, "The federal energy administration"; Federal Energy Administration, "Overview of the FEA," manuscript, n.d., but probably written in January 1977.

14. Susan R. Abbasi, "Federal energy organization," Congressional Research Service, Library of Congress, May 4, 1975, revised September 24, 1976.

15. George Gallup, "Oil companies, government, Nixon, and U.S. consumer blamed about equally for crisis," The Gallup Poll, January 10, 1974.

16. Nixon, "Proposals to deal with the energy crisis," January 23, 1974, in SCEN, *Energy Documents*, 119-141; Dixy Lee Ray, *The Nation's Energy Future*, Wash-1281, Dec. 1, 1973 (Washington, DC, 1973).

9

State Management of Petroleum Resources

Texas, 1910-1940

EDWARD W. CONSTANT II

This study focuses on the way esoteric scientific or technical knowledge is incorporated into public policy. For present purposes, I want to narrow that focus to the process by which the federal judiciary first rejected and then wholeheartedly adopted the emerging understanding of subsurface petroleum reservoirs as the foundation for oil policy in Texas. Because, however, these concerns relate to a broader, ongoing study of the development of petroleum engineering and its utilization in regulatory processes, I would like to cast the historical issues involved in the broadest possible terms.

At the risk of being provocative or argumentative, let me advance four assertions of the most general character. First, new scientific or technical information never emerges in a social void. It always engages prior values, ideological commitments, and real interests, social and economic. For the period under consideration here, it emerges within well-defined, well-developed institutional contexts that are themselves expressions or embodiments of relevant values, commitments, and interest. This much I think is both plausible and agreeable to historians.

But the social or historical process so neatly tucked away in the phrase "engages" needs much fuller characterization, which leads to my remaining assertions. The second of these is that initially, new scientific or technological information typically redefines, sometimes radically, the behavioral specification or expression of broadly held values without much changing the values themselves. What are changed initially I think are the "correspondence rules" between higher-level values and lower-level, mundane behavior. Moreover, I suspect that these initial changes most often occur in specialized or differentiated institutional contexts where their gross implications are by-and-large little realized.

Over extended intervals, however, and this is my third point, I think esoteric knowledge reifies and transforms values and radically alters their institutional embodiment. Values come to mean something different from their original meaning, and sometimes something entirely novel. Pursuant to these changes, institutions assume or develop powers or commitments sometimes diametrically opposed to their original purposes or intentions. We are still "utilitarians"; we still have a quasi-religious "respect for nature"; some people still believe that "cleanliness is next to godliness." But understanding oil deposits changes the meaning of utility; new ecological insight changes "respect for nature"; and the germ theory of disease redefines clean—none of these means what it did a century ago. And certainly the organizational forms we have for tending to these things far transcend nineteenth-century notions of proper democratic institutions.

Fourth and finally, I believe that in real time these changes, that is, behavioral redefinition, value reification, and institutional reorientation, all occur by what Herbert Simon calls "satisficing," a search process that is always lazy, limited, and suboptimal. At any point in time, people will tend to change as little as possible to accommodate new information or new environmental contingencies. The result is a slow, meandering, often ex post irrational social adjustment process, the outcome of which may seemingly only imperfectly express "scientific" knowledge. History is inductive and synthetic, hardly ever analytic or deductive.

The present study exemplifies these general assertions with reference to a specific historical instance: the evolution of the Texas Railroad Commission's prorationing policy and its relationship to reservoir engineering. But first, I need to do two things: specify what the objective nature of the problem of oil production is and define some historical background.

Petroleum hydrocarbons are commonly found as liquid deposits within porous, subsurface, sedimentary rock strata. Such deposits are usually called reservoirs, pools, or fields. In almost all cases, natural gas and salt water are found in the same strata as oil. Gas is found in solution in the oil, and the oil-gas solution is frequently mixed with salt water in the strata. The ease with which petroleum may be produced (be allowed to flow freely or be pumped from a well) is a function of the porosity and density of the strata, the viscosity of the oil (which is reduced by dissolved gas), and the presence of free gas caps or underlying salt water which may serve to force the oil toward the well. Because of these factors, each oil well has a maximum rate at which oil may be produced from it and still secure the maximum total recovery of oil from the pool. If oil is produced too rapidly, pressure may be depleted, oil viscosity may be increased through loss of connate gas, or salt water may intrude into the region of the well. Any of these events will cause premature abandonment of the well and subsurface waste in the form of unrecoverable oil. Under even conscientious management, about 30-40 percent of the total oil in a pool is not recovered, although secondary or tertiary recovery methods may reduce that percentage.

Each field is unique in its particular geological structure and in the nature of its primary production mechanism or "drive." Oil may be forced to the surface by a free gas cap, by dissolved or connate gas, by water intrusion, or by some combination of these mechanisms. Furthermore, different field management strategies derived from different assumptions about the controlling drive mechanism may have radically different implications for individual wells. Given the diversity of well ownership within a common pool, production policies designed to maximize total recovery from the pool may adversely affect the interests of some, while greatly benefiting others. These aspects of the nature of petroleum reservoirs and of production were not widely understood until the period from 1924 to 1930, and general acceptance of petroleum engineering practice giving them quantitative expression did not occur until well into the 1930s.

Prior to 1929, the ownership of oil normally was governed by the common law doctrine of the "rule of capture," the same rule applied to wild game. Oil, this "vagrant mineral," as one judge termed it, belonged to whomever could punch a hole in the ground and capture it. Texas law, however, also recognized the fee interest of landowners in the oil and gas actually in place beneath their property, although that interest remained contingent upon their ability to produce oil and the ability of others to drain it away. These legal doctrines led to several important consequences. The number of wells drilled into a pool depended upon the ownership of the land surface and was unrelated to the extent or physical nature of the subsurface pool. Since all that really mattered was capture, wells were produced wide open, with oil being stored in wooden or steel tanks, or frequently in earthen pits. Natural gas was commonly flared or simply vented into the air. These practices resulted in the rapid and premature depletion of new fields, and in great surface and subsurface waste.

Equally troublesome was the market instability resulting from such practices. Because the sudden discovery and sudden depletion of oil fields were essentially stochastic (but with the size of each major field such that it constituted a significant proportion of total national production), and because oil storage capacity was limited, massive overproduction alternated with shortage, and prices fluctuated widely in the face of a relatively inelastic demand.

Both corporate and government policy makers recognized the severity of these problems during the 1920s, but were unable to arrive at any consensus about corrective action. While I do not plan to wander off into the vicissitudes of public policy debates during the Twenties, I do want to make two points that I think are well established in the literature.

First, interests and opinions in the oil industry were (and are) extraordinarily diverse, complex, and sometimes peculiar. At one extreme was a group of progressive "planners" who, enamoured of the World War I experience, sought flat federal government regulation, price and quantity, of the oil industry. At the other extreme, and in much greater numbers, were the small, independent producers who saw any attempt to control anything by anybody as a monopolistic threat to their economic existence. In between were the scientific, management-oriented professionals in large integrated firms who fully understood the necessity of sound reservoir management and the desirability of orderly marketing practices, but who feared both government control and public resentment of any appearance of monopolistic behavior. Interests and opinions were complicated even more by the fact that some firms were fully integrated producer-marketers, some were refiners only, and some, especially outside the East, were mostly producers. These cleavages characterized both the American oil industry generally and the "oil fraternity" in Texas particularly.

Second, private and public research during the 1920s, especially that associated with the Federal Oil Conservation Board and with the Petroleum Division of the U.S. Bureau of Mines, did establish a secure, if not fully formulated, understanding of subsurface reservoirs. By 1930, that understanding rested on three sets of data: empirical studies of existent oil fields, including histories of past pressure-decline curves and, after 1926, experiences with unitized pressure maintenance; laboratory experiments with flow in simulated aquifers; and "quasi-experimental" results, some quite unintentional, from the management or mismanagement of new fields.

With all this as background, let me briefly sketch the evolution of prorationing policy in Texas. First, prorationing refers to the policy by which the Railroad Commission of the State of Texas fixes the production of every well in the state, i.e., assigns to it its prorata share of total state production. The Railroad Commission itself was originally created as a late-nineteenth-century Populist-Progressive reform agency to regulate railroad rates and practices. As pipelines began to supplant tank cars for oil transportation during the first decade of the twentieth century, the Railroad Commission's authority was extended to include pipeline regulation. In 1917, and more emphatically in 1919, the commission was empowered to regulate waste and pollution attending oil exploration and production.

The authority to regulate pipelines opened a Pandora's Box. Within a new oil field, access to a pipeline often meant the difference between a market and no market at all. The Railroad Commission therefore tried to require equal access for all field producers to pipeline connections by declaring the pipelines to be common carriers. That attempt, in turn, ran headlong into the rule of capture: In order to meet his obligations to his lessor, an oil operator (producer) had to flow his well at its maximum rate to avoid drainage to an adjacent well on a different tract. Such flush production usually produced more oil than a given pipeline could carry or purchasers wanted to buy. As a result, by the late 1920s, the Railroad Commission began, ineffectually, to try to ration production (by giving each well a prorata share of total field production) in individual oil fields in Texas. The commission tried to divide up total production among wells in a pool, even though it then had no scientifically rational method of doing so.

In 1929, an amendment to the enabling legislation permitted the Railroad Commission to control "physical waste" but not "economic waste," that is, production in excess of "reasonable demand." "Physical waste" was explicitly defined as "surface waste," such as production beyond available transportation, which necessitated losses in the storage or flaring of natural gas, and "subsurface waste," such as operation in a manner which would deplete reservoir pressure.[1]

Then came East Texas. Discovered in late 1930, by the early summer of 1931 the giant field, still the world's third largest, contained 700 wells and was producing more than 600,000 barrels of oil a day. Some forty miles long and six to eight miles wide, by 1933 the field would contain over 12,000 wells (27,000 by 1938) and be capable of producing oil equivalent to the entire nation's consumption. In 1931, the price of oil fell from a dollar a barrel to twenty cents to ten cents, with one firm (the Texas Company) offering a nickel a barrel.

Size aside, the East Texas field is unique in two respects. Its production depends on a pure water drive, moving west to east, which makes the entire field extraordinarily sensitive to depletion of total reservoir pressure. Second, due to the distribution of land ownership, with a multitude of small tracts, the twenty largest lease holders in East Texas controlled less than 50 percent of the production. The remainder was controlled by small independents, many of whom were highly leveraged, "shoe-string" operators. Thus, voluntary unitization or even restraint was unlikely, to put it mildly.

Rather than recount the travails of Texas oil policy during the 1930s chronologically and in detail, let me, in the interest of brevity, simply recount some of the more implausible turnabouts during the period. First, the Governor of Texas in 1931, Ross Sterling, was a former president of the Humble Oil Company, although he retained no financial interest in the industry. He was by conviction a rational manager, in the sense that he both understood and supported scientific development and cooperative exploitation of petroleum reservoirs. Simultaneously, however, he adamantly opposed price-fixing or any of the other trappings of monopolistic practice, and therefore rejected any attempt to use the authority of the state to limit oil production to "market demand." Furthermore, as might be expected of a Southern Democrat in 1931, Sterling believed in the strict constitutional limitation of all governmental powers.

Yet in mid-1931, when faced with a judicial injunction against the Railroad Commission's prorationing orders and with what he perceived to be imminent insurrection in East Texas, Sterling imposed martial law, and for nearly fourteen months single-handedly assumed control of the East Texas Field—until the Supreme Court of the United States ruled his action unconstitutional. In desperation, Sterling then supported a strong market demand statute as the only way of bringing order to the oil industry. The state legislature meanwhile moved from lukewarm support for conservation and laissez-faire opposition to market demand regulation to support for market demand limitation as the only way of preventing physical waste. Expected industry alignments were likewise jumbled. Some large independent oil producers like Roy Cullen, who stood to benefit most from price stability, were opposed to any government intervention at all. Other independents, hardly less conservative (such as H. L. Hunt), actively supported market demand regulation. Most major integrated producer-refiners, like Humble and the Texas Company, supported prorationing (at the state level), but some, notably Gulf, were initially opposed.

Judicial gyrations proved even stranger. Texas state courts upheld prorationing orders based on the original, non-market demand statute of 1929, even though prevention of subsurface waste did have an acknowledged and substantial effect on price. Neither in Texas nor anywhere else, however, was prorationing universally acclaimed. The Chief Justice of the Oklahoma Supreme Court, in a 1933 dissenting opinion, wrote that prorationing "was born of monopoly, sired by arbitrary power, and its progeny (such as these orders) is the deformed child whose playmates are graft, theft, bribery, and corruption."[2]

Yet the ultimate test of prorationing came not in state but in federal courts. And it is to their deliberate (if tardy) acceptance of petroleum engineering as the foundation of policy that I now want to turn, for I think the experience of the federal courts exemplifies in microcosm the processes of value reification and institutional reorientation described above.

While cases brought in federal court against the Railroad Commission of Texas commonly involved a whole menagerie of allegations—that the statute was invalid because it comprised an unconstitutional delegation of legislative authority to an administrative body, because it was unconstitutionally vague, because it effectively subjected state sovereignty to the National Recovery Administration, and so on—the only challenges seriously entertained by the federal courts were those based on the Fourteenth Amendment. Although there was some variation from case to case, as will be noted below, the essential complaint was that the Railroad Commission, under the guise of prorationing to conserve natural resources, in fact denied plaintiffs due process of law and arbitrarily and capriciously confiscated their property.

Both state and federal courts had promptly recognized the power of the state of Texas to regulate the use of its natural resources, the power of the Texas legislature to delegate wide discretionary authority to the Railroad Commission, and the prima facie validity of Railroad Commission orders. But for twelve years, federal judges maintained their watchdog role over constitutional guarantees of due process.

During the first two and one-half years of attempted state-wide prorationing, federal court challenges were uniformly successful. After that, they were not, and I want to examine in detail the basis of that transition.

The decision that shattered initial attempts at proration, MacMillan v. Railroad Commission of Texas, was rendered July 28, 1931.[3] MacMillan owned wells in East Texas, where the commission had sharply curtailed production and allocated allowable production on a 20- or a 40-acre unit basis, that is, independent of the number of wells per unit. MacMillan alleged that his wells were capable of producing 50,000 barrels of oil per day but were allowed only 1445 barrels daily, and charged that the Railroad Commission order had nothing to do with the conservation of resources or the prevention of waste; it was, "a mere arbitrary order designed to control the output, price, and market of crude oil by reducing the supply of oil to the demand for it" (p. 401).

The Railroad Commission said it wasn't so. While freely acknowledging their deep concern for the stability of the oil industry and the great public clamor for them to do something to bring it about, the commission contended that the effect of their orders was to prevent physical waste, surface and subsurface, as mandated in the Texas statutes, and that any other purpose or motivation shown for the orders could not thereby invalidate them.

In an extraordinarily angry and harshly worded opinion, the three-judge federal panel ruled for the plaintiffs. Circuit Judge Joseph C. Hutcheson, Jr., described as clearly "the dominant personality" on the court, wrote the opinion. He quickly disposed of the scientific issues raised by the Railroad Commission's expert witnesses:

Plaintiff further established that though there was evidence that the proration plan of ratable and moderate withdrawls would, if properly applied, have some effect to prolong the life of a field by delaying the intrusion of water and thus to enable more oil ultimately to be obtained, in the light of present knowledge this was largely theory and speculation, and that such plan could only be properly applied in each field after careful test and experimentation there [p. 402].

After noting that no such actual test or experimentation had been performed in East Texas, Hutcheson agreed with the plaintiff's contention that the Railroad Commission's orders were arbitrary and unreasonable, and that whatever effect on waste they might have was purely accidental.

Although acknowledging the validity of the Texas conservation statutes and of the powers of the Railroad Commission, Hutcheson noted:

Presumptively valid though such acts are, courts, bound to give effect not to fictions, but to realities, may not, in construing them, close their eyes to what all men can see. Disregarding pretense, subterfuge, and chicane, courts must, looking through form to substance, ascertain the true purpose of a statute not from its recitals of purpose, but from the operation and effect of it as applied and enforced [p. 404].

The commission, so Hutcheson concluded, had operated under the "thinly veiled pretense" of preventing physical waste, while its real purpose had been "to control the delicate adjustment of market supply and demand" in an attempt to bring oil prices up and keep them at a high level (pp. 404-405). Hutcheson and the court were clearly appalled by the apparent price-fixing conspiracy entered into by the Railroad Commission, even asserting: "It would serve no useful purpose to burden this opinion with a summary of the evidence on which these opinions rest," it being, "so known to every man."[4]

In terms of the adaptive search model presented above, the court turned to well-established interpretations of law and to completely traditional values in formulating its opinion, while virtually ignoring any novelty that in fact might have appertained to the situation. More importantly here, in rejecting the concepts of petroleum engineering as "mere theory and speculation," it quite unconsciously embraced a totally conventional, craft-derived notion of oil, its ownership and production. It still implicitly thought of oil in terms of individual wells with individual "potential production" on individual leases held by individuals, rather than as taps into a common pool. The court in MacMillan v. Railroad Commission was so swept away by the despicable motivation so obvious to "every man," that it felt compelled to search no further, and does not seem to have seriously examined the scientific issues at all.

The Railroad Commission, however, stuck to its guns. It did acknowledge, in the preface to its new orders for East Texas issued on February 24, 1932, that as of the previous summer, "engineers and operators in the field were not in possession of such complete data on the field as would enable them to bring to the commission conclusive testimony as to what should be done.[5] But the commission adamantly denied that it had ever entered proration orders for the purpose of price-fixing[6] and maintained that its sole purpose had always been and continued to be the prevention of the physical waste of oil and natural gas. It argued that its prior rules had in fact conserved gas-energy in the field, and "were further designed to provide for the most efficient utilization of the water drive or hydrostatic pressure arising from the approach of water from the west side of the field, and to increase the ultimate recovery of oil from the producing sands."[7] Moreover, the commission asserted that it had become evident since the hearing of the past August that a great deal of further information was available.

Since that time, "much valuable information" concerning pressures, pressure declines, oil-gas ratios, the movement of the water table, and other engineering data had been accumulated and compiled, and as a result, engineers at the hearing in February 1932 were able to testify with assurance and certainty as to what was going on underground in the oil field.[8] On the basis of the new evidence then available, the commission therefore concluded:

> that reservoir pressures have not been maintained as effectively as they should be in order to prevent liberation of "free gas" and consequent high oil-gas ratios and resulting gas waste; that the two lifting agencies (gas energy and water drive) have not been properly conserved and coordinated, that in said field there is a notable deficiency of gas, which in fact demands not only the most effective plan of orderly production of oil to conserve gas energy but a proper use of the water drive by withdrawals of oil at such slow rates and under such conditions as will permit the water to come in gradually and effectually displace the oil; that the maximum ultimate recovery of oil per acre of the field has not been but can be attained only by the maintenance of an orderly, gradual oil production rate.[9]

The commission consequently fixed a maximum daily production for the field of 300,000 barrels and a flat maximum allowable of 75 barrels a day for each well in the field.

Three items are significant about these orders. First, the Railroad Commission was clearly focusing on maximizing total ultimate recovery from the East Texas field as a unitary whole. Second, pursuant to that goal, they were embracing policies predicated on maximum utilization of "water drive," which necessitated gradual, modulated oil withdrawals. Third, they were searching for some allowable formula that was both possible to administer and acceptable to the courts: having orders based on acreage overturned, they turned to a flat, per-well rate.

The afternoon the new orders were issued, courts all across Texas were inundated with complaints in equity. The most important of the cases were tried together as People's Petroleum Producers v. Smith et al., decision on which was rendered by a three-judge federal panel on October 24, 1932.[10] Hutcheson once again presided and wrote the court's opinion. The plaintiffs once again charged that the Railroad Commission had promulgated orders under the guise of conservation which were arbitrary, unreasonable, and confiscatory, which thereby violated due process, and which were in fact designed solely to maintain the price of crude oil. Moreover, the plaintiffs also introduced testimony from their own experts purporting to show that East Texas was under gas drive rather than water drive, and that the orders of the Railroad Commission therefore promoted rather than prevented waste.

Once again, the court faced conflicting theories about East Texas, and once again it flatly refused to resolve the scientific issues, noting:

> In fact, so radical are their differences, and so contrary their opinions, so voluble, so volatile are most of the witnesses in advancing them, and so equal are they all in cocksureness, that form of knowing which easily mistakes certitude for certainty, that, if we assume, as we suppose on this record we should, them all to have equal theoretical knowledge and an equal absence of intention to deceive, the theories as such might best be held to counterbalance, leaving the question of the validity of the orders to be determined, not upon disputed theories, but by a consideration of the physical facts and their admitted consequences, and the common sense conclusions which that consideration compels. . . . We think that too little is definitely known about these theories, and there is too large a body of undisputed controlling physical facts to permit opinion evidence to determine, either before the commission or us, the real and substantial rights here in question [p. 363].

The court then proceeded to contradict itself, embracing elements of one and then the other of the competing theories. It first adopted the traditional separate-well notion, finding that

> complaintants' wells are nearly in the middle of the field, with oil saturated sands of the maximum thickness, but no water underlying, and they can produce large quantities of oil without waste [p. 363].

The court then turned around and embraced a consequence of the water drive hypothesis, finding that:

> if the present condition is maintained, plaintiffs will lose oil to which they are entitled to the wells on the east, and, long prior to the exhaustion of the oil and gas in the reservoir, the rise in the water will saturate plaintiffs' wells, drowning them out, and the sands lying to the east will produce the oil which has been driven from the plaintiffs' lands to them [p. 364].

Yet the court neglected the other consequence of the water-drive theory, that such operation would maximize total recovery from the pool, merely noting instead that the commission had never made the experiments, tests, or inquiries that would have been necessary to ascertain the greatest amount of oil which each producer might take from his wells without injury to the field (p. 364).

Next, rather than pursue the logic of its position, that is, that the Railroad Commission should make tests and then prorate production so as to maximize total recovery from the pool and protect the property rights of individual owners, the court instead hippity-hopped to price-fixing. After expressing classic laissez-faire faith that the "enlightened self-interest" of the East Texas producers could be counted upon to devise ways and means of obtaining the greatest ultimate yield from the pool, the court held that "no reasonable mind" could believe that the orders entered by the Railroad Commission were either designed to have, or in fact had, any real relation to the public need to conserve oil (p. 365). Hutcheson then concluded the court's opinion by quoting verbatim the vitiating price-fixing finding of the MacMillan case.

As in the MacMillan case, although with more confusion and difficulty, the court had once again refused to deal directly with scientific issues. It chose instead to concoct its own basically traditional potpourri of notions about oil wells, find those notions largely irrelevant, and then decide the case on the old price-fixing grounds.

Ironically, the first genuine success in federal court for the Railroad Commission came not in an East Texas case but in one originating in the vast Panhandle gas field (125 miles long by 15 miles wide). In Danciger Oil & Refining Co. v. Smith et al.,[11] decided in August of 1933, Hutcheson, again writing for a three-judge federal court, refused to invalidate a Railroad Commission prorationing order. Hutcheson carefully noted two major, determinant differences between the Danciger case and MacMillan and People's. First, allowable was "fixed at a very large proportion of the potential of the field," and second, in apportioning allowed production, an effort had been made "to fairly allocate to each producer that portion of the production which the situation and nature of his properties entitles him to have" (p. 237). Then, in a remarkable backhanded opinion, the court made a ruling that is worth quoting:

Impressed as we are with the strength of plaintiffs' contention, and inclined as we might be to hold that upon the very clear, vigorous, and convincing affidavits which they have furnished the preponderance of the evidence is with them on the issue that the best, the most reasonable way to prevent waste in that field, in view of all the conditions there, would be to produce each well at its proper gas-oil ratio, abandoning all attempts at proration or ratable taking, it must be kept in mind that the case is not before us for trial de novo of that issue on the preponderance of the evidence. The issue before us is one of a claimed confiscation through arbitrary and unreasonable orders. In reaching our conclusion upon that issue we are only authorized, we are only trying, to determine whether the evidence is such as that we must say that reasonable minds, charged with the duty of protecting the state's natural resources in that field, could not reasonably have reached the conclusion which the commission reached, that the order it entered would have at least some effect to fairly prevent waste. . . . We are clear that the evidence has not overcome the presumption of validity attending the commission's orders [p. 239].

Four factors seemed to have swayed the court. First, the degree of production limitation in the Panhandle field was moderate compared to East Texas. Second, Danciger had been permitted to operate unimpeded for the previous two years, and the court sought to strike a balance between "threatened injuries" and "benefits received."[12] Third, the Railroad Commission's limitation of production to minimize gas-oil ratios was in accord with traditional wisdom and presented none of the problems of scientific interpretation present in the dispute over water drive in East Texas. Fourth, and perhaps most significantly, the court finally seems to have begun to recognize the magnitude of the difficulties faced by the Railroad Commission, for it concluded:

whether in our opinion wise or unwise, they [the orders] represent an exercise, neither unreasonable nor arbitrary, of the judgment and discretion of the commission in the discharge of the difficult administrative duties which the statute has imposed upon them [pp. 239-240].

The great irony of course is that the Railroad Commission was finally permitted to prevent waste in the very field in which the most egregious waste in Texas history would occur over the next two years. Many producers in the Panhandle field had no market for natural gas; from May of 1933 to December of 1935, the Texas legislature, in a benighted attempt to fairly adjust the rights of those who did and did not have gas pipeline connections, permitted the "stripping" of natural gasoline from natural gas. Natural gas so stripped was then "popped" or vented into the air. The vented gas normally comprised more than 95 percent of the fuel energy withdrawn from the reservoir. Such practices peaked in 1934, when more than a billion cubic feet of gas per day were wasted, more than the then entire domestic consumption of natural gas in the United States.[13]

Yet some judicial principle that recognized the scientific and legal complexities of oil regulation was slowly emerging. The turning point in this evolution came in Amazon Petroleum Corporation v. Railroad Commission of Texas,[14] in which a decision was rendered by a three-judge federal panel on February 12, 1934. The law firm of Saye, Smead & Saye of Longview, Texas, who had made a virtual career of hauling the Railroad Commission into federal court, decided, in the immortal words of Darrel Royal, "to dance with who they brung." The plaintiffs once more alleged that Railroad Commission orders were arbitrary, capricious, and confiscatory; that they indeed promoted rather than inhibited physical waste underground; and that their sole true purpose was the forbidden one of price-fixing.[15]

The same experts reciting the same evidence that had confounded the Railroad Commission in the People's case appeared for Amazon.[16] Those experts once again maintained that East Texas was a conventional oil field in which the dominant force for producing oil was the expansion of dissolved gas, or gas drive, and that the optimum method of producing oil under such conditions was to minimize gas-oil ratios and to maximize, by high rates of production, the lifting or expulsive energy of the gas. They cited the high gas-oil ratios of wells which were produced intermittently at low rates compared to the low gas-oil ratios of wells which were allowed to produce at very high rates, as conclusive evidence that only unrestrained production would in fact prevent underground waste and waste of reservoir energy. The plaintiffs' experts adamantly denied that any significant water intrusion had occurred, arguing that on any reasonable set of assumptions about strata porosity, no rise in the salt water level in the field even remotely proportional to known oil withdrawals had occurred. They concluded that the oil itself had expanded, as it would if saturated with gas in a gas-driven field, and that any substantial role for water drive or "hydrostatic control" was, in a field like East Texas, purely mythical. Railroad Commission orders, which limited most wells to 4 percent of their potential production as determined by Railroad Commission tests, while allowing "marginal" or "stripper" wells (those capable of producing only twenty barrels a day or less) to produce freely, were therefore asserted to be totally without scientific foundation.

Two things are striking about Amazon's expert evidence. First, it is largely ad hoc and unsystematized. It depends for the most part on reports of surface potentials, practical gas-oil ratios, and water intrusion, all under widely varying conditions, for a large number of individual wells. Other than making the bald assertion that almost all known oil fields are gas driven, and that therefore East Texas must be, and issuing a blanket denunciation of Railroad Commission claims about water drive, little systematic analysis was offered. In fact, the only telling points concerned water levels in the field and gas-oil ratios. Second, virtually all of the plaintiffs' presumably expert witnesses were either practioners with wide practical experience but little or no formal training, or they were men educated either in geology or in some branch of engineering before 1922. None had any formal training in petroleum engineering or had graduated after 1922.

The Railroad Commission, in contrast, presented the most complete, systematic, and sophisticated scientific analysis of East Texas to that time—and one that has stood since with virtually no major revision. The core of their case rested on the work of two men: Ben F. Lindsley and Carl E. Reistle, Jr. Lindsley was Senior Petroleum Engineer, U.S. Bureau of Mines, Petroleum Experiment Station, Bartlesville, Oklahoma, but from mid-1931 had worked in a laboratory in Kilgore, Texas built by Shell Oil for the exlusive use of the Bureau of Mines. After the BOM budget was drastically reduced in July, 1932, a consortium of some 41 East Texas producers supported completion of the BOM studies.[17] Reistle had graduated as a petroleum technologist from the Chemical Engineering School of the University of Oklahoma in 1922, and from then until September 1933 worked for the Bureau of Mines. He then took a year's leave to work for the East Texas Engineering Association. In notable contrast to Amazon's witnesses, virtually all of the Railroad Commission's experts were similarly qualified.

To sustain the Railroad Commission's orders, expert testimony had to establish four points: first, that the East Texas field was in fact under water drive; second, that Railroad Commission prorationing orders were essential to efficient, non-wasteful recovery; third, that the alternative theory of dissolved-gas drive was not scientifically founded; and fourth, that alternative strategies of field management were therefore inappropriate and wasteful. In order to make their case, Lindsley, Reistle, and other petroleum engineers employed either by the Railroad Commission or, more often, by interested firms, conducted large-scale laboratory and field investigations in East Texas.[18]

First, Lindsley ascertained actual reservoir, that is, bottom hole conditions: the actual temperature, viscosity, and gas saturation of reservoir fluids in place, as opposed to their being inferred from measurements taken at the surface. Lindsley could command such information because he had access to two new technological innovations: a bottom-hole sampling device developed by Reistle for the Bureau of Mines, and a "lightweight portable well-measuring and sounding apparatus" developed by Halliburton, which made it possible for the first time to conveniently drop and retrieve the bottom-hole sampler.

Lindsley found East Texas crude to be undersaturated with gas at reservoir temperatures (146° F) and pressures (1200-1400 lbs./sq. in.), and that gas did not begin to come out of solution until pressure dropped to 755 lbs./sq. in. East Texas crude suffered a shrinkage of 20 percent between the bottom of the hole (3600 feet down) and the time it went into the storage tanks on the surface, as a result of thermal shrinkage and of liberation of connate gas. Lindsley also noted that East Texas oil at reservoir conditions was only negligibly compressible.

These findings had several critical implications. There was no gas drive in East Texas—oil was undersaturated at reservoir pressures and would not expand appreciably; no free gas cap could form above 755 lbs./sq. in. It was, however, essential to maintain reservoir pressure to keep gas in solution; otherwise, oil viscosity would increase and whatever aid gas-lift could provide in getting oil up the casing would be lost. The apparent variations in gas-oil ratios with rate of production resulted from dissolved gas being liberated below 755 lbs./sq. in. in the casing of shut-in wells, and in no way reflected actual reservoir conditions. Furthermore, the shrinkage of East Texas oil meant that it occupied 20 percent more space in the reservoir than at the surface, which in turn implied that correlations between surface volumes of oil produced and alleged rates of water intrusion were completely spurious, and that in fact the observed rise in the water level in East Texas wells was fully consistent with a pure water-drive mechanism under existent conditions. Finally, given his data on shrinkage and compressibility, Lindsley showed that any gas drive or reservoir fluid expansion theory of East Texas required assumptions about total reservoir volume that were totally absurd, and that therefore some other mechanism had to be present, namely, water drive.[19]

Reistle, for his part, conducted tests on "some 200 wells scattered in a representative fashion throughout the field." Using these and other data made available to him, he prepared a careful and precise graphical analysis correlating rates of production, total reservoir pressure decline, and rates of water intrusion.[20] He clearly demonstrated that actual observed pressures could only occur in the presence of water drive. He showed conclusively the precipitous rate of pressure decline at high rates of production and the absolute necessity of controlled, limited withdrawals in order to maximize total recovery from the pool.

The Railroad Commission had its case, a classic of scientific reasoning. Their experts had shown that all data, experimental and observational, were perfectly consistent with the water-drive theory of the East Texas field, and that competing theories either required absurd assumptions or led to patently false conclusions. There could be no reasonable doubt.

Judge Hutcheson, again writing for the court and ruling in favor of the Railroad Commission, nevertheless did not accept the theory of the Commission's scientists. After tortuously trying to show the objective differences in circumstance as well as the legal consistency in interpretation in the MacMillan, People's, and Danciger cases, Hutcheson took note of the recently passed "market demand" statute in Texas:

> Unfortunately for the plaintiffs, the spirit of the times making for collectivism against individualism has so warred against their contentions that the march of the statute law, which stands with us for public opinion and within constitutional limits determines the public policy of the state, has been with the restrictionists, the market demandists [p. 637].

Oddly enough, however, the case did not hinge on market demand at all. The Railroad Commission's order clearly stood on the pattern of distribution in East Texas and on considerations of physical waste. The commission's prima facie case, he said, was not rebutted by any testimony, but was

> reinforced by the great mass of it offered in its support, of experiments and tests made in the field, and of conclusions reached by engineers of at least equal standing with those offered by plaintiffs. The testimony taken in the cases we tried in 1932 fully developed the then known conditions in the East Texas field, and those assumed in the opinions of the engineers based on experiments and tests up to that time made there. Since then many experiments and tests have been made under field and under laboratory conditions, many opinions have been tested and tried, and some found wanting.

The result of all this work undertaken since 1932 was the common recognition that restriction was essential in the production of that field, and that free and unlimited production could not be tolerated (p. 638).

Thus the scientific evidence, Hutcheson seems to be saying, was largely responsible for the shift in public attitudes, resulting in the recent "market demand" statute. But his conclusion is notable:

> We have examined with the greatest care this mass of evidence, voluminous, ponderable, pretending to scientific accuracy, as to physical conditions in East Texas, and the relation of the restrictions to the prevention of waste there. We are impressed, but not aided, by the fact that scientific men of standing, integrity, and ability can so radically disagree. However much we may be disappointed in finding ourselves unable to determine to what extent interest in the result makes for these differences of opinion, and to what extent the questions are insoluble, we do find outselves so situated that we are bound to say that all this vast amount of evidence, submitted in favor of the commission's findings, is too ponderable to be brushed aside as no evidence at all. We find ourselves wholly unable to say that the conclusion the commission reached is not one which reasonable minds could entertain [pp. 638-639].

What has happened here is subtle and extraordinary. Hutcheson embraced not the particular scientific theory advanced by the Railroad Commission, but foreswearing even consideration of the issues of market demand and price-fixing, which had been so compelling in earlier cases, embraced instead the process of science, of scientific inquiry itself. Hutcheson let stand the prorationing orders of the Railroad Commission, not because he could determine that their theory was unquestionably right, which it was and which obviously bulked large in his decision, but because the process was clearly reasonable. The brute dominance of scientific issues had redefined both "reasonable" and "due process."

As should be obvious by now, I think the path followed by the courts was never clear and direct, but rather meandered in a "satisficing" search process that was sometimes random, sometimes confused, and sometimes desperate. In the MacMillan case can be seen traditional conceptions of due process, private property, and legitimate administrative behavior rampant and enraged. In the muddle of the People's opinion, and especially in Danciger, appears the dawning realization that behavioral change in the management of petroleum resources was absolutely essential, although old values and old interpretations were still held fast. Only in the Amazon case did recognition finally come that old values in fact meant something very new and that profound institutional reorientation was imperative.

NOTES

1. 39th *Annual Report of the Railroad Commission for the Year 1930.*

2. York Young Willbern, "Administrative control of petroleum production in Texas." Ph.D. dissertation, University of Texas, Austin, 1943.

3. MacMillan v. Railroad Commission of Texas, 51 F. (2d.) 400 (1931).

4. Willbern, "Administrative control of petroleum production in Texas."

5. Railroad Commission of Texas, Oil and Gas Division. Oil and Gas Docket No. 120 (1932).

6. MacMillan v. Ross S. Sterling, Governor of Texas, et al. Answer No. 395 (1932).

7. Railroad Commission order, February 27, 1932.

8. Ibid.

9. Ibid.

10. People's Petroleum Producers v. Smith, 1 F Supp 361 (1932).

11. Danciger Oil & Refining Co. v. Smith et al., 4 F Supp 239 (1933).

12. Letter from DuVal West to Joseph C. Hutcheson, Jr. (1933).

13. Willbern, "Administrative control of petroleum production in Texas," 75-76.

14. Amazon Petroleum Co. v. Railroad Commission of Texas, 5 F. Supp. 633 (February 12, 1934).

15. Amazon complaint, 6.

16. Amazon transcript, 506.

17. Lindsley, BOM RI 3212, Amazon transcript affidavit, 1334-1380.

18. Lindsley, BOM RI 3212.

19. Ibid., 1374-1375.

20. Reistle, affidavit, 1381-1391.

REFERENCES

BRANNIGAN, A. "The reification of Mendel," *Social Studies of Science* 9 (1979), 423-454.

GIEBELHAUS, A. W. *Business and Government in the Oil Industry: A Case Study of Sun Oil, 1876-1945* (Greenwich, CT, 1980).

HARDWICKE, R. E. "Legal history of conservation of oil in Texas," in *Legal History of Conservation of Oil and Gas,* The Section of Mineral Law of the American Bar Association (Chicago, 1939).

HURT, H. III "New oil: the Giddings gamble," *Texas Monthly* (Februay 1981).

McDONALD, S. L. *Petroleum Conservation in the United States: An Economic Analysis* (Baltimore, 1971).

MILLS, W. E., Jr. *Martial Law in East Texas,* Inter-University Case Program (Birmingham, AL, 1960).

MITCHELL, A. C. *Market Demand and Proration of Texas Crude Petroleum* (Austin, 1964).

PART III

Responses
Ideology, Culture, Organizations, and Politics

10

Urban Planning and Technological Development

Responses to the Modern City, 1909-1945

EUGENIE LADNER BIRCH

In the fifty years between 1870 and 1920, American cities experienced unprecedented demographic and physical growth. 'In the East, for example, New York City's population of less than a million multiplied to five and one-half million.[1] At the same time, its territory expanded from 22 to almost 300 square miles.[2] Chicago, Los Angeles, Washington, DC, Pittsburgh, Cleveland, and San Francisco all repeated the pattern, though on a smaller scale.[3]

Immigration and industrialization were the twin causes of this urban explosion, drawing labor and industry to the centrally located markets these cities became. In addition, technological advances in engineering, transportation, and energy production—creating the skyscraper, the motorized vehicle, and public and private electric lighting—enabled the cities to accommodate burgeoning populations and expanding economies. By the turn of the century, the American city had assumed its thoroughly modern character as a large, densely populated metropolis.

This growth and change did not occur painlessly. Nineteenth-century cities, built for smaller, less mobile economies, became the containers for much larger operations. To accommodate the transformation, they relied on ad hoc solutions for housing, transportation, and trade. Ultimately, these accommodations yielded negative results: Congestion, inefficiency, and threats to health and personal safety became routine urban characteristics. So dreadful were these factors in many cities that community leaders began to search for coordinated and broad-scale solutions to the most pressing problems. Out of this concern came the modern planning movement, one portion of larger turn-of-the-century activities labeled progressive reforms. As it emerged at this time, urban planning was to encompass the development of long-term strategies to guide and improve urban development.

The planning movement attracted supporters who assumed that cities could be efficiently arranged and serviced, physically attractive, rationally managed (from the point of view of municipal capital investment), and environmentally healthy. In general, planning advocates envisioned the management and harnessing of technological systems such as transport and energy as the means to achieve this objective. At its inception, city planning drew its supporters from a variety of urban boosters. Included among them were those involved with local municipal art organizations, housing reform, landscape architecture, architecture and municipal engineering, real estate development, and law and public administration.[4]

In the first decade of the twentieth century, this unusual alliance worked in a number of cities with a view toward securing adoption of urban planning. At the same time, early planners promoted public understanding of the idea. To this end, in 1909 they founded the National Conference on City Planning (NCCP). Similar to other progressive groups of the period, the NCCP met annually, published its own journal, and thus provided a focus and forum for the American planning movement. Later, in 1917, as planning became more widespread, a self-proclaimed group of professionals would break away from the NCCP to create the American City Planning Institute (ACPI). Its aim was to undertake more frequent and detailed technical investigations to advance what they called "the art of the science" of city planning. The ACPI would form the core of mainstream planners and establish the dominant planning ideology of the United States.[5]

The separation of the two groups was entirely logical, for as early planning practices developed, there were essentially four sets of actors. They were: local citizens who provided political support for planning; municipal planning commission members drawn from the community and serving in a volunteer capacity; town government officials encouraged but not required to implement planning commission proposals; and professional advisors hired by a locality to accomplish the technical work of planning. In general, the NCCP membership tended to encompass the first three groups, while the ACPI included the last. Basically, the NCCP looked to the ACPI for leadership in the development of the form and content of urban planning.

All agreed, however, that the tenement, the crowded intersection, the skyscraper, and the blighted area, all results of American energy and transport developments in particular, and of industrial prosperity in general, threatened to destroy the very cities where the nation's economic strength was centered. Early planners expressed this argument in monetary terms, estimating damages. In Boston, for example, they claimed that the loss of life from disease could be calculated at eight million dollars. In Manhattan, they maintained that businessmen lost half a million dollars daily due to inefficiencies in the transportation system.[6]

The planner's diagnosis of the problems as efficiency and cost issues naturally determined the nature of their solutions. As city planning was less developed in the United States then abroad, they adapted European techniques for American consumption. Among their suggestions were: German zoning, which included the legal designation of acceptable land uses in a municipality; British garden city concepts, which focused on the establishment of small, self-contained satellite towns adjacent to congested metropolises; Italian renaissance urban design, especially the use of monumental architectonic groupings symmetrically arranged to create, in the American experience, the civic center; and French boulevard and infrastructure construction, where the emphasis was on the remodeling of existing urban transportation and service systems to accommodate larger populations as had been accomplished by Napoleon III in Paris in the late nineteenth century.[7] All of these devices, they argued, could contribute to the creation of the ideal modern city which, in their view, would serve as a container for a safe, convenient, prosperous, and comfortable life for its citizens.

Ultimately, leaders of the planning movement settled on a hybrid. They developed an ideal of a long-range comprehensive plan whose major elements would be a monumental civic or central business district, a park system with recreational areas linked by parkways, and a massive circulation scheme to facilitate municipal and regional movement. In 1909, all of these characteristics had been brought together in the Chicago Plan, a widely publicized project sponsored by the wealthy industrialists and businessmen who were members of the Commercial Club. Architect Daniel H. Burnham had shaped the Chicago Plan, drawing upon antecedents such as the layout of the Chicago World's Fair (1893), the McMillan Plan for Washington, DC (1902), the Cleveland Group Plan (1903), and the San Francisco Plan (1905) (see Figure 10.1).[8]

Although Burnham, failing in health and in semi-retirement, did not personally participate in the organizational development of the planning movement, his Chicago Plan formed the basis of the practitioners' primary

Figure 10.1

product. Known over the years by various titles—the master, general, or comprehensive plan—this document would contain the three essential elements—schemes for central city renewal, public spaces, and circulation of traffic and people.

After 1909, innovations in transport technology such as the electric trolley and the automobile could be linked to the demand of downtown businessmen for improved traffic circulation and that of neighborhood residents for solitude, predictability, and plenty of urban services, such as sewers, electricity, and highways. What planners had in mind was to channel popular preference for the speed and mobility of the trolley and automobile into a set of technical and rational solutions for urban problems. Although planners and their plans included plenty of sewers, trollies, and other municipal services, the highway, and later the express highway, was their most popular idea. The Chicago Plan, with its local and regional highway routes, was the model for thought and plans along these lines, and during the course of the next twenty years, proposals for physical reform and redevelopment in other large cities followed it (see Figures 10.2 and 10.3). This vision ultimately dominated the field of city planning up to the 1960s. On the one hand, it was limited, conservative, and ameliorative; on the other, it was realizable, useful, and practical.

The central business district, with its offices, warehouses, depots, hotels, and department stores, stood as the symbol and economic reality that planners and their schemes for highways served. This commitment entailed making downtowns accessible to outlying areas through the imposition of radial arteries into the street pattern; keeping automobiles and trucks separate to streamline traffic flow; and eliminating unnecessary downtown vehicular traffic by providing circumferential bypass routes. Nearly equal in importance was the notion that residential areas should be kept clear of heavy traffic; that express traffic must be accommodated by grade separations and limited access highways; and that the entire circulation pattern should be regarded as a system, organized hierarchically by function (see Figures 10.4 and 10.5).

The planners' faith in their transportation improvements was further strengthened by the fact that these schemes were more frequently translated into public action than their other suggestions. In city after city, municipal governments undertook street widenings, expressway construction, and intersection improvements. Highly visible, easily financed through bond issues, and extremely effective, improved circulation was popular with politician and citizen alike.

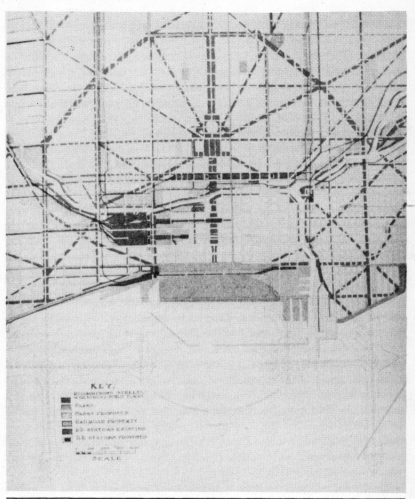

Figure 10.2

Their plans were attractive because not only did they provide effective programs for moving traffic, but also because they were profitable. Improved accessibility created higher downtown land values and heightened the development potential of adjacent property. This increase elevated assessed valuations and resulted in healthier municipal tax bases. In

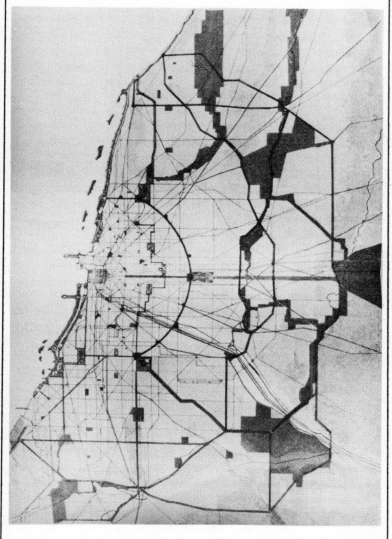

Figure 10.3

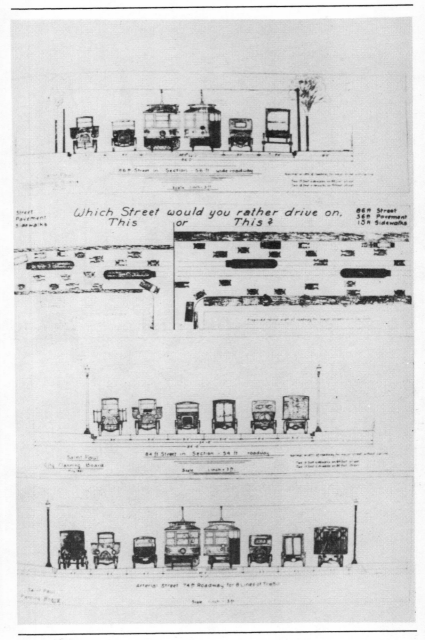

Figure 10.4

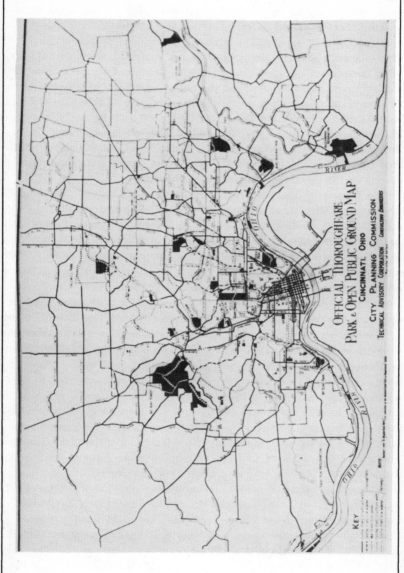

Figure 10.5

Chicago, for example, the completion of Wacker Drive according to the Plan led to a five- to sixfold increase in the prices of neighboring real estate, while in St. Louis, the widening of one major thoroughfare reaped a sevenfold benefit to the tax rolls.[9]

Relishing such measures of success as enhanced property values, the early planners realized that transportation programs, along with selected other devices, such as zoning, were among the best selling products in their stock. In contrast, they observed the failure of others, namely the unexecuted architectural or city beautiful schemes such as those for Phoenix, Arizona, and Lincoln, Nebraska (see Figure 10.6).[10] By 1929, they had learned the lesson thoroughly. Concluding that "planning commissions and their advisors will do well to make the plan as far as possible arise from the economic and social fabric of the city," they gambled their professional destiny on the proven set of transportation solutions.[11]

The Progressive Era planners passed on these teachings to their successors. In 1929, Harvard established the first planning degree program. Other universities soon followed. Additionally, increasing numbers of municipalities established planning departments and commissioned planning studies. (By 1942, over half of the nation's large cities had master plans.)[12] The output was predictable. A review of the general plans during this period reveals the same kind of solutions as in the earlier period (Figure 10.7). During the early years of professional city planning, then, planners relied upon the popularity of the auto as a strategy for marketing highway plans.

The training of planners in the technical arts reinforced their inclination to propose solutions such as highways. Drawn largely from the mechanical professions—architecture, landscape architecture, and engineering—they were accustomed to dealing with specific spatial problems such as street widths or lot lines. They had no background in addressing the broader factors of urban growth and change and therefore were not particularly interested in dwelling upon the implications of their recommendations. Lacking the skills and opportunity to meditate on the city as, say, a multiple ecology, only a rare soul attempted to pose alternative systems for community planning and for transportation in particular.[13]

While early twentieth-century planning was dominated by the private consultant who primarily needed to provide a marketable product, a minority tradition did develop. Predictably enough, the proponents of these approaches were those who did not depend upon meeting the demands of municipal-political clients for their livelihood. Instead, they were subsidized by private foundations, enlightened capitalists, or government funds earmarked for broader missions. A few examples of this type

Figure 10.6 Like the ill-fated civic center design for San Francisco (1903) pictured above, plans featuring grandiose public construction were infrequently implemented.

189

190

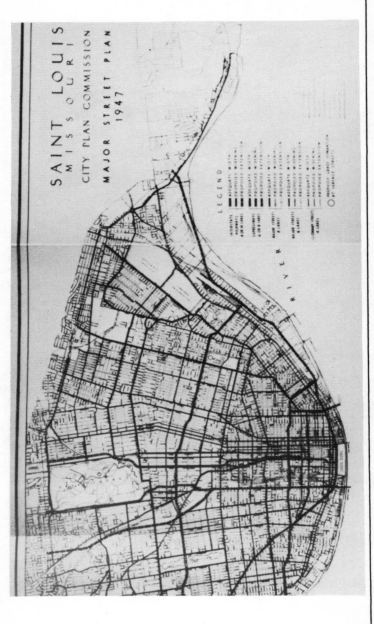

SAINT LOUIS
MISSOURI
CITY PLAN COMMISSION

MAJOR STREET PLAN
1947

LEGEND

RIVER

Figure 10.7

of pursuit are the work of the Regional Plan Association of New York, subsidized by the Russell Sage Foundation and directed by a few philanthropic businessmen; the ideas of the New York State Commission on Housing and Regional Planning; and the projects of the Regional Planning Association of America, especially in Radburn, New Jersey.

The most dramatic example of the approach of this minority was the plan for New York State, written by Henry Wright in 1926 under the auspices of the New York State Commission on Housing and Regional Planning. Wright was a member of the circle of like-minded architects and writers that included Clarence Stein, Lewis Mumford, Edith Elmer Wood, and Catherine Bauer. They were heavily influenced by the British planning tradition and synthesized the writings of garden city advocate Ebenezer Howard and regional planning proponent Patrick Geddes to create their own brand of analysis and solutions.[14] Unlike their colleagues in mainstream planning, they probed deeply into the relationship between technology and society to understand the roots of urban problems. Consequently, they gave far less attention to the details of particular issues than to the lack of equilibrium in urban systems. Isolating two factors, energy and transportation, they traced their influence on settlement patterns. Ultimately, they called for the harnessing of the modern expression of two items—electricity and automobiles—to yield a state plan featuring grouped urban settlements of medium density and large areas of land in conservation (Figure 10.8).[15]

The plan was brilliant. Unfortunately, it was never implemented. Not only did it have no real sponsor—it had been included in the agenda of a state commission whose real purpose was to study the Empire State's rent control laws—but it also had no natural allies. Unlike the executed municipal transportation plans of mainstream planning, it did not supply a politically palatable remedy for extreme conditions, and it did not parallel existing trends. In sum, it did not prove to be a practical document for the times. It was too rational and too intellectual to become a viable alternative in the period in which it had been conceived.

The proposed city of Radburn, New Jersey, was another product of this minority group of planners. Radburn was envisioned as a model town for the motor age. The most unusual features of the plan were its use of the neighborhood unit, the superblock, and a hierarchically arranged street system with separate functional roads for vehicles and pedestrians (Figure 10.9).[16] The depression-caused financial downturn aborted the construction of Radburn, and consequently only fragments appeared. Nonetheless, so highly publicized and so appealing in its rationality to planners was the

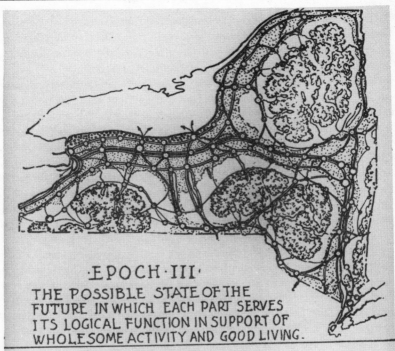

·EPOCH·III·
THE POSSIBLE STATE OF THE
FUTURE IN WHICH EACH PART SERVES
ITS LOGICAL FUNCTION IN SUPPORT OF
WHOLESOME ACTIVITY AND GOOD LIVING·

PLATE LVI

Comparable in importance with the railroad and the steam engine in determining the character of development in the second industrial epoch are the modern factors of the automobile, good road and electric transmission line. These modern forces do not portend a return to the widely distributed development of the first epoch. Rather they will lend themselves to a more effective utilization of all of the economic resources of the State and to the most favorable development of areas especially adapted to industry, agriculture, recreation, water supply and forest reserve.

Figure 10.8

Radburn concept that in the long run it became a theoretical success. It would be promoted in planning literature (Figure 10.10), taught in planning schools, upheld in government manuals for replication (Figure 10.11), and adapted to several federally sponsored projects of the New Deal and later periods (Figure 10.12).[17] Like the New York State Plan, the Radburn idea was highly rational and technically exceptional. However intellectually appealing the plan was, though, it was never adopted on a large

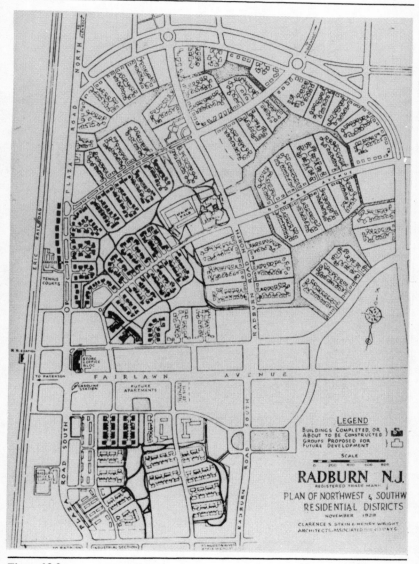

Figure 10.9

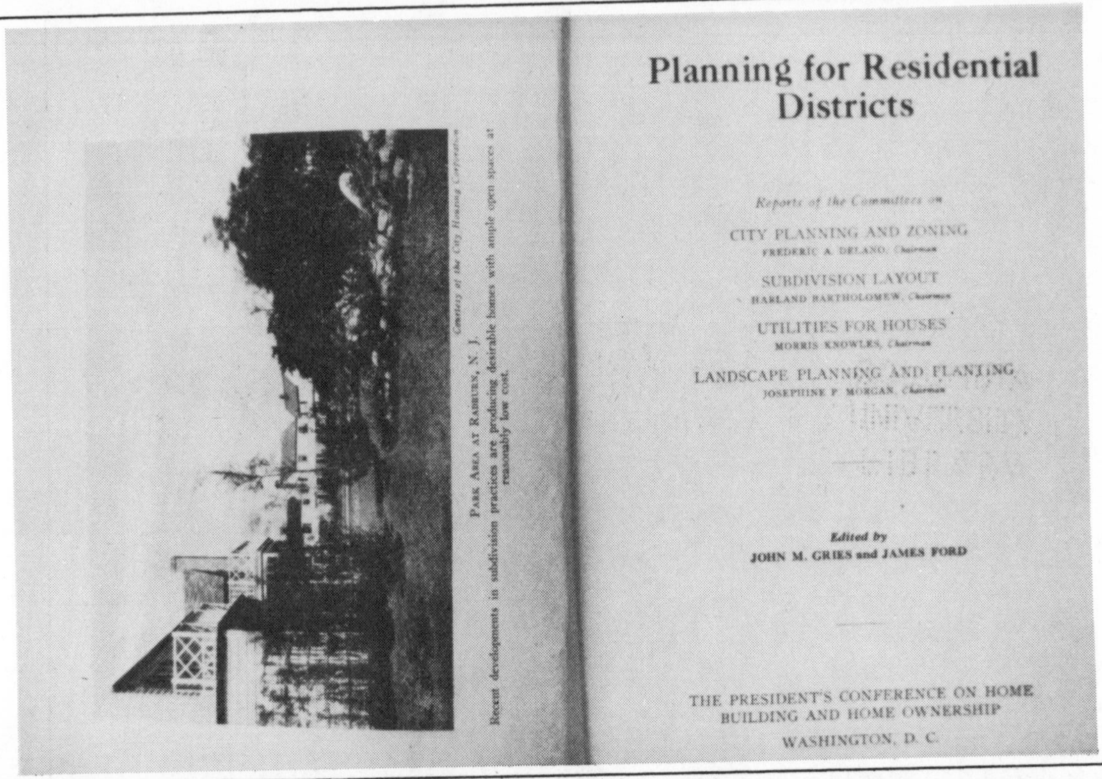

Courtesy of the City Housing Corporation

PARK AREA AT RADBURN, N. J.

Recent developments in subdivision practices are producing desirable homes with ample open spaces at reasonably low cost.

Planning for Residential Districts

Reports of the Committees on

CITY PLANNING AND ZONING
FREDERIC A. DELANO, *Chairman*

SUBDIVISION LAYOUT
HARLAND BARTHOLOMEW, *Chairman*

UTILITIES FOR HOUSES
MORRIS KNOWLES, *Chairman*

LANDSCAPE PLANNING AND PLANTING
JOSEPHINE F. MORGAN, *Chairman*

Edited by
JOHN M. GRIES and JAMES FORD

THE PRESIDENT'S CONFERENCE ON HOME BUILDING AND HOME OWNERSHIP
WASHINGTON, D. C.

Figure 10.10

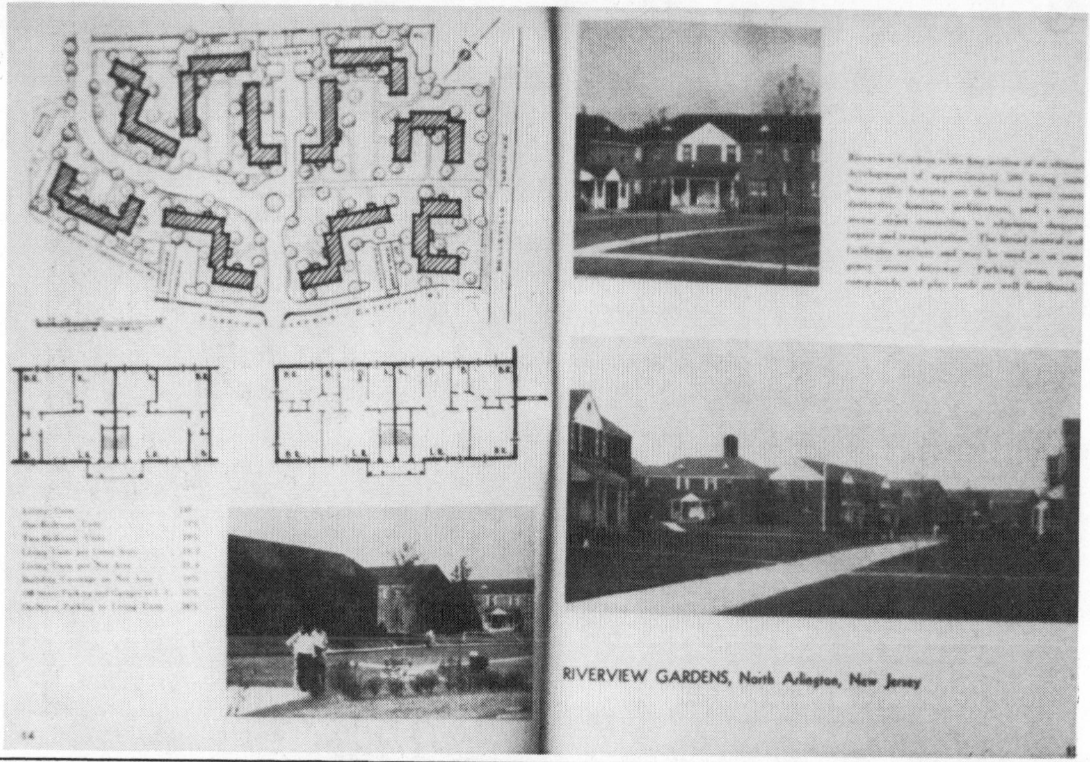

RIVERVIEW GARDENS, North Arlington, New Jersey

Figure 10.11

Figure 10.12

scale by the nation's major housing developers. It was a failure because it was not marketable. This phenomenon can be attributed to a simple economic fact: Its main thrust was contrary to American real estate traditions, with their emphasis on a grid-system of streets.

Although the two examples of New York State and Radburn are but a few of the minority planning alternatives advanced in the early developmental period for planning, their failure to be adopted, as well as the omnipresence of the standard set of solutions discussed earlier in this chapter, can be attributed to several factors: first, the peculiar nature of planning in the American system; second, the pervasive strength of consumer preferences in a market economy; and third, the defensive character of the planning profession, whose major product was a negotiable and marketable master plan.

Ultimately, the American city changed rapidly, but did so without much by way of formal guidance. Indeed, urbanites themselves planned their own cities in haphazard fashion as they selected sites for the location of stores, homes, and plants. The directors of urban utilities such as transit, electricity, and gas made their own private plans, but generally they followed the best markets outward to the urban periphery.[18] Such, at least, was the case up to approval by Congress in 1954 of legislation to require a master plan in order to qualify for urban renewal funds.

Even so, the planning process after 1954 remained a municipal activity, dependent upon the economic and political support of elected and non-elected leaders of a given city. Therefore, the planners continued to produce master plans that reflected many of the same client-oriented concerns that had been articulated as early as 1909: central city business revitalization, transportation efficiency, and relief of population congestion. They reinforced trends that had been barely perceptible at the turn of the century but that had become dominant by mid-century. The familiar solution, radial arteries and expressways, became standard practice as city after city took on the same appearance (Figure 10.13).[19]

The standard formula of central cities linked to outlying residential areas did not become the dominant urban mode because planners had made technical recommendations for this scenario. The rising standard of living, the popularity of the automobile and suburban home, and dramatic changes in the American economy from industrial to service production created conditions for which the planners' mainstream solutions were particularly suited.

Finally, the defensive posture of planners as professionals also contributed to the contemporary urban proposals. Professional planners were

Figure 10.13

always few in number. As a group, they grew slowly from the original 52-charter members of 1917, to the post-World War II roster of 240, to the mid-Sixties tally of about 3000. Furthermore, they were never secure about the definition of their profession. From the time of their inception to the present, they have increased their area of claimed expertise. Although they have expanded their horizons, they have not worked to pin down their own professional territory, as have other groups, like architects, physicians, and lawyers. Internal strife concerning licensing and registration, which reached a peak in the mid-Sixties, as well as the constant work of other professions to undermine them, have left them with empty claims to expertise. For example, even in the Twenties, when they exercised superior transportation knowledge, municipalities were already taking responsibility for traffic management out of planning departments and placing it in newly established, separate traffic departments. Thus, the distinctive nature of the American planning profession and the climate in which it has operated led to the situation where the only planning recommendations executed were those that coincided with the agenda of the political and economical dicision-makers of the jurisdiction in question. With this state of affairs, then, it is quite easy to understand why alternative planning policies have never been particularly well received in the United States.

NOTES

1. Bayrd Still, *Urban America, A History with Documents* (Boston, 1974), 210.

2. Kenneth T. Jackson, "Metropolitan government versus political autonomy: politics in the crabgrass frontier," in Kenneth T. Jackson and Stanley K. Schultz, eds., *Cities in American History* (New York, 1972), 443, 445.

3. Data for these other selected cities are as follows:

City	1870 pop.	area (sq. mi.)	1920 pop.	area*
Chicago	298,997	36	2,701,705	185
Los Angeles	5,728	29	576,673	85
Washington	109,199	60	437,571	60
Pittsburgh	139,256	23	588,343	40
Cleveland	92,829	12	796,841	46
San Francisco	149,473	42	506,676	42

*Data for 1910
Sources: Still, *Urban America,* 210; Jackson, "Metropolitan government," 443, 445.

4. For details about the early city planning movement, see Jon A. Peterson, "The origins of the comprehensive planning ideal in the United States, 1840-1911." Ph.d dissertation, Harvard University, 1967.

5. Eugenie Ladner Birch, "Advancing the art and science of planning: planners and their organizations, 1909-1980," *Journal of the American Planning Association* (January, 1980), 22-49.

6. Proceedings of the First National Conference on City Planning, Washington, DC, May 21-22, 1909 (Reprint, Chicago, 1967), 104; Theodora Kimball Hubbard and Henry Vincent Hubbard, *Our Cities Today and Tomorrow* (Cambridge, MA, 1929), 192.

7. For further discussion of the origins of city planning, see Mel Scott, *American City Planning Since 1890* (Berkeley, 1969).

8. Thomas S. Hines, in *Burnham of Chicago* (New York, 1974), provides a definitive study of Burnham's influence. John Reps's *Monumental Washington* (Princeton, 1967) is an excellent account of the development of the McMillan Plan.

9. Hubbard and Hubbard, *Our Cities*, 216-217.

10. Ibid, 264.

11. Ibid, 135.

12. "Status of planning in cities over 25,000," *ASPO Newsletter* 8 (February 1942), 30.

13. Birch, "Advancing the art and science," 26.

14. For a detailed discussion of the Regional Planning Association of America, see Roy Lubove, *Community Planning in the 1920's: The Contributions of the Regional Planning Association of America* (Pittsburgh, 1962); Clarence Stein, *Towards New Towns for America* (Cambridge, MA, 1973); and Carl Sussman, ed., *Planning the Fourth Migration: The Neglected Vision of the Regional Planning Association of America* (Cambridge, MA, 1976).

15. *Report of the Commission of Housing and Regional Planning to Governor Alfred E. Smith* (Albany, 1926).

16. Stein, *Towards New Towns*, 68-72.

17. See E. L. Birch, "Radburn and the American planning movement: the persistence of an idea," *Journal of the American Planning Association* (October 1980), 424-439, for further development of this idea.

18. For further discussion of this point, see Mark H. Rose and John G. Clark, "Light, heat and power: energy choices in Kansas City, Wichita and Denver, 1900-1935," *Journal of Urban History* 5 (May 1979), 340-364; Stanley K. Schultz and Clay McShane, "To engineer a metropolis: sewers, sanitation and city planning in late nineteenth century America," *Journal of American History* 65 (September 1978), 389-411.

19. See Alan A. Altshuler, *The City Planning Process* (Ithaca, NY, 1965), for illustration of this point.

11

Household Energy Consumption, 1900-1980

A Quantitative History

BONNIE MAAS MORRISON

Introduction: Some Scenes

Scene I, 1900:   After the five-mile walk from the schoolhouse, the children were happy to warm their hands, feet and noses in front of the crackling fire, a fire that also provided the heat under the big kettle where a hearty stew bubbled, issuing forth delicious smells and the promise of supper.

Scene II, 1920:   Out of the big cast iron stove, Mother lifted four pies and six loaves of bread. Into it she immediately placed the noon meal for our family of seven and the hired hand. Mornings were always busy in the farm kitchen, but the heat from the stove made it warm and a wonderful place to be on a cold November day.

Scene III, 1940:   It was 5:30 on a windy January morning, and sounds could be heard from the cellar. The sounds were like an alarm clock heard only during the winter months. Dad was shaking last night's clinkers from the furnace grate before shoveling in more coal. Reluctantly, I crawled out of my cozy bed, knowing it would be some time before the house would really feel warm again.

Scene IV, 1970:   As I left for the office, I glanced at the thermostat. It read 72 degrees. I also checked the timer on the electric oven to make sure it was set for 4:30 p.m. Pushing the button for the garage door opener, I thought to myself how safe and secure modern conveniences had made my life. I could be gone all day and return home to a warm house and a piping hot meal.

Scene V, 1980:   Now that the house is fully insulated and the wood stove in operation, we find we are using a lot less oil, except on the very coldest days. A blessing considering the price of oil! However, we still have to scream at the boys to get the wood in from beside the house, even after we talked to them about the necessity of keeping the wood fire going in order to save both energy and the cost of fuel.

The Good Old Days

The foregoing scenes were developed to depict a strongly pervasive notion which suggests that households in the past used less energy. The implied conclusion is that by returning to the "good old days" (turn of the century or so) of past energy resources and use patterns, American households could be rescued from present-day energy problems. Despite its surface plausibility and its widespread acceptance, this particular notion is not based on substantial evidence. The assumption that past generations of households used energy more conservatively than today is just that, an assumption—with little basis in fact. The wider and more serious implication of using this untested assumption is, of course, the fact that many household energy policies and programs at the national, state, and local levels (including household conservation activities) have been initiated without thorough testing or even close examination.

In my own research on contemporary household energy consumption patterns (from the Arab Embargo of 1973),[1] it has become more and more apparent that a national as well as a historical context for household energy research and policy making has been largely missing. Short-term quantitative histories of household energy use have been done; however, these studies (dating back no further than the 1950s) have neither lent support to the "good old days" notion nor tested the assumption that past generations of households (turn of the century or so) used less energy.[2] Thus, the most compelling reasons I saw for undertaking the research reported here were the following:

(1) the need for a quantitative history of household- and national-level energy consumption dating back to the turn of the century, which would allow statistical comparisons; and

(2) the need to test the assumption that households in generations past used less energy; that is, a test of the "good old days" notion.

The quantitative history of household- and national-level energy consumption, as well as an informal test of the "good old days" notion, accounts for most of the research reported here.[3] Beyond discovering *how* household- and national-level energy consumption patterns (types of energy and amounts) changed over time, I also felt strongly that having a quantitative measurement of household and national energy consumption patterns would provide the basis for understanding *why* the changes had taken place. In other words, having the quantitative measurement of energy consumption at the outset would provide the framework for adding a rich qualitative history of household energy consumption at some later time.

Plan for the Quantitative Analysis

Initially, I set out to describe energy consumption patterns generally (i.e., national-level as well as household-level) in order to determine what fuel sources were used, how their use and composition changed over time, the magnitude of the changes, and what the relationships were between national and household trends. Then, in more specific terms, I focused on household energy consumption, attempting to describe and understand patterns and changes in patterns over time. This was done first by looking at aggregate household energy use (all households over the eighty years), and then by looking at per-household use over eighty years. This descriptive analysis required the development of a vast energy consumption data base[4] for both national- and household-level uses, in addition to the development of a second data base to allow the description of households.[5] The study is thus both a year-by-year and an eight-decade study of national-level and household-level energy consumption. The year 1900 was selected as a starting date because by that time the United States was well on its way to becoming a nation committed to industrialization, with all the attendant energy demands. The research related to the causes for the energy patterns and changes is still in progress; however, I will discuss some speculative conclusions from both the findings and from the ongoing qualitative research.

The Quantitative Analysis

The fuel sources analyzed are:

(1) Fuel Wood
(2) Anthracite Coal (Hard coal)
(3) Bituminous Coal (Soft coal)
(4) Natural Gas (Dry)
(5) Direct Electricity
(6) Petroleum
(7) Natural Gas (Liquid)

The analysis further includes national-level energy consumption for all sectors of the economy, including households, as well as household-level energy consumption (termed "residential" in the data used). Household analysis included all types of housing, from single-family to multiple dwelling.[6] Analysis for each fuel source was done in a comparative fashion: national compared to household consumption (converted to British thermal units), including the most noteworthy statistics, years of statistical and meaningful increases or decreases, years of peak use or greatest decline, and years when changes in use were particularly interesting.

The last descriptive analysis was a look at household numbers and percentage changes, comparing them to total fuel use changes, and finally a look at per-household and per-person/per-household energy consumption of all fuel sources, again reported in British thermal units.[7]

Fuel Wood

Fuel wood data are reported for the period between 1900 and 1973 for national-level consumption and between 1900 and 1977 for households (see Figure 11.1).

The use of fuel wood declined substantially for both national- and household-level use from 1900-1973. National use of fuel wood was reduced by a total of 81 percent between 1900 and 1973, whereas household use was reduced by 90 percent for the same years. From the

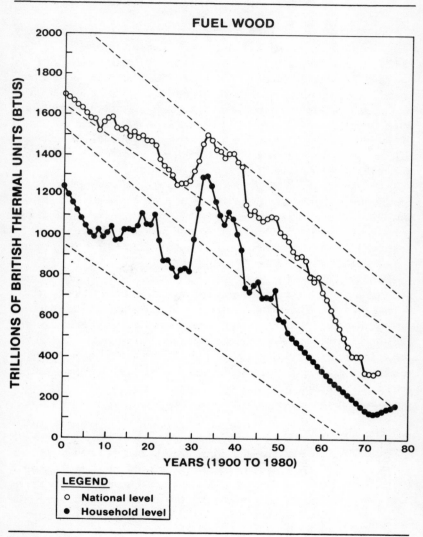

Figure 11.1

figure, it is possible to see year-by-year fluctuations, with 1942 and 1970 being the years of greatest overall reduction from the previous year (–14 percent and –20 percent, respectively) at the national level. For households, the largest reductions took place in 1942 and 1950 from previous years, both at −20 percent.

Prior to 1900, wood was a very important fuel source for all energy needs (national and household); that is, until sometime between 1875 and 1880,[8] when coal began to outpace wood use at the national level.

The peak year of fuel wood use was 1933 for both national and household consumption (statistically significant at the .025 level). This peak comes after nearly thirty years of declining use at both levels. There was a 17 percent increase from 1929 to 1933 at the national level, and a 49 percent increase in household use for the same period. It would appear that fuel wood was being substituted for other more expensive fuel sources during the Depression years (1929 to 1933).

During World War II, slight increases in fuel wood use were also noted. Furthermore, after nearly twenty years of decline, the use of fuel wood was observed once again to be increasing both nationally and in households, starting in 1973 (+3 percent increase nationally and +5 percent for households, from the previous year), perhaps as a result of the increased prices of other energy forms.

Based on Figure 11.1, there appears to be a distinct parallel between national and household energy uses. The patterns of use are closely related in magnitude and fluctuate in very consistent patterns. This tends to suggest that there were not many uses of wood beyond household uses, and that what affects the national level affects household uses and vice versa. The influences may range from the human energy and time needed to gather the wood, to the introduction of other energy sources and the attendant technology, to the socioeconomic and political forces that that condition the demand for wood as a fuel source.

Anthracite Coal

Anthracite coal is a very hard, long-burning, clean coal which produces a high intensity heat. This form of coal is primarily mined in the state of Pennsylvania and is considered a precious fuel because natural reserves have always been limited, as compared to the softer bituminous and lignite coals, vast reserves of which are found in several regions of the country.

As illustrated by Figure 11.2, anthracite has some of the same consumption characteristics as fuel wood. For example, there has been a general decline in its use, particularly since 1917-18. Major peaks in use were related to World Wars I and II. Like fuel wood, anthracite coal uses at the national and household levels were very similar in patterning and closely related in terms of Btus. In other words, household use makes up

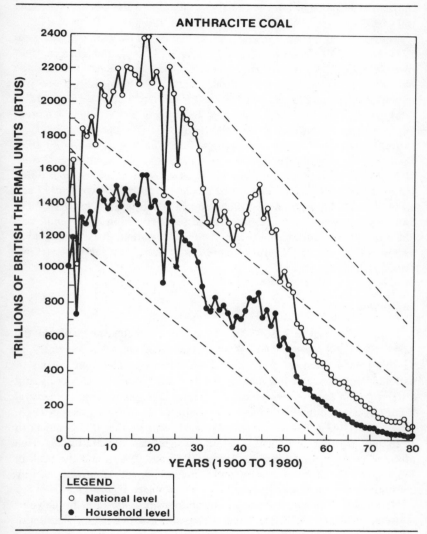

ANTHRACITE COAL

Figure 11.2

the largest proportion of anthracite use (approximately 80 percent in the early 1900s to approximately 60 percent in the 1970s).[9]

On the other hand, the sharp declines noted (unlike fuel wood) were generally related to strikes in the coal mines. The years of the most substantial declines in both national and household use of anthracite coal were 1902 (-38 percent), 1922 (-31 percent), and 1949 (-25 percent).

The peak years of anthracite use nationally and for households were 1917 and 1918 (statistically significant at .025 level), and again in 1944 (not statistically significant). Between 1941 and 1944, a national increase of 19 percent was noted; for households, a 21 percent increase was measured. Both major peaks in the use of anthracite coal were related to World Wars, stemming from the added demands of war production nationally and fuel substitutions at the household level.

Increases in anthracite consumption since the Arab embargo in 1973 have only recently been noted. Declines have generally been the case since 1950, both nationally and for households. However, an increase was noted nationally in 1978, with a 12 percent increase measured between 1977 and 1978. Household anthracite use also increased 18 percent between 1979 and 1980. Newspaper accounts of increased coal use in households, particularly in the northeastern regions of the nation, have suggested a resubstitution of coal for other, more costly petroleum fuels (New York Times, January 22, 1981).

Bituminous Coal

Bituminous coal is a soft coal mined in 26 states, primarily in the Appalachian, Midwestern, and Western Plains regions of this country. It has long been plentiful and relatively inexpensive. The comparisons of national-level use with household-level for this form of coal were vastly different than for fuel wood and anthracite coal. Nationally, the general trend has been an increase in use, with major peaks of use coming in 1918, 1926, and 1943 (1918 is statistically significant at the .025 level; both 1926 and 1943 are just slightly below the significance level of .025). Two of these peaks were during war years (1918 and 1943), and the peak in 1926 was related to increasing industrialization and improved railway consumption of coal just prior to the Depression (see Figure 11.3).

Nationally, the deepest decline in bituminous coal use came in the years between 1929 and 1933 (the Great Depression), with a total reduction of -47 percent in bituminous coal consumption. Both the increasing use of bituminous coal during the war years and the vast decreased use during the Depression helps to explain the increased fuel wood and anthracite coal consumption measured for the same periods. Fuel wood and anthracite coal were either supplements to or substitutes for bituminous coal during times of drastically changing energy needs at the national level. The largest

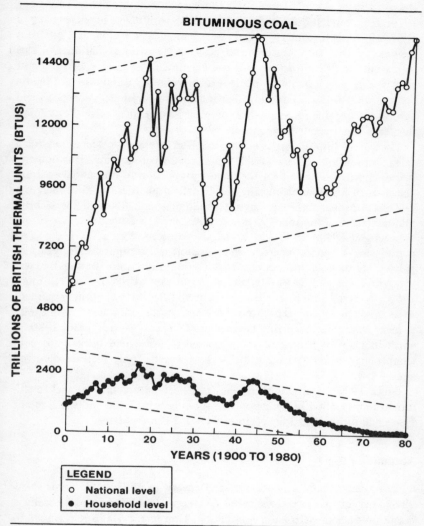

Figure 11.3

unbroken period of increasing bituminous coal use at the national level was between 1939 and 1943, when a 61 percent increase was noted.

Since the Arab oil embargo, there has been a general trend of increasing use of bituminous coal at the national level, with consumption matching and surpassing the 1917 peak of 57 million short tons, particularly since 1976. This trend started as far back as 1960, with minor breaks coming in 1967, 1971, 1972, and 1978. Between 1978 and 1980 alone, a 12 percent increase in the use of bituminous coal has been noted nationally. This increasing use of bituminous coal was encouraged by the resubstitution of coal in electrical generating plants (76 percent of bituminous and lignite consumption in 1978) and in other industrial operations. As fuel oil and natural gas become more costly (and even illegal) for use by the utilities, this trend is anticipated to continue.

Household bituminous coal consumption has always accounted for a small proportion of the total bituminous coal consumed nationally. Anthracite has provided for the largest proportion of household coal use "because of its superior burning and handling qualities."[10] Thus there is a vast proportional difference between national- and household-level bituminous coal consumption. At the national level, a general increase in use between 1900 and 1980 was noted; despite some fluctuations, the same period saw a general decrease in household consumption. The years of greatest household bituminous coal consumption were during the war years of 1917 and 1944 (statistically significant at the .025 level). Since 1953, the trend in household use has been a decrease of from -4 percent to as much as -92 percent from the 1900 consumption level, with a -97 percent reduction occurring between 1917 (peak use year) and 1980. A small increase of 6 percent was observed in household bituminous consumption between 1973 and 1974. This was the only increase observed since 1953.

Since 1973, bituminous coal has not become a source of fuel substitution or transition in households, as it has become in the industrial sector (particularly for generating electricity) in the United States.

Natural Gas (Dry)

For many years after its initial discovery in 1821 in Fredonia, New York, natural gas was considered dangerous (explosive) and basically a waste product of petroleum production. Late in the 1800s it was used to light streets, and shortly thereafter it became used for household lighting. Not until the 1920s was natural gas generally accepted as a cooking fuel in households.[11] It took the development of vast pipelines and related technology, mainly after World War II, for natural gas to become a popular, cheap, clean substitute for coal and wood for cooking, heating, and power generation. Once natural gas was fully accepted and an infrastructure was in place for its distribution, its use increased both nationally and at the household levels at near exponential rates. With few exceptions (mainly in 1921, -6 percent, and between 1931 and 1933, -7 percent), natural gas consumption has grown rapidly at the national level; that is, until the Arab oil embargo of 1973, when the first decrease in thirty years was observed. Natural gas use at the national level increased 11,200 percent between 1900 and 1972 (the year of peak consumption nationally). The 1980 natural gas consumption levels were still 9 percent below the 1972 peak, although some slight increases have been noted in the years 1976 (+5 percent) and 1979 (+3 percent) at the national level (see Figure 11.4).

Household natural gas consumption in general follows increases in use found at the national level (a 16,000 percent increase for households, 1900-1972); however, it is never more than 25 percent of the total national use. Until 1973, there was only one year of a decrease of more than 6 percent. That year was 1921, when a decrease of 14 percent was noted. Since the peak year of 1972 (same for national consumption), small decreases of use in household natural gas have been recorded (-7 percent in 1974 from 1972, -5 percent in 1977 from 1976, -4 percent 1980 from 1979). Therefore, it appears that household consumption of natural gas has been holding around the 1972 peak year, with small reductions.[12]

Electricity (Direct)

Electricity is the only energy form discussed that is not a primary fuel but rather a power source generated by other fuels (including coal, hydro, fuel oil, natural gas, nuclear, and even wood). Electricity is a power source that can do many things, from heating, cooling, and lighting to running motors for both industrial production and home appliances. Because electricity is generated at central utilities using other sources of fuel, then transmitted to the place of use, there are conversion and transmission losses that occur before the energy is used. Therefore, electricity has both an indirect measurement (taking into account conversion and transmission losses) and a direct measurement (measure of use directly at the place of use). Conversion and transmission losses account for approximately 70 percent of the total energy in electrical production, and thus 30 percent is useful as an energy source.

The measure used within this study is the *direct* measure of electricity.[13] This was done for reasons of compatibility with other energy sources used in this report. This is to say, all the other sources of energy

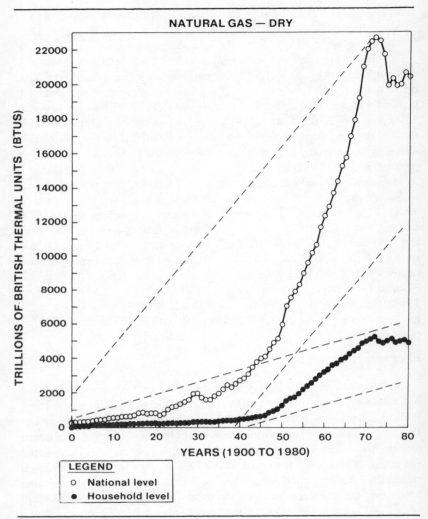

Figure 11.4

consumption in this chapter are measures of direct uses; therefore, they do not reflect losses in production and transportation to the place of use.[14]

Generally, electricity consumption has been on the increase since the earliest records of use (1903 nationally and 1910 for households), with few exceptions. In only seven years of electrical use at the national level

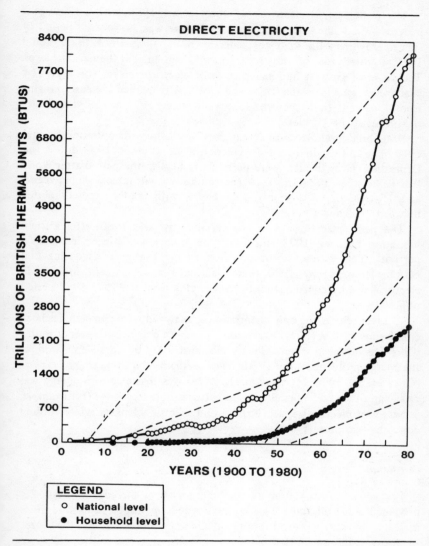

Figure 11.5

has reduction ever occurred (1921, 1930, 1931 and 1932, 1938, 1945 and 1946). The largest reduction of 16 percent occurred between 1930 and 1933 (during the Depression). Other reductions have been minor compared to this (see Figure 11.5).

The peak year of electrical use thus far was 1980, with a 17 percent increase noted since the Arab embargo. There was, however, a period of slower growth in the increases generally noted since 1973. In 1974 and 1975, a growth rate of only 1 percent was measured at the national level. The years of greatest national growth of electrical power (on a year by year basis) were between 1938 and 1959, with annual increases ranging from 1 percent to 15 percent. The years since 1977 are all statistically significant at the .025 level.

Household-level electrical energy uses have increased continuously since 1910. The only reduction (−2 percent) in use came in 1933 during the Depression. Growth rates were particularly high in the period after World War II, between 1944 and 1954 (percentage growth rates were between 9 and 15 percent on a year-by-year basis), with another growth period between 1968 and 1969.

The peak year for household electrical use was 1980, after a slight hesitation between 1973 and 1974 (percentage increase of less than 1 percent). This was, of course, related to the energy crisis during that period. However, by 1980 there had been a 23 percent increase in electrical energy consumption by households from the 1973-1974 period of hesitation.

Electricity is the only energy source analyzed where growth has been continuous with very few exceptions. Furthermore, it is an energy source which has not been affected in any substantial way by wars, depression, or the energy problems of the 1970s. The speculation by some energy experts (Grier et. al., 1976; Morrison et al., 1979) was that electrical energy was replacing other fuel sources as they became more expensive (for example, using room electrical space heaters and electric blankets while turning down the thermostat).

Petroleum

Petroleum consumption at the national level includes domestically produced crude oil, natural gas liquid, condensate, imported oil, and other products. In other words, it is not just an energy source but also the source of many byproducts that do everything from greasing the wheels of industry to relieving headaches. The growth of petroleum consumption at the national level was therefore more than a measure of its energy content and uses. Generally, the consumption of petroleum (like natural gas and electricity) has been growing at a steady rate.

Since 1900, there were eleven years where a reduction in consumption was recorded. The largest of these reductions (20 percent) came in the Depression years, 1931 and 1932. Other years when reductions occurred were: 1906 (−9 percent from 1905), 1924 (−7 percent from 1923), 1942 (−7 percent from 1941), 1974 and 1975 (−6 percent from 1973), and 1980 (−8 percent from 1979). The peak year of petroleum consumption came in 1978 (1973, 1977, 1978, 1979, and 1980 were all statistically significant at the .025 level); however, a 9.4 percent reduction occurred between 1978, the peak year nationally, and 1980 (see Figure 11.6).

Of all the energy sources analyzed in this study, petroleum has come to be of particular importance since 1973. The Arab embargo affected oil shipments to the United States and other nations. Industry in the United States is highly dependent on cheap and plentiful petroleum for its very operations; therfore, any decrease in supply and/or increase in price slows its operation while making its products more costly. Since the United States produced only 16.2 percent of the world's crude oil in 1980, and since domestic crude production has not kept pace with U.S. consumption, imports make up the important shortfalls. By 1980, for example, imports were equivalent to about 40 percent of the national consumption,[15] thus making the United States particularly vulnerable to cut-offs or fluctuations in import supplies and/or price increases.

Household-level petroleum consumption includes only heating oil (distillates 1, 2 and 4), plus range oil (in the early years, 1930s to 1950s) and kerosene. These fuels are mainly used for heating and cooking functions within households. Although household petroleum consumption has generally increased since its earliest recorded date of 1935, the increase has not been as dramatic as that for national-level consumption, nor has it been anywhere near the national level of use. Household consumption has never been more than about 7 percent of the consumption of petroleum nationally. Reductions of household petroleum use came during World War II, 1942 and 1943 (−6 percent from 1941). Reductions totaling −14 percent were also recorded during the period after the Arab embargo, 1973 to 1975, with a very substantial reduction of −32 percent occurring between 1977 and 1980.

The peak year of use was 1972; however, levels of household petroleum consumption varied only slightly during the 1960s. The years of greatest growth in the use of petroleum by households were between 1944 and 1958, when increases averaging 11 percent were noted. After the end of World War II, the increase in the number of households, particularly in

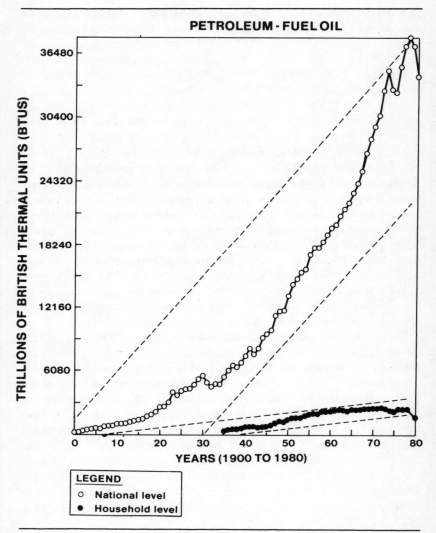

Figure 11.6

suburban areas (especially before natural gas pipelines were laid), would account for the increase in fuel oil (petroleum) consumption during that period. After 1960, almost every small town had natural gas, thus confining the household consumption of petroleum mainly to the rural areas, where natural gas was still not accessible.

Natural Gas (Liquid)

Natural Gas Liquid is a product obtained in the processing of natural gas. Thus, this energy source is one of several byproduct or useable waste products of natural gas cycling and fractionation. Included are such byproducts as ethane, liquid petroleum gas (LPG), natural gasoline, and plant condensate. For the purposes of this study, the liquefied petroleum gases (LPG), including propane, butane, and propane-butane mixtures, were measured. These liquid fuels are generally used for heating and cooking, and some processes in industry (welding, for example).

Liquid petroleum gas consumption was not measured until 1922, and at the national level dramatically increased each year without exception until 1974, when the first decrease in use was experienced (-8 percent between 1974 and 1975, -1 percent between 1977 and 1978, and -7 percent between 1979 and 1980). Since the initial peak of year of 1973 (year of the Arab oil embargo), there has been a rally in use, with a new peak established in 1979 (9 percent higher than 1973). Even the 1980 level was 2 percent higher than 1973 (initial peak year).

The years of greatest growth in the use of liquid petroleum gases at the national level were between 1939 and 1959, with growth rates averaging 23 percent. The Depression had no effect on decreasing the consumption of LPG, and during World War II a 167 percent increase was noted from 1941 through 1945, with an increase of 58 percent experienced between 1943 and 1944 alone. Obviously, LPG became a useful and cheap replacement energy source during the Depression years and a vital energy source in the war industry during World War II (see Figure 11.7).

Household use of liquid petroleum gas has been mainly limited to heating and cooking needs, especially in rural areas (also in vacation and mobile homes). Household use has also increased dramatically, though never accounting for more than 8 percent of total household energy use when all fuel sources are considered. The peak year of use for households was 1979, which showed a 9 percent increase over the initial peak year of 1973. There was a 16 percent decrease between 1973 and 1975, and a 7 percent decrease between 1979 and 1980 in household use, indicating that in spite of generally increasing use, some adjustments to price increases were being seen.

Households and Energy Consumption

Over the eighty years of this study, household energy consumption patterns have changed. Table 11.1 shows a comparison by decades of the

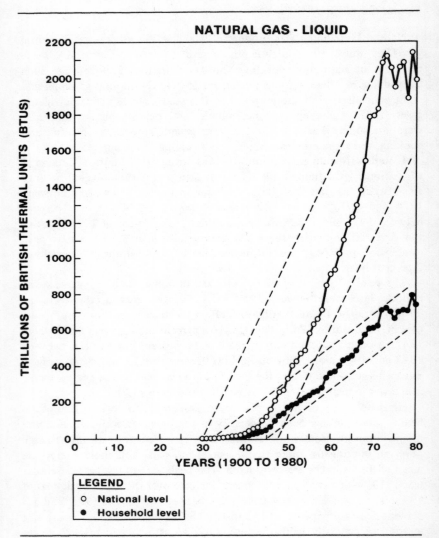

Figure 11.7

various energy sources, each as a percentage of total household consumption. In 1900, for example, 99 percent of the energy use was provided by coal and wood. Wood provided 37 percent, whereas coal provided 62 percent (anthracite 30 percent, bituminous 32 percent). Natural gas (used

TABLE 11.1 Household Energy Consumption by Decades, 1900 to 1980: Each Energy Source as a Percentage of Total Household Energy Consumption

DECADES	ANTHRACITE COAL %	BITUMINOUS COAL %	FUEL WOOD %	NATURAL GAS (DRY) %	ELECTRICITY (DIRECT) %	FUEL OIL %	LIQUID GAS (LPG) %
				SOURCES			
1900	30	32	37	1	--	--	--
1910	31	43	22	3	--	--	---
1920	28	46	21	5	--	--	--
1930	25	44	23	7	1	--	--
1940	16	32	23	10	2	16	--
1950	10	25	10	22	4	25	3
1960	3	7	4	43	9	30	5
1970	1	2	1	50	15	25	6
1980	0.3	0.7	3	48	25	16	7

PERCENTAGES MAY NOT EQUAL 100 DUE TO ROUNDING

Source: *Household Energy History: 1900-1980.* Data compiled by Bonnie Maas Morrison during a period as Visiting Scholar, Historian's Office, U.S. Department of Energy. Michigan Agricultural Experiment Station Project 1375, College fo Human Ecology, Michigan State University.

mainly for lighting but also for cooking in some cities near gas pools) accounted for 1 percent. During the decades between 1910 and 1930, coal continued to be an important source of household fuel, increasing to 75 percent in 1910 and 1920, but decreasing to 69 percent by 1930, considering both anthracite and bituminous. Wood use for these same years dropped, however, to average about 22 percent, whereas natural gas (dry) increased from 3 percent in 1910 to 7 percent by 1930. By 1930, electricity accounted for 1 percent of household use.

By 1940, a greater variety of energy sources became available to households. Although coal still dominated the energy mix (48 percent, considering both anthracite and bituminous) and wood remained at 23 percent, natural gas and fuel oil combined accounted for 26 percent, and electricity for 2 percent.

In the post-World War II years of the 1950s, the energy mix for households changed once again with the addition of LPG, and the proportions within the mix also changed quite drastically. In 1950, total coal accounted for 35 percent, fuel wood 10 percent (more than a 50 percent reduction between 1930 and 1940), natural gas and fuel oil became dominant for the first time at 47 percent (22 percent for natural gas, 25 percent for fuel oil), electricity had increased to 4 percent, and LPG to 3 percent.

The 1960 household energy consumption mix, however, showed the greatest single change in proportional energy source uses. By 1960, coal (combined anthracite and bituminous) only accounted for 19 percent and wood 4 percent, whereas natural gas by itself had increased to 43 percent and fuel oil to 30 percent. Electricity had increased in household use to 9 percent of the total, and LPG to 6 percent.

The last year of the study, 1980, finds coal almost non-existent as an energy source in households; it had been reduced from its all time high in 1910 and 1920 of 75 percent to 1 percent. Fuel wood use had increased to 3 percent by 1980, following a trend to use wood as a substitute for natural gas and fuel oil (New York Times, February 1, 1981, 16). Natural gas use decreased by 1980 to 48 percent of total household use from its 1970 high of 50 percent. Electricity appears to be becoming an energy source of the future for households, capturing 25 percent of total household use. Fuel oil consumption was reduced to 16 percent of total household use by 1980, matching the level of use found in the 1940s. Fuel oil has been the energy most affected by the increasing energy prices and threats to a stable supply since the Arab oil embargo. Thus, either households are finding substitutes for it, or simply using less of it through

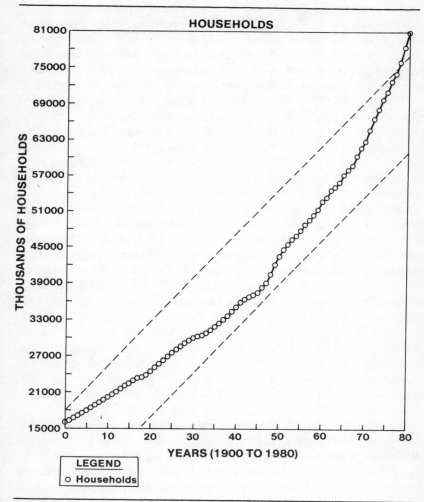

Figure 11.8

conservation practices. Household consumption of liquid petroleum gas (LPG) had increased to 7 percent of total household consumption by 1980.

Household numbers have continuously increased since 1900 (see Figure 11.8). There has not been a year when an increase in household numbers has not been noted; however, there have been some years of slowed growth (between 1930 and 1933), particularly during the Depression and again during the period of both World Wars. At each of these periods, growth rates of only 1 and 2 percent were noted. The years after World War II, particularly between 1947 and 1958, were years of notable increases in household numbers (between 5 and 9 percent). However, 1970 and 1971 were the years of the largest percentage increase in household numbers on a yearly basis (both years increased 12 percent). This trend was noticeable by the late 1960s and continued through 1980.

Between 1900 and 1980 there has been a 373 percent increase in household numbers in this country. Energy consumption (see Figure 11.9) by the aggregate number of households has increased by only 223 percent between 1900 and 1976 (the peak year of total household energy use). The percentage increase in energy consumption by households was not as substantial as the increase in household numbers, nor has it been as steady. After a peak in total household energy use in 1917, a more or less steady decline was noted until 1932. Levels of total household energy consumption by 1932 had declined to levels approximating levels of consumption in the early part of the century. After 1932, total household energy consumption increased, with few exceptions (these included 1937-38, 1945-46, 1949, 1953, and 1957). For fifteen years, from 1957 to 1973, increases averaging 3 percent were noted. This period was the longest unbroken trend of increases in household energy consumption over the eighty-year period. Since 1973, however, reductions of −5 percent occurred between 1974 and 1975, and −1 percent between 1976 and 1977. The all-time peak year of total household energy consumption was 1976; a −5 percent reduction was noted between 1976 and 1980.

Energy consumption of all fuel sources analyzed on a per household (see Figure 11.10) and a per household/per person basis are the final ways the historical household energy consumption study will be discussed.

As mentioned in the initial statements of this chapter, an assumption of continuous growth in household energy consumption has prevailed, thus suggesting that perhaps a return to some of the fuel sources of the past (fuel wood and coal in particular) might help resolve the present energy problems, i.e., the "good old days" notion of past energy consumption.

This assumption was partially refuted by the data presented in Figure 11.9, which indicated that some substantial fluctuations in total household energy used had occurred, particularly between 1900 and 1930, and further, that the road to the peak energy use by households in 1976 was not without valleys along the way (minor though they were).

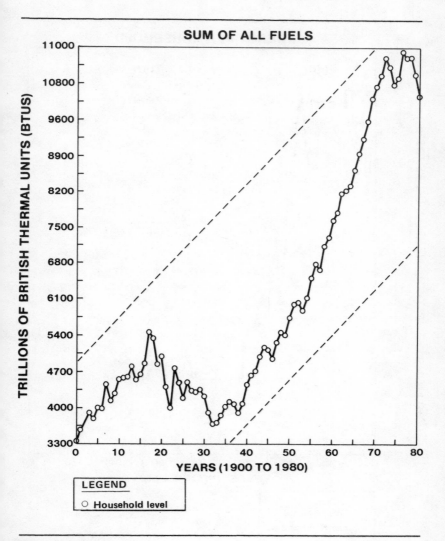

Figure 11.9

On a per household basis,[16] however, the assumptions about growth in household energy consumption were completely unsupported (see Figure 11.10). It becomes apparent that on a per-household basis, total energy consumption has been substantially reduced since the early parts of the

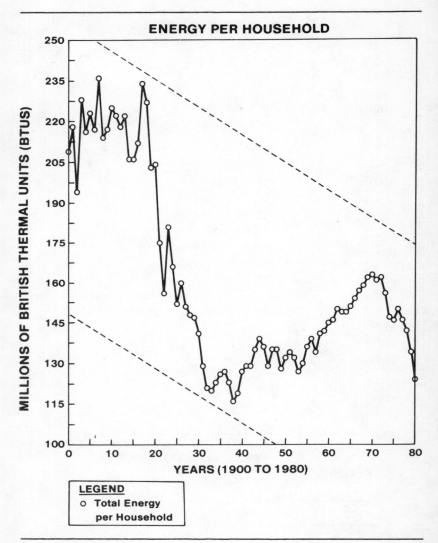

Figure 11.10

century, and further, that total energy consumption on a per-household basis is still far below the peak uses found in 1907 (236 million Btus) and 1917 (234 million Btus), even when secondary peak use in the late 1960s and early 1970s was reached (163 million Btus for 1969 and 1970).

TABLE 11.2   Household Energy Consumption, 1900 to 1980: Average Millions of Btus per Household and Average Millions of Btus per Person/per Household

| YEARS | AVERAGE BTU IN MILLIONS | | AVERAGE HOUSEHOLD SIZE |
	PER HOUSEHOLD	PER PERSON/ PER HOUSEHOLD	
1900	209	43.9	4.76
1910	225	49.6	4.54
1920	204	47.0	4.34
1930	141	34.3	4.11
1940	127	34.6	3.67
1950	132	39.2	3.37
1960	145	43.5	3.33
1970	163	51.4	3.17
1971	162	51.6	3.14
1972	162	52.9	3.06
1973	155	51.5	3.01
1974	146	49.2	2.97
1975	145	49.3	2.94
1976	149	51.6	2.89
1977	144	50.3	2.86
1980	127	46.4	2.76

373 PERCENT INCREASE IN NUMBERS OF HOUSEHOLDS SINCE 1900

Source: *Household Energy History: 1900-1980.* Data compiled by Bonnie Maas Morrison during a period as Visiting Scholar, Historian's Office, U.S. Department of Energy. Michigan Agricultural Experiment Station Project 1375, College of Human Ecology, Michigan State University.

Total energy consumption on a per-household level decreased 52 percent between 1907 and 1938, and nearly 51 percent between 1917 and 1938. With 116 million Btus measured, 1938 is obviously the year of least per-household energy consumption. The peak total per-household energy consumption levels of 1969 and 1970 (163 million Btus) were still 31 percent below the all-time peak of 1907. In fact, it was about the same level of energy consumption noted in 1923. By 1980, total energy consumption per household was reduced even further from the 1969-70 peak, matching exactly levels observed in 1936. Table 11.2 is a decade-by-decade analysis of these changes in per-household energy consumption (in millions of Btus), with year by year analysis between 1970 and 1980 (except years 1978 and 1979).

Table 11.2 also indicates the per-person/per-household energy consumption for the same decades and years. On a per-person/per-household basis, it was interesting to note that the magnitude of difference in energy use was not great. It ranges on a per-person/per-household basis from lows of 43.9 million Btus in 1900 and 43.5 million Btus in 1960, to a high of 52.9 million Btus in 1972. This amounts to approximately a nine million Btu average difference over the eighty years. The per-person/per-household Btus consumed in 1980 are on about the same level as in 1920.

Some Speculations

Why has total household energy consumption increased generally over eighty years? Why were the changes in energy consumption on a per-household basis so surprising (50 percent reduction between 1907 and 1938 and a 32 percent reduction between 1907 and 1980)? And finally, why has the per-person/per-household energy consumption been so stable?

The answers to these questions are the basis for the historical quantitative and qualitative analysis that is presently ongoing; therefore, my comments in answer to these questions will simply be of a speculative nature. These speculations are becoming the research hypotheses guiding the final phases of this research.

The forecast volume of the U.S. Department of Energy's *Annual Report to Congress* (1980) suggests that energy consumption in the residential sector of the economy is determined by the interaction of these factors:

- energy prices and availability
- macroeconomic conditions, especially per-capita income
- population and the number and type of households
- the number and characteristics of energy-using equipment
- energy use habits
- government energy policy and conservation programs (DOE/EIA-9173 [80]/3, 148).

To this list I would add:

- the type of housing and its energy efficiency

- the technical efficiency of energy sources
- the technical efficiency of the energy-using equipment
- the activities of the households (production activities as compared to consumption activities)

The aggregate household energy consumption over the eighty years of this study has increased approximately twofold, while household numbers have increased threefold. Thus, it would appear that number of households is at least in some measure an indicator for how *much* total energy (all fuel sources) was consumed by households at the aggregate level (i.e., the more households, the more energy used).

It has been speculated that the price of energy in real terms affects the amount of energy demanded, whereas energy availability and price relative to each source affects the mix of various sources. Price has not been a factor in the analysis to this point; however, at the household level, a fourfold increase in the fuel oil price appears to have been instrumental in the 36 percent reduction measured between 1973 and 1980. Or was it? Was it price or was it price relative to spendable income? Or was it price, price relative to expendable income, and an almost psychological reaction to a perceived threat to continuing supplies? Or was it price plus a conservation ethic? These are examples of the kinds of questions and the kinds of interdependencies that make the answer to the question of why household energy consumption has increased/decreased so difficult, so complex, and requiring further study.

Why were the changes in energy consumption over the eighty years on a per-household basis so surprising? Some speculative answers to this question have to do with our present assumptions about energy use per household, particularly, how household energy use has been viewed in the absence of a historical quantitative measure. The assumption has been that present-day individual households are highly energy intensive, especially when compared to the early years of the century. On logical grounds, for example, it is easy to think of the human energy and time that has been replaced in each household through the purchase and use of a plethora of mechanical devices: from automatic furnaces to electric can openers, TVs, stereos, garage door openers, the amount and kinds of specialized lighting, and the specialized cooking devices, from electric frying pans to ranges to microwave ovens. All of the physical evidence of human energy-using devices prepares one to believe that more energy is being used today by each household than ever before in history. However, in the speculative comparison of household energy uses over time, what we tend to think of is the replacement of human energy by convenience devices, not how energy-intensive (in fuel energy terms) the household activities of the past might have been. That is, even in a time when household work was mainly a task done by human energy (rather than mechanized energy), other fuel sources (fuel wood and coal mainly) were being used for heating and cooking and other activities.

Perhaps looking at some of the aspects of household energy use at the turn of the century can help us overcome our fixation on the replacement of human energy only.

Households were large in size (4.76 in 1900 compared to 2.76 in 1980), and this required housing large enough to accommodate them. No accurate measure of house size (i.e., number of rooms or amount of square feet) exists for years prior to 1940; however, in 1900, 60 percent of all households were rural, which is a good indicator of single-family dwellings, and many farmhouses were large to accommodate large families, perhaps some relatives, and some hired hands.

Heating was accomplished in fireplaces, often in individual rooms. Central heating with coal did not become prevalent until after World War I.[17] Fireplaces (even today) are not an energy-efficient heat source. They lose 90 percent or more of their usable heat up the chimney.

Cooking was also sometimes done in the fireplace, but even with the use of dutch ovens, the same loss of heat was suffered. Cooking, however, was usually done in or on large cast iron stoves, and cooking went on year in year out, day in day out, using heat from wood or coal. Although more energy-efficient than the fireplace, these cast iron stoves lost much of their heat (even in the summer) to the atmosphere or the interior spaces. The constant need to use wood or coal energy for cooking in the early years of the century prompted separate outbuildings (particularly in the South) to house the task, but nonetheless the task still went on. Later, summer kitchens were added with kerosene stoves, so that the wood and coal stoves could be retired in the summer months. Perhaps this was one of the steps in the reduction of energy use on a per-household basis noted between the early 1900s and 1932.

The sources of fuel themselves were not highly efficient heat sources. The average technical efficiency of energy had increased from 9 percent to 35 percent by 1974[18] in response to both the kinds of energy sources used conventionally and the efficiency of the equipment in which they were used. Households did production tasks at least to some extent in the early part of the 1900s. Although some of these tasks required mainly human energy (weaving, sewing, quilt-making, and the like), others required fuels (baking, canning, preserving, ironing, hot water heating for bathing, cleaning, and clothes washing, as well as meal preparation for large families). Most of the products of these tasks were, of course, used in the household, but some margin of them were used for trade, barter, or sale. Production tasks such as those mentioned have largely (since around the 1920s) been done outside the household, with the household becoming a consuming unit in the wake of commercially manufactured products.

Therefore, from a speculative perspective, several factors may have influenced the per-household energy consumption patterns noted in the early part of the 1900s. Others could help explain the reduced energy use observed per household since 1930. Some of the factors that could be mentioned are: decrease in household size; urbanization, with the attendant use of multiple dwellings; smaller homes; more efficient fuels used in more efficient equipment; and less household production. Only further analysis and further research into the history of households, and equipment will substantiate these speculations.

Why has the energy consumption per person/per household remained within the narrow margin of nine million Btus? At this point, the only explanation that can be gained from the research is related to the number of persons in each household. With more persons sharing the various fuels used in the earlier parts of the 1900s, there may have been less use per person. As energy consumption became more efficient (i.e., more efficient fuel sources, more efficient household equipment, smaller houses, and smaller households), fewer persons shared a smaller amount of energy. These factors appear (at least on the surface) to have stabilized the energy use observed on a per-person/per-household basis over the eighty years studied here.

Summary with Policy Implications

This research was implemented for two purposes: first, to establish a quantitative energy consumption data bank that was historical in nature and which allowed comparisons between household- and national-level energy consumption, as well as comparisons between household energy uses (year by year, decade by decade); second, to test (at least in a preliminary fashion) the prevailing assumptions that households in the past (turn of the century or so) used less energy than households today. These objectives have been accomplished, and the findings have implications for future energy policies, especially with regard to households.

The most prevalent energy sources at the turn of the century and up until the 1920s or so were fuel wood and coal. Fuel wood and anthracite coal, in particular, were similar in patterning and amount of use for both household- and national-level uses. This was not so for the other energy sources examined. The implication is that there were few uses of wood fuel or anthracite coal beyond the household uses, and that they were inefficient fuels used in inefficient equipment. Furthermore, when aggregated household and per-household energy consumption for all energy sources was analyzed, it was found that between 1917 and 1938, a substantial reduction in energy uses occurred (−28.6 percent for all households and −51 percent on a per-household basis). Given this evidence, it is possible to say that the assumption of continuous growth in household energy consumption since the turn of the century was at least partly refuted.

When a longer-term historical perspective on a household energy use basis was taken, it was both unexpected and surprising to find that on a per-household basis (considering the total amount of energy each household used), households in 1980 consumed the same amount of total energy as households in 1940 (127 million Btus per household), and further, that a reduction of 52 percent in total household energy was recorded between 1907 (peak year of per-household energy use) and 1938, on a per-household basis. Given this evidence and the evidence that households in 1980 (in fact, in any period since 1938) were still not using energy on a per-household level that was anywhere near the levels recorded between 1900 and 1917, it would seem that the assumption that households in past generations (near the turn of the century) used less energy than do individual households today is completely refuted by the evidence presented.

From this evidence then, the following generalization can be drawn:

(1) If energy sources such as fuel wood and coal are promoted on a large scale as a substitution for the more costly energy sources now being used, there is a strong possibility that energy use will be increased rather than reduced on a per-household basis.

(2) If energy sources such as fuel wood and coal are promoted for future household use, without increasing the efficiency of the energy-using equipment and the housing structure, there is an added possibility that the increased energy use per household would be substantial.

(3) If individual households were encouraged to reformulate rather than to continue to undouble (as has been the case since the

1960s), it would promote greater energy efficiency. The situation would be one of using the already more efficient energy resource even more effectively. More persons using present levels of household energy (on a per-household basis) would mean less energy (on the aggregate) would be used by the housing sector of the economy, than is being used today.

The policy implications from these generalizations could be synthesized to the following:

(1) Do not promote the use of fuel wood or coal in particular, if energy reduction on a per-household basis is desired.
(2) Promote more efficient energy using equipment and housing structures, if fuel wood and coal were to be encouraged.
(3) Discourage new household formation. The more persons within a household using the energy sources available today, the less energy on the aggregate will be consumed.

Back to the Good Old Days

It would appear from the foregoing discussion that perhaps there were no "good old days," when energy was used more effectively than it is today. This is so, especially when a long-term historical view is taken (turn of the century or so). The conclusion drawn (given the evidence) is that as romantic as the idea might be of returning to the era of the crackling wood fire in the fireplace or the warmth and glow of the potbellied coal stove, it will not, by itself, resolve the household energy problems of today.

NOTES

1. The author has been a member of a transdiciplinary research team, called the "Family Energy Project," since 1973. Their research is conducted in the Institute for Family and Child Study, College of Human Ecology.

2. An extensive work by Schurr et al., *Energy in the American Economy: 1850-1975* (Baltimore, 1960), uses 1955 as the year to extrapolate household energy uses to 1975. Eric Hirst and Jerry Jackson, "Historical patterns of household and commercial energy use," *Energy* 2 (1977), 131-140, use 1950 as their historical point of reference. See also U.S. Department of Energy, *Federal Energy Data System (FEDS): Statistical Summary* (Washington, DC, DOE/EIA-0031/2, February 1978), 324-465.

3. The data for this study were compiled during a sabbatical leave from Michigan State University while the author was a Visiting Scholar in the Historian's

Office, U.S. Department of Energy (October 1978-August 1979). The analysis was funded by the Michigan Agricultural Experiment Station (Project 1375). This chapter is Michigan Agricultural Experiment Station journal article 10348.

4. The data sources most used for energy consumption were:

(a) Schurr et al., *Energy in the American Economy: 1850-1975* (1960).
(b) *Historical Statistics of the United States,* Vols. I & II (1976).
(c) *Minerals Yearbook,* U.S. Bureau of Mines (selected years).
(d) *Department of Energy Annual Reports to Congress* (1977-1980).
(e) *Historical Statistics of the Electric Utility Industry: Through 1970,* Edison Electric Institute.
(f) *Statistical Yearbook of the Electrical Utilities Industry,* Edison Electric Institute (1977-1980).

5. *Statistical Abstracts of the United States* (1900-1980).

6. Energy consumption data for multiple dwellings are often reported in the data used under commercial/residential. This is particularly so for fuel oil, natural gas, and electricity. The decision rule used to separate household from commercial was developed by Steve Cohn in *Fuel Choices and Aggregate Energy Demand in the Commercial Sector,* ORNL/CON-27 (1978), 29, 33, 36. The percentages developed by Cohn were used for electricity, fuel oil, and natural gas for all years of the study.

7. According to the 1970 Census Bureau definition, "a household comprises all persons who occupy a 'housing unit'." Average household size is the average number of persons per housing unit (total population divided by number of household heads). *Historical Statistics of the United States,* Vol. I (1976), 6.

8. Series M, 84-85 and 92, *Historical Statistics of the United States* (1976), 588.

9. Calculation formula from 1900 to 1960 was done with advice of Jack Alterman, Senior Researcher, Resources for the Future (personal consultation and memo, July 9, 1979), and after consultation with Herbert Foster, National Coal Association (August 3, 1979). Calculation formula from 1960 to 1980 was from *FEDS Technical Documentation,* DOE/EIA-0031/1 (June 1978), 15.

10. *Annual Report to Congress,* Vol. III (1978), 87.

11. There were a few exceptions, especially in cities located near large pools of gas such as Tulsa, where natural gas was used for both cooking and heating shortly after 1900.

12. Natural gas price deregulation is scheduled for 1985.

13. Indirect electrical measure has been compiled as a part of the data bank in this historical study. They were simply not used here for the reasons given above.

14. The price of all energy sources used in this study would, however, reflect the indirect costs of all points in the process of getting the energy to the sources of use. Price was not a major consideration in the analysis at this time, whereas useful energy content was.

15. Energy Information Administration, *Annual Report to Congress,* Vol. II, (1980), 45.

16. Per-household energy consumption was calculated by dividing:

$$\frac{\text{Total household Btus*/year}}{\text{Total number of households**/year}}$$

*Btus are in trillions of British thermal units
**Household numbers in thousands

17. E. S. Keene, *Mechanics of the Household* (New York, 1918).

18. Michael G. Lacy, "Why has energy consumption increased?" Presented at the annual meetings of the Midwest Sociological Society, Milwaukee, Wisconsin (April 1980), 23.

REFERENCES

COHN, S. *Fuel Choices and Aggregate Energy Demand in the Commercial Sector,* Oak Ridge National Laboratory ORL/CON-27 (December 1978).

Edison Electric Institute, *Advance Release of Data for the 1980 Statistical Yearbook of the Electric Utility Industry,* Economic and Finance Group (1981).

——— *Statistical Yearbook for the Electrical Utility Industry* (1977 and 1980).

——— *Historical Statistics of the Electric Utility Industry: through 1970* (1971).

GRIER, E. S. "Changing patterns of energy consumption and costs in U.S. households." Presented to the Allied Social Sciences Association, Atlantic City (September 1976).

HERSHEY, R. D. "Study of institute finds wood fuel surpasses nuclear power in nation," New York *Times* (February 1, 1981), 16.

HIRST, E. and J. JACKSON "Historical patterns of residential and commercial energy uses," *Energy* (1977), 131-140.

JESTER, J. F. and W. A. JESTER "Energy: past, present and future," Pennsylvania State University, mimeograph (June 1977).

KEENE, E. S. *Mechanics of the Household* (New York, 1918).

KNIGHT, M. "Renewed use of coal in Northeast causes shortages," New York *Times* (January 22, 1981), 1, 8.

LACY, M. G. "Why has energy consumption increased?" Presented at the annual meetings of the Midwest Sociological Society, Milwaukee, Wisconsin (April 1980).

MORRISON, B. M. et al., "Impacts of household energy consumption: an empirical study of Michigan families," in Unseld, Morrison, Sills and Wolf, eds., *Sociopolitical Impacts of Energy Use and Policy Content* (Washington, DC, 1979).

SCHURR, S. H. et al., *Energy in the American Economy: 1850-1975* (Baltimore, 1960).

U.S. Department of Commerce *Statistical Abstracts of the United States* (1900-1980).

——— *Historical Statistics of the United States: Colonial Times to 1970,* Bureau of the Census, Vols. I & II (1975).

U.S. Department of Energy *Annual Report to Congress* (Washington, DC, 1977-1980).

——— *Annual Report to Congress* Vol. III (Washington, DC, 1980).

——— *Federal Energy Data System (FEDS): Statistical Summary* (Washington, DC, DOE/EIA-0031/2, UC-12, February 1978), 324-465.

——— *FEDS Technical Documentation* (Washington, DC, DOE/EIA-0031/1, June 1978).

U.S. Department of Interior *Minerals Yearbook,* U.S. Bureau of Mines (selected years, 1900-1977).

12

The Barn is His, The House is Mine

Agricultural Technology and Sex Roles

CORLANN G. BUSH

While rural people may be the most studied and analyzed people in America, and while many history books discuss the agricultural revolution wrought by mechanization, very little has been written about the effect of agricultural technology on the family lives and roles of farm men and women.[1] However, this oversight pales in comparison to the lack of attention paid to the effects that more general technologies such as electricity and transportation have had on the lives of rural consumers.[2]

In fact, power and transportation technology have had dramatically *different* consequences for men and women in farm families and rural communities. The availability of cheap forms of energy—electricity and fossil fuels—and their concomitant technologies have fundamentally altered the balance and equality that characterized the work of men and women in rural societies in the first decades of this century.

Between 1930 and 1970, changes from horse-drawn to diesel-powered machinery, such as combines and threshers, and equally significant changes in household technology, including convection ovens, automatic washing

AUTHOR'S NOTE: This chapter has been developed through discussions with the late Lilly Hermann, a farmer in Genesee, Idaho, and Isabel Miller, of Moscow, Idaho, both of whom worked with me on the Rural Women's History Project. Dr. Susan Armitage, Professor of History and Women's Studies at Washington State University, has been an invaluable and crucial collaborator. I am indebted to them all for their inspiration, criticism, and encouragement.

machines, and refrigerators, had profound effects on the lives of rural men and women. The introduction of household technology eliminated much of women's traditional work that was formerly crucial to the economic functioning of the family, at the same time that agricultural technology enhanced the importance of men's activities. Thus, the value or *"crucialness"* of men's and women's traditional roles was differentially affected by changes in agricultural and domestic technology.

As used here, the term crucialness describes the cumulative effect of an individual's actions and decisions on the economic functioning of the family unit. Activities and decisions are crucial to the degree that they risk the survival or continuance of the family as an economic unit. By comparing men's and women's economic activities before mechanization and electrification, and by contrasting these with men's and women's work today, this chapter will present a model for analyzing and understanding crucialness as a description of the effects of technological change on individuals.

Several factors affect the crucialness of an act or decision. These include complexity, risk, scale, diversity, access to alternate or substitute providers, and discretion about the use of one's time.[3] *Complexity* describes the number and difficulty of factors that must be considered or included in a decision or activity. *Risk* describes the degree of harm that will result from an erroneous decision, while *scale* is a measure of the scope of the enterprise as a whole. *Diversity* refers to the number of components on which the enterprise of activity is based. *Access to alternate or substitute providers* is a concept that describes the "safety net" available if an activity or decision fails, and *discretion about one's time* refers to the degree to which an individual has control over deciding what to do and when to do it.

For ease in understanding crucialness and its components, it is useful to express their relationships "algebraically":

$$C = f \; \frac{Cx \cdot r \cdot Sc \cdot Td}{d \cdot Ap}$$

where crucialness (C) is a direct function of complexity (Cx), risk (r), scale (Sc), and discretion about time (Td). Crucialness varies inversely with diversity (d) and access to alternate providers (Ap).

Agriculture in the Palouse

In order to explain and substantiate the model of crucialness presented above, this chapter will look specifically at men and women living on farms and in rural communities in northern Idaho and eastern Washington from approximately 1900 to 1975. This region, which is called the Palouse, has several attributes that recommend it for a study of this kind. First, it was settled relatively late in the nineteenth century, so that individuals who remember their own and their parents' homesteading days are still alive. Second, the region is a discrete geographic area: The Palouse hills are bounded to the east by the foothills of the Bitterroot Mountains and to the west by the Palouse River. The land lies in steep, loess-covered hills; the soil is fertile and, with 20-24 inches of rainfall per year, amazingly productive for dry land farming of peas, lentils, and soft winter wheat. There has not, for example, been a region-wide crop failure for eighty years, and yields of over 60 bushels of wheat per acre have been common since 1940, while yields of 80-85 bushels per acre have been the norm since the late 1960s. Forests in the higher elevations produce harvests of white pine and western red cedar. The lumbering industry makes the second most important contribution to the regional economy; many families living in the foothills combine logging, small-scale farming, and hunting to earn a marginal living. Interspersed throughout the Palouse are numerous small communities that once featured a thriving business district but which now serve to house the post office, the school, a cooperative-run gas station, the seed or grower's company office, and several bars.

Third, agriculture in the Palouse region has always been relatively large-scale. Farm operations averaged 420 acres in 1920 and 1200 acres in 1974, but over 95 percent were and still are privately-owned family or family partnership farms.[4] The large size of farms, the early specialization in cash crops, and the steepness of the terrain have meant that farmers have continually had to invest in machinery in order to make their operations as efficient and competitive as possible. This, in turn, has meant that technological innovations and their concomitant economies of scale have been welcomed and pursued rather than distrusted and resisted, as has sometimes been the case in areas where smaller-scale, more traditional agricultural practices have prevailed.

The history of farming in the Palouse is divided into three discrete technological phases: (1) the period of early settlement from 1870-1900, which was characterized by small-scale, subsistence farming and the use of simple, manually operated equipment such as the "footburner" plow and the stump puller; (2) the period from 1900-1930, called the "horse interlude," in which horses provided the energy supply for what was, according to the standards of the time, large-scale, cash crop agriculture; and (3) the era of mechanization, which began in approximately 1930 and which saw the conversion from horse-drawn to diesel-powered machinery.

In regard to this progression from settlement to mechanization, agriculture in the Palouse represents a microcosm of the stages of development that have characterized agriculture in the nation as a whole, except that the time scale has been significantly shortened. Men and women who pioneered the area are still living today, as, of course, are farmers who remember the horse-farming era. Their experiences as told in oral histories and in memoirs and diaries provide valuable insights into the history of agriculture and the effects of technological change on lifestyles and values. Thus, the Palouse region, with its abbreviated time scale, its tradition of large-scale farming, and its retention of family-owned and -operated farms, provides a unique laboratory for the study of social change in rural areas.

From 1974 through 1976, I was involved with other staff of the Rural Women's History Project (RWHP) in interviewing women throughout northern Idaho.[5] Over 100 interviews were completed with respondents ranging in age from 19 to 94. Respondents were demographically typical of rural women throughout the country: 87 percent had married, 9 percent had remained single, and 3 percent had divorced. Of those who had been married, 30 percent were widowed at the time of the interview. Place of residence was also typical of the rural population at large: 14 percent were residing on farms, 40 percent lived in small towns or villages of less than 500 population, 30 percent lived in towns with a population between 500 and 1500, and 16 percent were elderly emigrants to larger cities.

Several truths about rural life emerged from both the literature and from our interviews. First, the gender-based division of labor that has long characterized the work of men and women in agricultural societies was the norm in the Palouse. Men traditionally worked in the fields and with the animals; women worked in the home with the children. One of our RWHP respondents, Edna Cochrane, stated this extremely well: "My husband, he always went ahead and made his decisions. He was outside, I was inside; the barn was his, the house was mine." Men's work was entrepreneurial; women's work was domestic. Women rarely worked in the fields, and when they did it was to "help out," for women were not responsible for the planting, harvesting, or selling of the crop. Because harvesting was the most important activity on the farm, everyone lent his or her best efforts to ensure its success. In fact, it is the essence of our agricultural heritage that farm and family overlapped; the farm woman was an active partner in the family's common work. On the traditional farm, the family itself was an economic unit.

I use the past tense here because the congruence of work and family lives that once characterized rural life has been steadily disappearing under pressure from technology and industrialization. A brief description of women's and men's farm work in 1920 will serve to illustrate what has changed.

The Horse-Farming Era

Traditional agricultural technology was based on manpower and horse power. The 1920 census in Whitman County, Washington—one of several counties in the Palouse—recorded 40,000 horses and mules. Dividing by the 2,597 farms, we get an average of thirteen horses per farm[6] that had to be stabled, fed, and cared for throughout the year. The first combines required at least 32 horse power—in other words 32 horses or mules—to pull them through the fields. Farmers had to pool their animals and equipment in order to get the harvesting done. It was not uncommon for a combine to be hitched to a team of 33 or more draft animals. There are numerous instances of farmers using three, four, or even five horse-drawn combines in the same field at the same time.

Unfortunately, multiple horse teams hitched with standard "dead hitch" harness had one inherent disadvantage: The horses did not share the load equally or efficiently. Lazy horses would let other horses do their work; wheel horses pulled more load than those hitched in the middle of a span. Equalizing the load for multiple teams was necessary, because only then could 32 horses provide the necessary horse power. The Schandoney Equalizing Hitch solved these problems and, in so doing, changed the scale of agriculture in the Palouse.

Patented in 1892 by Peter Schandoney,[7] the equalizing hitch was one of those deceptively simple innovations, like the horse collar and the water wheel, that revolutionized an entire technological and social system. The Schandoney hitch was made of iron and shaped like a slightly elongated cloverleaf at least twelve inches long and at most twelve inches wide. It was attached with clevices at the center-ends of a three-horse triple tree. Figure 12.1 shows the combined harvester pulled by a team of 32 horses—the minimum required to pull the machine through the fields. Depending on the terrain, farmers sometimes used three lead horses to help with turning and to increase their control.[8] Figure 12.2 shows a cross-sectional view of the first nine horses of a 33-horse team hitched using the Schandoney hitch.

Harvest required almost as many workers as it did horses, and even with neighbors helping neighbors there were not enough hands to perform all

Figure 12.1 A 32-Horse Team Hitched to a Combined Harvester
Source: Kirby Brumfield, *This Was Wheat Farming*, 120.

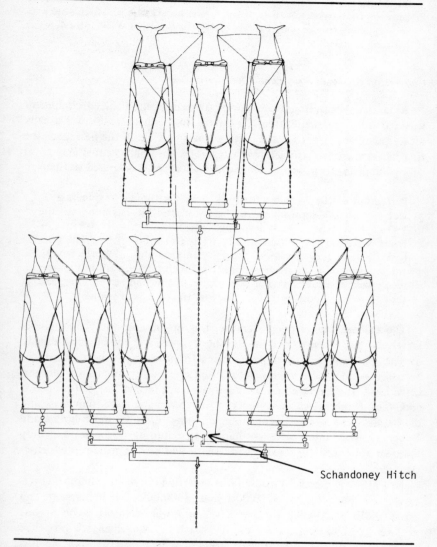

Schandoney Hitch

Figure 12.2 Section of Horses Using the Schandoney Equalizing Hitch
Source: Thomas B. Keith, *The Horse Interlude*, 92.

many as 22 or 23 people, and, of course, until my boys got big enough, I chopped my own wood. I was here alone so much that I had to learn to do it or I'd freeze [Betty Smith, RWHP interview, November, 1975].

Conversion to Diesel Power and Electricity

A farmer's transition from horse-powered to mechanized equipment was marked by his acquisition of a tractor. In the Palouse, this was usually a caterpillar or crawler tractor because the steepness of the hills made the first wheel tractors inefficient and dangerous. Caterpillars could crawl over soft ground on steep slopes, while early wheel tractors tended to tip over.

Perfection of the farm tractor took time. [Although engineers were working on these problems in the 1860's] . . . it was not until the 1930's that [they] had developed and refined the tractor to the point where it could consistently outperform horses. . . . The tractors triumph over the horse became complete during World War II, when farm labor was in short supply throughout the nation. Farmers recognized the labor saving advantages of mechanized farming and they were eager customers for whatever tractors were available.[13]

The Palouse farmer bought crawler tractors because they could immediately be put to use to pull the threshers, plows, and combines he already owned. He was thus saved the expense of investing in new machinery because, in effect, he merely substituted one power supply for another. Only later, and as he could afford it, would a farmer buy self-propelled combines. Nonetheless, the effects of the conversion were immediate and dramatic. Some farmers went from requiring thirty or more horses and fifteen or more hired men one harvest to requiring no horses and only three or four men the next. Productivity and profits soared as expenses dropped.

In 1975, a successful Palouse farm operation (land and equipment) was capitalized at between $220,000 and $300,000 for equipment and $600,000 to $1,200,000 for land. The equipment inventory included: one or two 225-280 horsepower crawler tractors, two small self-propelled combines or one large one, three drills or seeders, one ten-bottom flex beam plow, one 22-foot chisel plow, one 42-foot field cultivator, one 36-40-foot rod weeder, one tine or peg harrow, one 40-foot rower, one tough. . . . You go out with one of those teams . . . and maybe plow five, six acres a day, gosh, it took a lot of time to plow. That was a big job. You really had to make the hours count. It was time. You had to be out there because you just couldn't speed it up, you had to put in lots of time.[11]

In addition, the horse-based technology supported numerous ancillary occupations, such as blacksmithing, harness making, and milling, in adjacent communities.

What was the farm woman doing while her husband and sons worked in the fields and barns? She and her daughters were cooking. She cooked for the family and for the hired hands, whose average wages of $45 per month were supplemented by the board she provided. Had women not done this, farmers would surely have had to increase wages, and thus incur increased costs.

During harvest, women cooked an average of five meals per day (breakfast, lunch, and late supper were sitdown meals, and mid-morning and late afternoon snacks of sandwiches and lemonade were brought to the fields). Their day would begin before dawn and end only after the last pan had been washed and the table reset for the next day. Women baked bread two or three times a day:

All would be bustle and hustle around the big kitchen for days before the crew arrived. Big tables had to be set up, with benches down the side to serve from 15 to 17 men. Bread, cakes, cookies, pies, hams and much other good, solid food was prepared. Always there were two hired girls to help mother and they usually went with the crew from house to house. As did the men, each one carried her own bedroll. Cooks arose at 3 a.m. to serve breakfast before dawn, as the boys had to be in the field by daybreak.[12]

When not working to feed harvest crews, a farm woman usually kept chickens, milked a cow and made butter, raised a garden, and canned the produce. In addition, she was responsible for the sewing and mending of the family wardrobe, and for the endless washing of clothes. To do this, farm women had to pump water, heat it on the woodstove, empty dirty water, and replace rinse water—all by hand. A survey conducted in 1929 of women in Washington found that they worked an average of 63 hours per week, 53 in homemaking tasks and the other ten in farm work,[13] although it is unclear from the study how gardening, milking and butter-making were categorized. Wayve Comstock summarized her experiences as a farm wife as follows:

> That was one of the things that was a little different in my life than in some others, we did have a lot of help, because it took a lot of help in those days to get the work done. It took five on the thresher crew and we hired a man to stay with me when the crew was away, and we had a lot of relatives that worked for us part time. And I was home with three little children, real small, and I had the chores to do, and the shopkeeper to wait on—he would come and get vegetables and butter and those fryers that I raised—and I also canned fruit in two-quart jars for the cookhouse and we had our own eggs. We had all the stuff we could possibly get from home to feed the people we got 'cus it cut down on the expenses, and nobody was making any money except a few like us that did extra jobs like thrashing and harvest. You can see how busy we were, very busy, but it was a happy life and we made it pay [Wayve Comstock, RWHP interview, June 1974].

Women felt themselves to be not just equal as partners but also equal to their husbands as providers of the goods and services necessary to the family's survival. Men provided expertise and decision-making about the management of the farming enterprise; women had responsibility for and authority over the management of the home. For example, she provided butter and egg money to purchase goods such as shoes, sugar, and kerosene that could not be produced on the farm. In addition, women provided medical care to their families and communities; this included everything from emergency first aid to injured field hands to full-time care of sick and elderly relatives. Occasionally, women were the only wage-earners upon whom a family could depend. Roberta Nygaard, for example, sacrificed an early marriage in order to keep her family on their land:

> My courtship was seven years long. Oh, we wanted to marry sooner but it was the Depression and I was a school teacher. They only hired single women to do the teaching and I was the only one in the family earning any cash money. If I'd got married, my Mom, Dad and sisters would have lost the farm, 'cause there wouldn't have been any money to pay the taxes [Roberta Nygaard, RWHP interview, June 1974].

While the foregoing descriptions of men's and women's work on the typical Palouse farm help us to understand how time-consuming, demanding, and exhausting farming was for both sexes, this is not the most important realization. What is significant is the value of the work. Although men and women had substantially different roles, performed different tasks, and had separate responsibilities, men's work and women's work were equally essential to the well-being and survival of the family. If men did not meet their responsibilities of caring for their animals and repairing their equipment, both their own harvest and their neighbors' would be adversely affected. Similarly, if women failed to get hearty meals prepared on time, the health, energy, and morale of the crew would be affected and the harvest operation jeopardized. The entire family depended upon the farmer's foresight in buying seed, in deciding what and when to plant, and in reading the weather to determine when to mow, combine, and summer-fallow. Likewise, the vegetables a woman planted in her garden, and the chickens she raised for eggs and meat, were often the margin of security that determined if her family would last out a hard winter. Just as the farmer's skill in selling his crop determined the family's yearly income, so too did his wife's butter and egg money provide the cash flow necessary to take care of daily, domestic expenses. It is not only that men's and women's work combined to make the farm a producing unit, it is even more that the work men and women did was equally crucial to the survival of that family unit.

Although they did not use this term, women and men recognized the crucialness of their roles: "Well, it just seemed to be my duty. There was no one else to do it" (Edna Cochrane). The ability to cope, to make do, is one of the aspects of their lives that women themselves took pride in: "You know, us women, they couldn't have done it without us" (Wayve Comstock). Indeed, women felt themselves to be full partners in the economic enterprise:

Well, I've done just a little bit of everything; when I was home I helped my dad in the fields. He didn't have a boy to help him so I did it and I drove a tractor in the hay field and when I was old enough I learned to drive grain and wheat trucks. I milked cows and did gardening; then later when I got married and had the five kids, so of course, I learned to cook and sew and I helped build our house. I put the roof on, put the floor in and what I could do and I like to do minor home repairs, wire light fixtures and plug ins and I like to overhaul lamps and things like that. I love to bake bread, I do all the painting here in the house and I like to sew, I made my drapes and I make a lot of my girls', and my own clothes. . . . Most of the time I'm pretty busy cooking for the hunters. In the fall, I cook for as the separate operations of feeding, harnessing, hauling, heading, threshing, binding, sacking, sack-sewing, and stacking that were required to harvest the wheat. Additional men had to be hired to work the harvest, and crews of 15-25 were typical. Most crews worked until eight or nine at night and were paid wages, room and board:

Wheat harvest was a backbreaking, filthy, dirty, job. . . . The population of the small farming communities swelled considerably during the harvest season. By July, each train into town, both freight and passenger, meant dozens of workers piling off and wandering up and down main street waiting for work. . . . Each man carried his own bedroll. It consisted of a blanket or two rolled inside lightweight canvas. . . . In addition to wages the men were given room and board but the room wasn't anything to brag about. It was the straw pile. Most outfits worked until eight or nine at night. When the day's work ended the workers didn't hit the hay, they hit the straw.[9]

When harvesting was completed in one area, crews would move on to the next one. As many as 10,000 transient laborers worked the harvest in the Palouse in the 1920s, and over $4 million was spent in labor.[10]

In addition, the farmer usually had at least one hired man who stayed permanently on the farm while larger landowners employed two or more hands to help them with the innumerable chores—feeding the horses, repairing machinery, farrowing, planting, making hay, and so forth—that kept farmers busy throughout the year:

I herded sheep, I herded cattle and did everything like that when I was old enough to ride a horse. And then of course, automation started maybe in the '20's, and, of course, I learned to drive an old Ford truck about those times. Just barely could look over the dashboard. But there was always work. I could rake, use a rake with a team. I remember I used to rake hay. We did a lot of haying and we put in about thirty days of haying because we had to provide all the feed, fill the barns to feed those animals all summer and winter. And it just took a lot of time. And I did chores, milked cows. Fed pigs. Always had pigs. Fatten up the hogs to sell them. . . . We would seed there the 20th of September and then we'd go and plow that ground that was harvested, all that fall, we'd plow way into Thanksgiving. We worked longer in those times, I remember plowing Thanksgiving; it was nothing to be plowing Thanksgiving. Now if we think we don't have it plowed by the last of October, we think we're late. It would be difficult, it would be wet and frozen, cold. It was

22-foot heavy duty disk, two or three grain trucks, and one or two pickup trucks.[14] Harvest now requires only four laborers: two to drive the combines and two to shuttle the grain trucks to and from the elevator.

The change from horse-drawn to diesel-powered farm machinery also created sudden and enormous changes for farm women: Instead of cooking five meals a day for fifteen hired men, she cooked three meals a day for her family and perhaps one or two extra hands; instead of planning and organizing large meals, she prepared smaller meals for workers who were not as hungry.

Farm women understood clearly the ways in which their lives were determined by the degree of mechanization of the farm on which they lived. In a brochure praising the advantages of the caterpillar tractor, entitled "At Last We Wives Can Have Vacations," women described the effect of purchasing a tractor on their own and their husbands' lives:

Before we had our tractor we farmed with 30 or 40 head of horses and mules and had four or five hired men to cook for all summer long and one, sometimes two, all winter. Now I have only two men in the summer and none at all in the winter. . . . I used to be tied down at home all the time cooking for a bunch of hired help and many times had to have a hired girl, which I don't need now since we have the "Caterpillar." It gives me more leisure time and I enjoy life more now than I ever have before. . . . Since my husband has no horses to care for he has more time to fix things up around the place. Painted the house and all such since we have the tractor, which he never thought of doing, or rather did not have the time to do before. . . . And the most important thing of all is that since my husband doesn't have to get up so early in the morning and tend to a bunch of horses before breakfast and work until late at night feeding and unharnessing, he isn't half so cranky as he used to be.[15]

These sentiments were echoed by Mrs. Con Fink:

I must say that up to now it is the most wonderful thing that has ever been used on our farm. It is not only convenient for the men, but for the women as well. It certainly saves a great amount of work and expense. There isn't always a meal to cook for hired help as before, which occupies the biggest part of a woman's time during the day. This also means that a woman has her weekends free. The men benefit as well, for there aren't any chores to do every day of the year.[16]

Mrs. F. R. Johnson stated the case more simply: "When we farmed with horses, I did most of the milking in the working season, because there was not time to lose—now I help milk if I want to. No hurry."[17]

Caterpillar tractors, combines, seeders, threshers, and other machines were readily accepted by Palouse area farmers, not only because they made men's and women's lives immediately and quantifiably easier, but also because they made the farm enterprise more productive and competitive in a rapidly changing agricultural economy. Less obvious and less well understood were the changes in values and crucialness that accompanied the changes in machinery and productivity.

Women's Roles on the Modern Farm

Historian Susan Armitage notes that, in the Palouse at least, electricity and labor-saving electrical appliances for women were purchased later than labor-saving agricultural technology, so that the time they freed and the increase in productivity they caused could not be effectively used to help the family economic enterprise. In other words, the farmer's technological improvements eliminated the basis for his wife's efforts.[18] Farm women did not need new appliances to feed farm workers more efficiently because diesel power had taken the place of horsepower and there were fewer workers to feed.

During the harvest in the Palouse today, you will find women not cooking, but driving: driving wheat trucks to the elevator; driving seventy miles round trip to get a replacement part; driving to the shopping mall for groceries; and driving the children to school activities. While it is almost as time-consuming, driving is not like cooking; it does not require physical work, engage a woman's creativity, or challenge her management skills. Nor does it result in closure ("Well, that's done") or feedback ("Gee, those pies were good").

The situation is little different during the rest of the year. Instead of sewing the family's clothes, a farm woman now buys them; instead of canning the produce from her garden, she buys food. In fact, it is cheaper for the farm wife to buy case lots of canned peaches than to put up the equivalent amount herself. Cash income, the availability of fresh produce, and good roads have removed the *economic* necessity of her doing anything beyond shopping. In addition, other functions she once provided alone are now performed by others: schools educate her children, television entertains them, ambulances provide emergency medical care, and social service agencies care for the needy. The rural woman who does not have paid employment contributes to the economic welfare and survival of the family in ways that are invisible, rather than visible: by reducing expenditures, cutting costs, and spending less. Consequently, the focus of the women's role has shifted from producing goods and services to consuming them, from managing domestic labor to managing the family's recreation. One of our respondents expressed this well:

A lot of the advantages that we have here are recreation: our fishing, our hunting, it's a small community, not a big city. The disadvantages, of course, you don't have the shopping like you do in the big city, so we go to Spokane to do a lot of that, which I think most everybody here does. It's only an hour and a half if you're going slow like me. We spend the day and come home; it's not bad. I enjoy fishing for recreation, just go behind the house. In the wintertime we have two snowmobiles and we can just go right out here in the field and have a ball. Anytime a person has enough snow to do it and it is fun. The kids enjoy it, we didn't have any time this year to go on any snowmobile trips, maybe next year. Our family does most everything together, snowcapping, fishing, picnicking or going to a show or something; we usually do that together or go to the lake or whatever [Linda Appel, RWHP interview, May, 1975].

Mrs. Appel's children also live lives that are remarkably different from the lives of children forty and fifty years ago. Chores such as feeding stock, chopping wood, carrying water, and driving tractors predominate in those early descriptions, while school activities are emphasized today:

Cheryl is fifteen and her interests are sewing, cooking and her band at the school, her band activities. Ginger is 14, she was active in youth club at the Presbyterian Church and the different things they did and in pep band and she loves the outdoors. Jackie she's 12, she's in band and she loves to be active in sports, they all seem to be active in sports. Wendy, she's 8, no 9, she likes the outdoor activities, none of them are really indoors or like to fool around inside; they like to get out and be active. Of course the baby, he's just whatever. He'll be 2, he loves it outside, he'd sleep out there if we let him [Linda Appel].

A mother must somehow keep up with all this; she drives the children to their activities, keeps track of their progress, provides a sympathetic ear to help them with their problems. She is, in short, responsive to the needs and decisions of others. Her time and desires must bend to accommodate theirs. Linda Appel, for example, is so busy coordinating her family's activities that she has little time for herself and her own interests: "Well, I haven't been in too many activities or projects. The home things pretty much take up most of my time, by the time supper and with the kids. . . . I have joined one club which is a good club but I quit because at night time I was so tired I don't think I was much good at all."

Almost everything the farm woman does can be and is done by someone else. It just costs less—since wives are not paid—to have her do it. This is especially true of keeping the books, the one area of women's traditional work on which farm women spend more time today than they did forty years ago. Yet here again she provides an ongoing maintenance function over which she has no real decision-making authority:

> In the days when I was growing up there were no books kept. There wasn't any income tax in those days. But since we've had books and there's a terrific amount of bookkeeping on a farm now days and especially in the partnership my husband is in. . . . Of course we have our income tax done by an accountant but then I have to get the books ready. Oh you just can't imagine the bookkeeping there is [Roberta Nygaard].

As Roberta Nygaard's and Linda Appel's accounts indicate, rural women are still busy. In fact, our research supports the well-documented proposition that they are busier than ever. Finding that rural women devoted five more hours per week to housework in 1965 than they did in 1926, researcher Joann Vanek states that "technological changes have increased women's productivity and shortened the hours necessary to do certain tasks (i.e., laundry), but the addition of new tasks and the creation of higher standards of cleanliness have meant that the hours necessary for housework have not noticeably changed."[19] Thus, it is not true that technology has freed women from their domestic responsibilities; changes in household technology have instead redefined the value of their domestic work, making luxuries out of what were once necessities, and making superfluous what was once crucial. Robert Smiths discusses this dynamic in his 1959 analysis, *Women and Work in America*, where he wrotes that:

> technology brought "new work" into the home but the amount of time spent in household maintenance did not decline. New work includes the happiness of others, the emotional development of children, interior decorating, gourmet cooking, chauffering, enter- taining and volunteering. *Whether these new duties of women are*

properly classified as work is a matter of definition [emphasis added].[20]

While none of our rural respondents had any doubt that what they were doing was work, Smiths has inadvertently hit upon the key to understanding what has happened to farm women: Their work is no less time-consuming than it ever was; it is simply less crucial.

Men's Roles on the Modern Farm

In contrast, men's farm work since 1930 has become, if anything, less time-consuming as it has become more crucial. Farmers have less and less margin for error; as the cash value of a crop increases, so do the costs and the risks. For example, Palouse farmers today concern themselves with decisions of how much acreage to plant, which pesticides and herbicides to use, when to schedule crop dusters, when to harvest and when to sell the crops, what methods of accounting and estate-planning to use to get the best tax advantages, and which growers' association or cooperative to affiliate with. About 10 percent of Palouse farmers are now growing wheat on contracts where crops are sold before they are planted. In addition, 95 percent of the area's wheat crop is exported to China and Japan where it must meet exacting standards defining permissible moisture content and levels of disease and impurities. These standards are set, not by the farmer, but by the buyer, who is frequently an official of a foreign country or a representative of an international conglomerate.

If everything goes well (and it usually does in the Palouse), the farmer will receive over $200,000 for his crop. With this money, the farmer must pay off his debts and buy all food, supplies, furnishings, clothes, fertilizer, seed, and fuel on which his family will depend next year. Indeed all that is left on the Palouse family farm is a man and his internal combustion machines. "Farming that was once a way of life, albeit a long and labored way, is now a business, geared to the machine as surely as any factory."[21] And while machines do not require the outlay of his time that horses once required, they have so increased the cost and scale of the enterprise that a farmer must now make complex decisions at every stage of the process.

Although the analogy is a popular one, the modern farmer is *not* a small businessman. In that he is responsible for but one aspect of a large, multifaceted institution, the modern farmer is more like a mid-level manager of a large, diverse corporation than a small businessman. He can do his part to greater or lesser efficiency but he can only do a part; he has no authority over the workings of agriculture as a whole. The modern farmer can do little to cut his costs or raise his prices, for he must buy in a seller's market and sell in a buyer's market. And, because he is producing crops for cash, he is powerless to withhold them and live off them until the price improves. There is, after all, a limit to how much wheat his family can consume.

Put another way, the context in which farmers farm has shifted dramatically from shared responsibility for an independent, self-sufficient unit to exclusive responsibility for an interdependent, income-producing one. For the farmer, this transition has meant increases in scale, complexity, and risk and a concomitant increase in the crucialness of his decisions. It has also meant that while he has more discretion over the use of his time—no horses to feed, groom, and stable—his enterprise is less diverse than it was when he could sell his hay or his horses if the wheat crop failed. In addition, there are fewer alternate providers, friends and neighbors, on whom he can rely if he is unable to work or make decisions. While a disabled farmer can hire custom cutters or prevail upon his neighbors to help him at harvest, no one would presume to decide for him what variety of wheat to plant or whether to disc or low-till his summer fallow. There is no "safety net"; the farmer who cannot make major decisions himself—for even the shortest time—is not a farmer.

Crucialness

For these reasons, the "crucialness" of men's traditional roles has increased dramatically since the horse-farming era, and technology has played a significant role because it has affected the scale and risk of farming and marketing decisions. Specialized cash crop agriculture has also increased the complexity of the factors to be considered in making a decision at the same time that it has decreased the diversity of the farming operation. As diversity decreases (or specialization increases), the number of people available to help the farmer in his decision-making also decreases. There is no margin for error as there was when farms were small-scale, diversified, and self-sufficient. This increase in crucialness is illustrated in Figure 12.3, which shows the relationship of crucialness to technological change.

It is interesting to note that where increasing risk has been the single area of greatest change for her husband, the farm woman's role has been most affected by changes in the availability of alternate providers and her

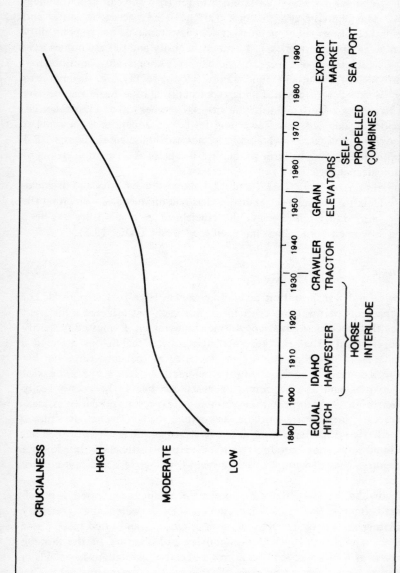

Figure 12.3 Changes in Farmer's Crucialness as a Function of Development of Agricultural Technology

253

family's access to them. Canned goods and frozen foods are now "provided" by supermarkets at costs much lower than she can produce them herself. The highway system "provides" her ready access to stores and supermarkets. Emergency medical services have removed her responsibility for knowing home remedies, just as social security and old age homes have eased her obligation of caring for the elderly. Schools provide education; TV provides entertainment; food stamps tide the family over through hard times. Most of her activities and responsibilities have been assumed by others in the society. The farm wife's work becomes less and less essential; her errors in judgment have fewer and fewer consequences as the number of people and agencies who can do her work increases. Figure 12.4 illustrates the decline in farm women's crucialness as a function, again, of technological change.

Superimposing Figures 12.3 and 12.4 shows the disparity and disequalizing effects that technological change has had on men and women on the family farm. Put euphoniously, the crucialness of men's roles has been loaded as women's crucialness has been eroded (see Figure 12.5).

Summary

Power and transportation technology are in large part responsible for these patterns of diverging crucialness, but each has affected a different part of the crucialness equations for men and women. Expressed primarily as the electricity that ran her appliances, power technology affected a woman's work by increasing her productivity at the same time that her husband's conversion to diesel power eliminated both the scope and risk of her activities and the economic necessity for her to be economically *productive* at all. Transportation technology, expressed primarily as inexpensive cars, inexpensive gasoline, and public roads, affected the crucialness of her work by facilitating access to other suppliers who provided her traditional services and products more cheaply and efficiently. In addition, the requirements of shopping and driving gave her less and less control over her time.

Meanwhile, back on the farm, power technology, expressed as diesel-powered tractors and self-propelled combines, affected the farmer by eliminating almost completely his need for horses and hired men. These changes, in turn, affected the productivity and diversity of the farming enterprise as the farmer sold his horses and cattle, planted his hay fields in cash crops, and invested in more machinery to increase his yield. This upwardly escalating spiral of machine-stimulated investments converted

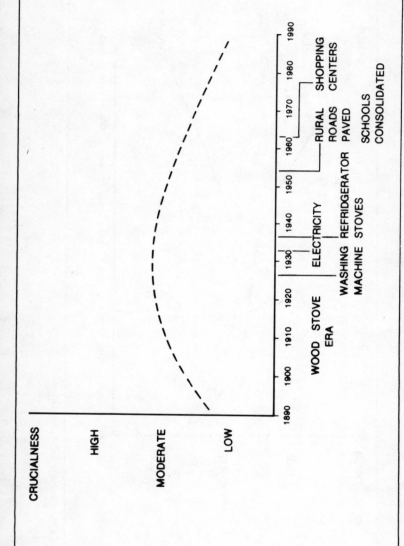

Figure 12.4 Changes in Farm Women's Crucialness as a Function of Development of Household and Transportation Technology

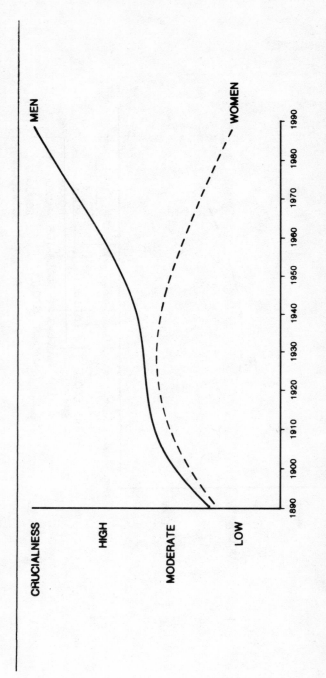

Figure 12.5 Changes in Farm Family Crucialness

the farm from a moderate-scale, diversified, self-sufficient, and labor-intensive enterprise to a large-scale, specialized, capital-intensive, income-producing one. The result was an enormous increase in crucialness.

Transportation technology, expressed primarily as grain trucks, grain elevators, railroad cars, and cargo ships, also affected farmers by providing access to national and international markets, thereby increasing the risks of low productivity. Improvements in grain varieties, in herbicides, and in pesticides further increased the complexity and risk of the farmer's decisions. Selling internationally has made farmers as vulnerable to market failure as to crop failure.

The key to understanding technology and its differential effect on crucialness is to remember that technology has magnified, not altered, the gender-based division of farm labor that has traditionally determined men's and women's roles and responsibilities. Technological innovation accepts and frequently exacerbates the norms of the society in which it is adopted; it seldom challenges or contradicts them.

Public Policy Implications

The public policy implications of this analysis of crucialness are many and profound, affecting technology assessment as well as social services and agricultural policy. For example, health care professionals, mental health workers, and social service agencies need to study their activities to analyze their impact on the crucialness equation and to become aware of the increased incidence of stress-related diseases among men and depression-related conditions among women. Further, the ever-widening gap between men's and women's crucialness is putting the traditional rural family under an enormous stress that is all the more damaging because it is so subtle: The accepted roles for men and women have not changed, but the content of the roles has. Therapies and services should be redirected to consider this.

In addition, educators at all levels, but particularly those in agricultural and cooperative extensions, should examine their policies and practices to evaluate the extent that they contribute to increased polarization and inequality in the farm families they serve. By providing resources and information on cooking, canning, sewing, gardening, and keeping books, cooperative extension agents only help women better fulfill traditional but increasingly empty roles. Farm women would be better served if they could acquire skills in making some of the technological and managerial decisions that modern farming requires. Agricultural economists, on the other hand, need to reorient their services. By providing endless workshops on how to improve farm practices, how to get tax breaks, and how to utilize ever newer strains and varieties, extension agents increase a farmer's critical knowledge, but they also increase his isolation and risk. In the future, the focus of all extension education efforts should be on helping farm families reestablish "crucialness equity" by helping women to become fully functioning, economically critical partners in the farm enterprise and by helping men to ease some of their burdens and responsibilities.

In addition, researchers and scholars who study the relationships between technological and social change need to examine the concept of crucialness and evaluate its applicability in other situations. If it proves generalizable, crucialness may provide a tool for expressing the ways in which technology changes the lives, values, and self-esteem of individuals.

Furthermore, the concept of crucialness leads to the realization that a given technological innovation loads some roles while it erodes others. This may prove useful in refining techniques of technology assessment, since a major fallacy permeating previous assessments has been the assumption that men and women are affected similarly by, and thus benefit equally from, technological change. Therefore, in addition to environmental impact reports, technology assessments and cost-benefit analysis should include a sex-role impact report. Such reports should examine closely the differential effects of an innovation on men and women and should propose strategies for eliminating consequent inequities.

Finally, the concept of crucialness can provide a model by which to understand the effects of technological change on individuals.

NOTES

1. Significant exceptions are the Cornell University *Farm Family Decision-Making Project,* a 14-year longitudinal study of families in upstate New York, and continuing work by Joann Vanek in a soon-to-be-published manuscript tentatively titled *Time and Women's Work.*

2. Michael Berger's *The Devil Wagon in God's Country: The Automobile and Social Change in Rural America, 1893-1929* (Hamden, CT, 1979) attempts to fill some of this void.

3. The definitions of complexity, scale, and risk proposed herein are based loosely on the job factor analysis prepared by Hay Associates of Chicago. They are currently used by government agencies, including the State of Idaho and the City of San Jose, California, to analyze job descriptions and salaries of employees.

4. U.S. *Agricultural Census* (1920, 1974).

5. Tapes, data sheets, and transcripts of interviews conducted by the Rural Women's History Project, are deposited in the archives of the University of Idaho library in Moscow, Idaho.

6. Susan Armitage, "Farm women and technological change." Presented at the 5th Berkshire Conference, Vassar College, Poughkeepsie, New York (June 16-17, 1981), 3.

7. Thomas B. Keith, *The Horse Interlude: A Pictorial History of Horse and Man In the Inland Northwest* (Moscow, Idaho, 1980), 67-68.

8. Ibid., 89-92.

9. Kirby Brumfield, *This Was Wheat Farming* (New York, 1968), 109.

10. Armitage, "Farm women and technological change," 3.

11. Elvin Hampton, interview by Sam Schrager for the Latah County Historical Society. From 1973 to 1975, staff of the Latah County Historical Society collected in-depth interviews with men and women who pioneered the county. These oral histories have been transcribed and are available for review at the Historical Society and at the archives of the University of Idaho library.

12. Brumfield, *This Was Wheat Farming,* 68.

13. Keith, *The Horse Interlude,* 167-168.

14. Art Helbling, August 19, 1981, personal communication. Mr. Helbling is an owner of Helbling Brothers, the largest farm equipment dealership in the Palouse. Helbling Brothers has been doing business in Moscow, Idaho, since 1939.

15. "At last we wives can have vacations." Pamphlet printed by the Caterpillar Tractor Company, Peoria, Illinois, 1930, and distributed by Hofus-Ferris Equipment Company, Spokane, Washington.

16. Ibid.

17. Ibid.

18. Armitage, "Farm women and technological change," 13.

19. Joann Vanek, "Time spent in housework," *Scientific American* (November 1974), 118.

20. Robert Smiths, *Women and Work in America* (New York, 1959), 28.

21. Brumfield, *This Was Wheat Farming,* 158.

13

Energy Regimes and
The Ideology of Efficiency

LANGDON WINNER

In his *Histories*, Herodotus tells of an ancient crisis in natural resources and its eventual resolution. A prolonged drought dried up all the water of the Psylli, a people who lived in North Africa. "The Psylli took counsel among themselves, and by common consent made war upon the south-wind. They went forth and reached the desert; but there the south-wind rose and buried them under heaps of sand."[1] As one follows today's conversations on energy and society, the plight of the Psylli seems prophetic. Obsessed with a resource problem and confused as to where the origin of that problem lies, our society is evidently prepared to take desperate measures, not even short of declaring war, to secure its precious energy supply. Whether or not we meet the same fate as the tribe in Herodotus' tale, those who read the statistics, analyses, and arguments of contemporary energy studies may have the feeling that we are already being buried in sand.

Taken on their own terms, the energy reports sponsored by the Ford Foundation, the Mellon Foundation, the National Research Council, and others during the past decade are formidable documents. Works such as *A Time to Choose, Nuclear Power Issues and Choices, Energy: The Next Twenty Years, Energy in Transition,* and *Energy in America's Future* contain what seems to be the most reliable information, the most sophisticated thinking and trustworthy advice that the nation can muster.[2] The reports give scrupulous attention to the circumstances that influence the demand for energy and equally careful review to factors that affect supply. Prospects for many possible energy sources and technologies are analyzed in detail. Elaborate "scenarios" showing the relationship between different levels of supply and demand, and different mixes of energy resources, are

AUTHOR'S NOTE: This chapter was prepared with the support of National Science Foundation grant OSS-8018089. Its views are those of the author and do not necessarily reflect those of NSF or NEH.

projected decades into the future. Important issues of national security, international relations, and environmental quality all receive judicious consideration. The possible roles of both government and business are compared as means for creating wise energy policy; invariably, an agreeable balance between the two is sought.

The findings and recommendations of the panels of experts who write the studies tend to agree on many central points. All of them reassure the reader that there is no energy "crisis" as such, no absolute shortage of energy, only a situation in which the price of energy will continue to rise. Conservation is usually found to be a better choice than conventional wisdom had previously suggested. By using presently available energy more efficiently, the country can and should consume less than historic trends of energy growth would indicate. A crucial policy, according to many of the panels and study groups, is to let prices rise to reflect the true value of the energy we use; hence, government price controls and subsidies that distort the workings of "the market" are frequently denounced as bad practice.

When it comes to the matter of evaluating various sources of energy, the recommendations are somewhat more scattered. All of the studies recognize that petroleum and natural gas now have relatively short horizons, but conclusions about the relative prospects for coal, nuclear, and solar energy differ widely. It is not uncommon to learn from today's energy studies that America ought to keep its nuclear "option" open, especially the future option of developing large-scale capacity in liquid metal fast-breeder reactors. Of course, that suggestion means something more than storing scientific and technical information on the LMFBR under an appropriate catalogue heading in the library; it means actually building at least one such reactor right away.

Whatever their agreements or disagreements on specific solutions, a prominent feature of contemporary energy reports is a remarkable uniformity in approach. The intellectual program of the research—evident in the various demand and supply estimates, the analyses of different alternatives, and so forth—is always roughly the same, as if guided by some deeply acknowledged but unseen format. As one turns from one volume to the next, it becomes evident that a strong consensus about both form and content of energy policy inquiries exists among experts in this field (at least those experts likely to be asked to join team research studies sponsored by the Ford Foundation, the Mellon Foundation, or the National Academy of Science). One encounters a wonderful set of fixed beliefs about how the world works and how things ought to be.

A Grand Consensus

The uniformity of world view among energy policy analysts was recently commented upon by Laura Nader, an anthropologist at the University of California, Berkeley. In the middle 1970s, she was invited, much to her surprise, to a conference on energy and the future attended by a number of the nation's leading authorities on the topic. "We were to talk about these different 'scenarios' for the future," she recalls, "but it became clear that there were already boundaries around those scenarios. You were to think freely—within those boundaries. When you went beyond them, someone would tell you, 'You're off the track.' Finally I told one fellow that we didn't know where the track was; that was why we were there." Professor Nader began to notice that a number of taboos prevailed within the discussions. "Solar was never mentioned by anybody other than myself, literally never mentioned. The possibility of dropping nuclear power as a future alternative wasn't even discussed. The social and political consequences of nuclear power were not discussed. Nobody used the word 'safety.' "

When she was later asked to join two energy study teams, Nader took the opportunity to observe the behavior of the participants from the perspective of her own discipline. She found groups of white, middle-aged, middle-class, male professionals involved in patterns of intense competition characteristic of same-sex groups in all cultures. In this case, the competition found its special magic in the display of numbers and computer statements. "Jack says to Bill, 'Bill, I like your numbers, they agreed with mine.' Bill beams and says, 'How about Jim? Has Jim generated any numbers yet?' Jack says, 'No. Why don't you send your numbers over to him before he gets his ego involved with generating his own.' " Speaking as an anthropologist, Nader writes of her work on the National Academy of Science-sponsored Committee on Nuclear and Alternative Energy Systems: "The CONAES project was the hardest field work I've ever done."[3]

The uniformity of today's energy studies is, of course, more than a reflection of cultural style. From beginning to end, almost all such reports produced in the United States during the past ten years are based upon the same explicitly acknowledged premise. Stated as a question, their concern is this: How much energy and what kind of energy will society require if economic growth is to continue? As the Resources for the Future National Energy Strategies Project put the issue: "We assume that there is a consensus for the idea that sustained real growth is essential if the United States is to meet the many domestic and international demands that press for attention. Even among those who accept the need for overall economic growth, however, there is no clear agreement on how much (if any) accompanying growth we need in energy consumption."[4] Even those participants in the debate who take relatively unorthodox positions—those who advocate extreme conservationism, solar energy, or soft energy paths—usually feel obliged to offer their proposals as fully compatible with economic growth. Thus, a report by the Union of Concerned Scientists, *Energy Strategies: Toward a Solar Future,* insists: "The United States can provide a high level of economic prosperity for all its citizens without the wastefully high levels of gross energy use characteristic of conventional government and industry projections. By increasing energy productivity and thereby deriving greater benefit from the energy we use, economic growth can be sustained with little or no growth in overall energy use."[5]

Along with this commitment to a common goal comes a closely related choice of intellectual, or perhaps one might better say ideological, persuasion. To be recognized as having a "serious position"[6] on this topic, one must embrace the wisdom of contemporary neoclassical economics. As the Ford Foundation's Nuclear Energy Policy Study Group has announced: "When analyzing energy, one must first decide whether ordinary rules of economics can be applied."[7] The group decides that, yes, energy is "an economic variable, rather than something requiring special analysis." It is always encouraging to see our leading experts getting back to first principles, always reassuring to learn that our problems do not require anything so drastic as "special analysis." On every page, the major energy studies make it clear that the concepts and models of economics, especially those that help us to compare the dollar costs of various energy choices, are the considerations (along with the constraints presented by physics and engineering) that truly matter.

Once again, participants who hold unorthodox viewpoints in the debate nevertheless find it necessary to recognize the primacy of this approach. Thus, Amory B. Lovins, leading proponent of soft energy paths, writes of his method: "While not under the illusion that facts are separable from values, I have tried . . . to separate my personal preferences from my analytic assumptions and to rely not on modes of discourse that might be viewed as overtly ideological, but rather on classical arguments of economic and engineering efficiency (which are only tacitly ideological)."[8] To Lovins's credit, he has consistently argued that the social consequences of energy choices are, in the last analysis, the most important aspects of energy policy making. But when the chips are down, his strategy (and it is probably a wise one, given his audience) has been to beat the establish-

ment energy analysts at their own game, marshaling figures about comparative costs that indicate that renewable sources are preferable to
nuclear and coal.

To be taken seriously in energy policy deliberations, therefore, every
concerned person must first bow down before the altar. One must swear to
God and country that what ultimately matters are questions of efficiency.
Something resembling an oath is taken that pledges one to examine all
possible alternatives to discover those which give the most energy per
dollar. It is possible to fiddle a bit with the specific definition of efficiency
one employs. Some hope to modify the ritual by arguing that we must
first identify and measure the end uses to which energy is put. But
suggestions of that kind, as helpful as they are in certain respects, do
nothing to change the fundamental nature of the discussion. One still puts
Btus or kilowatt-hours in the numerator and dollars in the denominator
and worships the resulting ratio as gospel.

A fascination with efficiency has a long history in American life,
announced early on, for example, in Benjamin Franklin's maxims about
the virtue of economizing on time, effort, and money. During the progressive era of the late nineteenth and twentieth centuries, efficiency became
something of an obsession among the well-educated in the United States.
Understood to be a criterion applicable to personal and social life as well
as to mechanical and economic systems, efficiency was upheld as a goal
valuable in its own right, one strongly linked to the progress of science, the
development of industry, the rise of professionalism, and the conservation
of natural resources. In politics, the rule of efficient, well-trained professionals was seen as a way of sanitizing government of the corruption of
party machines and eliminating the influence of selfish interest groups.
Throughout the progressive era and in decades since, an eagerness to define
important public issues as questions of efficiency has been a common
strategy; adherence to this norm has been welcomed as a way of achieving
the ends of democracy without having to deal with democracy as a living
process. Thus, it is not surprising to see efficiency reappear at the center of
today's energy debate. For Americans, to demonstrate the efficiency of a
course of action conveys a sense of scientific truth, political wisdom, social
consensus, and a compelling moral urgency.[9]

By calling attention to the goal of economic growth, the exclusive use
of neoclassical economic concepts, and the prevalence of efficiency as the
dominant consensus norm in energy policy discussions, I am not tacitly
arguing that a no-growth or steady-state society would be better than the
one we have, nor that economic analysis is not a powerful and useful tool,

nor that a critically defined notion of efficiency would not be of help to our thinking about energy. Each of those issues would have to be addressed separately in its own right; none of them is the point I am after here. Instead, what interests me is the extent to which the prevailing terms of debate tend to exclude other points of view that might be equally fruitful. Rich perspectives in the social sciences and humanities, indeed whole branches of learning, are somehow never consulted on the matter. In fact, an astonishing feature of today's energy projections and recommendations is how thoroughly devoid they are of any vision of history, how completely divorced from any theoretical grasp of the present situation other than that provided by neoclassical economics. When history is mentioned at all, it is typically represented on a set of graphs that show the rise and decline of various energy sources, rising or falling energy prices per unit consumed, and the relationship between energy use and gross national product over several decades. The history of the energy problem, it would seem, began in 1973, although some reports proudly point out that the cognoscenti had gotten wind of it three or four years earlier. If there is a story to be told about what it meant for modern society to adapt to the expanding use of hydropower, coal, natural gas, and petroleum, that story is never mentioned.

Similarly, the exclusive reliance upon the concepts and models of economic analysis in these reports is an intellectual stance of remarkable single-mindedness. Modern social theory, it turns out, did not begin (nor did it end) with Adam Smith. Perhaps because economics has succeeded in portraying itself as a scientific discipline, perhaps because its concepts and principles are so closely attuned to the workings of modern capitalism, economics is the only branch of the social sciences taken seriously in our time.

It is true, of course, that our society's commitment to economic growth as a central goal and to efficiency as an overriding social norm has both historical and theoretical significance. At a certain time in the development of American democracy, growth—also called prosperity, abundance, or progress—became a substitute for other shared ends. An unwavering faith in ever-expanding abundance became a way of ignoring some important questions about the shape of democratic society, questions about the structure of wealth and power. Because issues of this kind involve our energy systems as much as any other aspect of modern life, the origins of our faith in ever-growing material plenitude deserves a closer look.

Democracy, Abundance, and "Power"

Let us begin by remembering that at the time of the founding of the American republic, this was not a country that depended upon high levels of energy consumption or, for that matter, high standards of economic prosperity. In fact, during political discussions of the 1770s and 1780s, the possession of great wealth by a people was sometimes seen as a danger to freedom. Material well-being was associated with "luxury," a source of corruption in the body politic. According to one line of argument, a taste for "luxury"—what we today might call materialistic values—tended to subvert the morals of a people, making them less capable of genuine self-government. A speaker before the Continental Congress in 1775 called upon the citizenry to "banish the syren LUXURY with all her train of fascinating pleasures, idle dissipation, and expensive amusements from our borders" and to institute "honest industry, sober frugality, simplicity of manners, plain hospitality and christian benevolence."[10]

There are signs that a desire to shape economic development to accord with the principles of republican virtue continued to interest some Americans well into the nineteenth century. Attempts to include at least some elements of republican community in the building of a factory village in Lowell, Massachusetts in the 1820s show this idea at work.[11] But in an age that had tasted the fruits and pressures of industrialism, such efforts were short-lived. In the 1840s and decades since, the notion that industrial development might be shaped or limited by republican morality dropped out of common discourse.

By the middle of the nineteenth century, most Americans had embraced an idea that identified democratic freedom not in frugality, simplicity, self-restraint, and the activities of citizenship, but rather in the enjoyment of material abundance. The country was rich in land and resources, its people, liberated from the social hierarchies and status definitions of traditional societies, were given the opportunity to exploit that material bounty in whatever ways they could muster. In this context, new technologies, including energy technologies, were seen as unquestionably good because they enabled the treasures to be extracted more quickly. Factories, railroads, steamboats, telegraphs, and the like were greeted as the very essence of democratic freedom for the ways they rendered, as one mid-nineteenth-century writer exclaimed, "the conveniences and elegancies of life accessible to the many instead of the few."[12]

American society encouraged people to be self-determining, to pursue their own economic goals. That policy would work, it was widely believed, only if there was a surplus that guaranteed enough to go around. Class conflict, the scourge of democracy in the ancient world and in modern Europe, could be avoided in the United States because the inequalities present in society would not matter very much. Material abundance would make it possible for everybody to have enough to be perfectly happy. Eventually, Americans took this notion to be a generally applicable theory: Economic growth driven by the engine of technical improvement was the very essence of human freedom. Franklin D. Roosevelt reportedly remarked that if he could put one American book in the hands of every Russian, it would be the Sears, Roebuck catalogue.

In this way of looking at things, the form of the technology you adopt does not matter. If you have a cornucopia in your grasp, why worry about its shape? If, as a citizen of a free society, you find yourself served by a system of energy supply, there is no need to ponder its resource base, the design of its hardware, or the arrangement of the social institutions that build, own, and manage the operation. The appropriate thing to do is celebrate: applaud the abundance that modern industry has made available, rejoice in the liberation that accompanies the new machines, techniques, systems, products, and services.

An understanding of this kind has informed the greater share of American writings on energy technology for the past century and a half. Thus, an early twentieth-century journalist of science and industry proclaimed: "Steam proved the great liberator of mankind. Before we learned how to use steam, human energy was exploited for thousands of years. The steam-engine enabled men to use the energy locked up in coal, thereby releasing from drudgery, bondage, and misery an army of workmen."[13]

Notice the political language used to glorify these developments. The same writer argues that the coming of abaundant energy was a source of freedom much like that gained in the British, American, and French revolutions. To emphasize the point, he tells of a conversation that Matthew Boulton, eighteenth-century engineer and business partner of James Watt, evidently had with King George the Third.

"In what business are you engaged?" asked the King.

"I am engaged, your Majesty," said Boulton, "in the production of a commodity which is the desire of kings."

"And what is that? What is that?"

"Power, your Majesty," replied Boulton.[14]

An attractive feature of "power" of this kind (as perceived in American popular writings) is that unlike the power of kings and dictators, it does not need to be limited. As a benign and universal social blessing, it requires none of the checks and balances placed upon powers created by the U.S. Constitution. Ordinary people participate in this power. They do so, however, not by controlling the manner of its production or distribution, but by enjoying the wealth created by increasing energy use, by filling their lives with the various commodities—automobiles, heaters, radios, televisions, hair dryers, lawn mowers, and the like—that the economy makes available to everyone, regardless (so it is hoped) of social class. As one of the recent energy studies explains: "Progress, to most Americans has meant the widening of access to the 'good things of life.' These good things have included mobility, enhanced access to health care and education, reduced drudgery, more leisure, and more 'stuff.' For virtually everyone—the farmer, the housewife, the laborer, and the businessman—energy use has helped overcome obstacles of space and time. Ultimately, an industrial system fueled by abaundant energy was expected to overcome want by speeding the blessings enjoyed by the American upper and middle classes to all."[15]

Over many decades, the idea that freedom and social well-being could be achieved through sheer abundance has been a preeminent, almost unquestioned tenet of American political thinking. According to this notion, the ends of democracy and equality can be achieved without the struggle and sacrifice they might otherwise entail. Everything one might desire of the relationship between industrial technology and the conditions of a good society will be produced automatically.

Lost in the continuing chorus of hosannas, however, are a number of important questions about the structure of society as it relates to human well-being. To persist in looking for the most efficient energy path to sustained economic growth, to establish the lowest cost kilowatt-hour or Btu as a primary social goal, to talk as if everyone had an equal share in the achievement of these objectives—such an approach means that questions about the quality of human association as affected by the social organization of energy will forever be put aside.

One significant range of issues has to do with the distribution of wealth created at the time new energy systems are being designed, built, and introduced into widespread use. Should this wealth be instituted as private property, for example, or should it be considered a public trust whose ownership is in some way or another shared by the citizenry as a whole? If a society does choose arrangements of private ownership, what limits, if any, should be placed upon the extent of the enormous private wealth and privately exercised social power that accompanies the development of energy systems?

Another set of issues concerns the way in which energy systems themselves are organized. In both their operating hardware and the social institutions that administer them, what patterns should such systems be given? Because modes of energy production, conversion, and distribution are bound to become lasting fixtures of the material and institutional framework of society, what is sensible to prescribe for their structures? For example, should energy systems be relatively centralized or dispersed in their workings?

By and large, American society has side-stepped both kinds of issues, not only in energy but in other areas of institutional change related to new technology. The question we have, in effect, chosen to focus upon is the following: If the nation is *not* prepared to distribute wealth or decision-making power equally, how shall it maintain its claim to be a society dedicated to freedom and equality? The answer, as clearly stated in the energy studies as anywhere else, is familiar: The economy will grow. And the best course to pursue this end, the policy that will surely win the widest possible consensus, is presumed to be that which seeks the most efficient use of "our" resources.

Energy Regimes and Social Contracts

A number of recent writings have analyzed the political economy of energy, finding an extremely unequal distribution of wealth reflected in the ways energy is produced and consumed.[16] Indeed, an embarrassing moment in some of the major energy studies comes at the point in which the expert panels take up the topic of "equity." Discussing the significance of decontrolling oil prices, one report points out that decontrol would transfer about $5 billion from consumers to business corporations. "It should be emphasized," the report explains, "that while the general direction of this income transfer is from poorer to richer, it is not a transfer from the poor to the rich. It is a transfer from consumer generally, some of whom are poor, toward stockholders, not all of whom are rich. . . . Since the nonpoor consumers spend more on petroleum products than poor consumers, the larger burden of this transfer in dollar terms is from the nonpoor to the comparatively well to do."[17]

If nothing else, this explanation shows that structural inequalities in our economy can place a severe strain upon the English language.

As important as the distribution of wealth and income certainly is, however, it is not the only issue that ought to concern us. Equally significant, but less thoroughly studied, are the social and political dimensions of the structure of energy systems. It is that matter that I want to explore briefly here.

To provide the variety of goods and services that sustain them, modern societies have created elaborate sociotechnical systems that link production, distribution, and consumption in coherent patterns. Within such systems, the activities of work, management, finance, planning, marketing, and the like are coordinated in highly developed institutional arrangements. These institutions, together with the physical technologies they employ, can well be characterized, borrowing a term from political theory, as "regimes" under which people who use energy are obliged to live. Such regimes of instrumentality have meaning for the way we live not unlike regimes in politics as such. It is possible to examine the full range of structural features contained in a particular sociotechnical arrangement and to identify the qualities of its rules, roles, and relationships. Thus, there are a number of regimes of industrial and agricultural mass production—the one called "the automobile," for example—each with qualities that may be talked about as political phenomena. The existing system of broadcast television is another such regime, one being challenged at present by cable television, which is, of course, not merely a new set of instruments but a novel regime in its own right. If one were to identify and describe all of the regimes of instrumentality in our society and their complex interconnections, one would have a picture of a sociotechnical constitution, one that runs parallel to and occasionally overlaps the constitution of political society.[18]

In this light, if one looks at the ways our society organizes energy, one notices a number of different regimes of varying size and complexity, each one created to exploit a particular kind of energy resource, each one using appropriate instruments, techniques, and social relationships to do so. In New England, for example, the regime of deriving energy from wood is still alive and well. Its components include local wood cutters using chain saws and local distributors, often the cutters themselves. Their neighbors obtain the product through very flexibly defined exchanges that involve either money or barter or both. One can compare the structure of this regime to the one that exists in petroleum. Its enormous, world-wide networks of extraction, transportation, refining, marketing, advertising, litigating, and so forth can also manage to heat a home in New England. The renewed popularity of wood energy among those who have convenient access to it is not merely a consequence of the lower cost of wood as compared to oil. In fact, wood is sometimes preferred even though it costs more. Many people feel comfortable with the features of the regime of wood energy at the same time that they have become wary of the far-flung arrangements that tie them ultimately to the likes of Exxon and OPEC oil countries.

How far one ought to go in specifying the boundaries of the different energy regimes is an important analytical problem.[19] Obviously, there are many interactions—financial, technical, and social—between the systems that enable us to obtain and use energy; for instance, the links between the regime of petroleum and that of electricity or coal. For the purposes at hand, however, the sticky question of boundaries must temporarily be set aside.

For each sociotechnical regime, including those of energy, it is also helpful to consider the "social contract" upon which the regime is established and justified. Again, this is a concept taken from political theory. Social contracts in energy may be explicit or implicit, spelled out in law or simply acknowledged in common understanding. But it is usually possible to probe the historical circumstances under which a given system arose and to reveal the normative foundations upon which its structure rests. This foundation can be thought about in much the same way that Rousseau envisioned the social contract agreed upon, in theory at least, at the founding of any political society. Those who have come together to form a community spell out very carefully the lasting conditions of power, authority, justice, citizen rights, and the manner in which decisions shall be made and administered. Much the same can be said of the agreements that legitimate the building and operation of energy regimes. While there are, of course, many important differences between political constitutions and sociotechnical ones, they may be fruitfully compared for the ways they establish enduring frameworks of social order. If we are to go beyond the narrow focus upon economics and efficiency in contemporary energy analysis, we need to understand and evaluate the qualities of social life that any energy policy, public or private, entails.

The implicit social contract that has governed the development of energy systems in the United States during the past century can be stated fairly simply. Producers of energy agree to supply safe, reliable, abundant energy at a reasonable price. The rest of society agrees to pay the going rate and let producers go about their business. Within the terms of this understanding, the structure of the regimes created to fulfill the contract are, for reasons we have already seen, regarded as black boxes—input/output devices whose internal structure is of no particular public concern.

As long as the desired result is achieved—the supply of abundant energy at a relatively low cost—everyone is assumed to be satisfied. The fact that the building of each new energy system involves a partial reconstruction of society, broadscale changes in how people are able to live and work, has, in general, not been regarded as anything needing careful attention.

An illustration of a social contract that underlies a specific energy regime can be recognized in the development of the electric utilities. Recognized in law as "natural monopolies," such utilities are regarded as an industry "affected with a public interest" and therefore subject to certain kinds of governmental regulation. The social contract that provides legitimacy to privately owned, publicly regulated electric utilities has recently been described in this way: "As defined through various legislative, regulatory, and judicial channels, the terms of this contract have assured the utility investor that electric prices will be high enough to assure the credit worthiness of the utility and the safety of his investment. The consumer in turn has agreed to pay the electric rates necessary to assure this credit worthiness."[20] In this context, standards of service and utility rates are established under governmental authority and administered by state public utility commissions.

Although it would appear that the public is well protected by these measures, in historical practice the utilities have achieved considerable independence from public interference in their activities. From its beginnings early this century, the framework of regulation that governs the utilities has been one largely shaped by the companies themselves. While there have been skirmishes in which federal and state agencies tried to shape policies in this area, over many years the strength of public regulation has languished. "Planning and pricing decisions—how many plants, of what type, where and when they should be built, and who should be charged for them—were made largely by the industry itself, with little supervision by the government regulators. As long as rates were stable or declining and service was reliable, about the only people who paid any attention to state utility commissions were utility executives."[21]

Energy regimes built under social contracts of this sort have some interesting political features. They tend to be extremely large, complex, centralized, and hierarchically managed. Their enormous power is exercised on a wide variety of conditions in society which affect their operations; for example, continuing attempts to influence aggregate consumer demand. The most common justification for building energy systems on such a monolithic scale is that they are more efficient than smaller ones would be. Organizations in petroleum and electricity have grown to capture economies of scale. In this regard, Samuel Insull, president of Commonwealth Edison of Chicago in the early part of this century, can be recognized as the founding father of the electric utilities regime. He devised the institutional structures that enabled centrally generated electrical power to capture economies of scale, higher and better balanced load factors, and thus to develop larger and larger integrated systems. His great accomplishment, from one point of view, was to be able to lower prices and raise profits simultaneously. The American public has readily applauded the achievements of sociotechnical systems builders like Samuel Insull, for the populace has received what the social contract required here: cheap, reliable energy.

On occasion, however, the scale of our energy regimes has begun to seem reptilian. With the rise of the petroleum industry, American society was suddenly faced with The Standard Oil Company, an oppressive monopoly whose hold on that industry took decades to overcome. During the 1920s, the consolidation of control in electrical power systems, following Insull's wise formulas, had advanced to an alarming point at which only "fifty-seven systems delivered ninety percent of the nation's privately produced electricity and only twelve systems delivered more than fifty percent."[22] Public outcry over the abuse of power by privately owned utilities led to a number of New Deal programs—the Tennessee Valley Authority, the Rural Electrification Administration, the Electric Utility Holding Company Act, and others—that introduced a greater degree of public ownership and public control to the production and distribution of electricity.

In our own time, the structure of energy regimes has become a subject of widespread concern. The social dominance of the large petroleum companies has become so great that they seem all but impervious to public criticism, limitation, or direction. At the same time, the power of the electric utilities has once again arisen as an issue in conflicts like those surrounding the decision to build high voltage powerlines through the farmlands of Minnesota.[23] In places like Seabrook, New Hampshire and Diablo Canyon, California, attempts have been made to demonstrate that with enough police, national guard troops, and attack dogs, it will be possible to install nuclear power plants. In a wide-ranging series of discussions during the past decade, we have all been engaged in a process of choosing which new energy supplies and energy technologies this nation ought to sponsor.

The occasion for these renewed conversations and struggles is, it seems to me, that the social contract that has for decades justified our orientation to existing energy regimes has now been broken (or at least seriously weakened). What ordinary citizens were supposed to receive as their part of the bargain—cheap, reliable energy—no longer seems secure. For that reason, it is now possible to reconsider what energy producers have gotten in their half of the deal—the right to build huge organizations with enormous social power. Many have begun to suspect that the present agreement is less like a contract for continuing freedom and abundance, and more like a bill of goods whose surprise pay-off is an exaggerated, potentially restrictive dependency.

Crucially at stake in the debate about energy are choices about the shape of our society now and in the future. These are choices that concern the essential character of energy regimes: how large they will be, what energy sources they will employ, how they will be designed, how and by whom they will be run, and how they will affect the structure and texture of human life. Thus, two proposed energy regimes now on the drawing boards—those associated with breeder reactors on the one hand, and solar energy on the other—present very different possibilities. Liquid metal fast-breeder reactors, if introduced to us on a large scale, will almost certainly bring with them a set of drastically repressive social conditions. Their regime involves very high levels of capital investment, bureaucratic centralization, a further concentration of social power, and the need for strong police measures—not short of wiretaps, covert surveillance, lie detector tests, and the like—to protect the power plants and the plutonium they generate. "It is not impossible," one recent study of breeders concludes, "that America will find her children growing up in a society so stratified and regimented that it more nearly resembles fifteenth century Peru or nineteenth century Prussia than the twentieth century United States."[24] In contrast, it appears that a regime of solar energy has a good chance of being a flexible, forgiving, humanly agreeable setting under which to live. There is, of course, nothing necessary about that result; solar technologies are not, as some have suggested, inherently democratic. How they affect society will depend upon the configuration given to both their material and social components.

My point is, then, that the obsession with efficiency, economic growth, and lowest cost energy alternatives simply ignores what is most important in decisions before us now. To retain a democratic form of society means, among other things, that we seek to develop energy systems compatible with the continued existence of a free society. If we simply attend to questions of cost and efficiency, it may happen that we will create energy regimes so monolithic, powerful, and vulnerable that they present hazards to liberty.

When it comes to thinking about the structure of energy in society, however, we are still very easily persuaded to silence. They say every man has his price. Ours is now about $1.40 a gallon or 3¢ a kilowatt-hour.

NOTES

1. Herodotus, *The Histories of Herodotus*, Vol. I, George Rawlinson, trans. (New York, 1964), 355.

2. A representative selection of foundation-sponsored energy studies done during the 1970s would include the following: *A Time to Choose*, Energy Policy Project of the Ford Foundation (Cambridge, MA, 1974); *Nuclear Power Issues and Choices: Report*, Nuclear Energy Policy Study Group (Cambridge, MA, 1977); *Energy in America's Future: The Choices Before Us*, National Energy in America's Future: The Choices Before Us, National Energy Studies Project (Baltimore, 1979); *Energy: The Next Twenty Years*, Report of the Study Group Sponsored by the Ford Foundation and Administered by Resources for the Future; Hans H. Landsberg et al. (Cambridge, MA, 1979); *Energy in Transition, 1985-2010*, National Research Council Committee on Nuclear and Alternative Energy Systems (San Francisco, 1980).

3. Laura Nader, "Barriers to thinking new about energy," *Physics Today* (February 1981), 9, 99-104.

4. *Energy in America's Future*, 15.

5. Henry W. Kendall and Steven J. Nadis, eds., *Energy Strategies: Toward a Solar Future*, a report of the Union of Concerned Scientists (Cambridge, MA, 1980), 58.

6. *Nuclear Power: Issues and Choices*, xi.

7. *Nuclear Power: Issues and Choices*, 44, 41.

8. Amory B. Lovins, "Technology is the answer! (but what was the question?): energy as a case study of inappropriate technology." Presented at the Symposium on Social Values and Technological Change in an International Context, Racine, Wisconsin (June 1978), 1.

9. For a discussion of the wide-ranging significance of the idea of efficiency in American thought, see Samuel Haber, *Efficiency and Uplift: Scientific Management in the Progressive Era, 1890-1920* (Chicago, 1964); and Samuel P. Hays, *Conservation and the Gospel of Efficiency: The Progressive Conservation Movement, 1890-1920* (New York, 1959).

10. Quote in Gordon S. Wood, *The Creation of the American Republic, 1776-1787* (New York, 1972), 114.

11. See John Kasson, *Civilizing the Machine: Technology and Republican Values in America, 1776-1900* (New York, 1976).

12. Denison Olmsted, "On the democratic tendencies of science," *Barnard's Journal of Education* 1 (1855-1856), reprinted in Thomas Parke Hughes, ed., *Changing Attitudes Toward American Technology* (New York, 1975), 148.

13. W. F. Decker and Waldemar Kaempffert, "Putting steam to work," in Waldemar Kaempffert, ed., *A Popular History of American Invention.* Vol. I (New York, 1924), 468.

14. Ibid., 503.

15. *Energy in America's Future,* 403.

16. Some of the writings that have approached the political economy of energy from a critical point of view are the following: James Ridgeway, *The Last Play: The Struggle to Monopolize the World's Energy Resources* (New York, 1973); Michael Tanzer, *The Energy Crisis: World Struggle for Power and Wealth* (New York, 1975); John M. Blair, *The Control of Oil* (New York, 1976); Robert Engler, *The Brotherhood of Oil: Energy Policy and the Public Interest* (New York, 1978).

17. *Energy: The Next Twenty Years,* 197.

18. I develop this idea more fully in "Techne and politeia: the technical constitution of society," to appear in a forthcoming volume of Paul Durbin, ed., *Research in Philosophy and Technology.*

19. A strong analytical approach to ideas of this kind can be found in George Hoberg, "Electricity, decentralization, and society: the socio-political aspects of dispersed electric generating technologies," a Working Paper for the Office of Technology Assessment, January 1981.

20. Robert W. Gilmer and Richard E. Meunier, "Electric utilities and solar energy: the service contract in a new social context," *Mercer Law Review* 30 (1979), 383.

21. Douglas D. Anderson, "State regulation of electric utilities," in James Q. Wilson, ed., *The Politics of Regulation* (New York, 1980), 21.

22. Gilmer and Meunier, "Electric utilities and solar energy," 380.

23. See Barry M. Casper and Paul David Wellstone, *Powerline: The First Battle of America's Energy War* (Amherst, MA, 1981).

24. *Energy Choices in a Democratic Society,* Report of the Consumption, Location, and Occupational Patterns Resource Group Synthesis Panel of the Committee on Nuclear and Alternative Energy Systems, National Research Council (Washington, DC, 1980).

Index

About the Contributors

GEORGE BASALLA is Associate Professor of the History of Science and Technology at the University of Delaware. The author of numerous articles and books, including *The Rise of Modern Science: Internal or External Factors?*, Basalla is currently at work on two projects, one dealing with science, technology, and popular culture, and the other with civilization, technology, and science.

WARREN J. BELASCO is Assistant Professor of American Studies at the University of Maryland in Baltimore County. In 1982 he was awarded a fellowship by the National Endowment for the Humanities for research on aspects of popular culture. He is the author of papers, articles, and a book, *Americans on the Road: From Autocamp to Motel.*

EUGENIE LADNER BIRCH is Assistant Professor of Urban Planning at Hunter College. She is serving as the elected chair of Columbia University's Seminar on the City and is the author of numerous articles and papers and a forthcoming book, *Impatient Crusaders: Women and the Fight for Low Cost Housing in Britain and America, 1860-1970.*

CORLANN (CORKY) GEE BUSH is Assistant Dean for Student Advisory Services at the University of Idaho. She is the principal investigator for the Rural Women's History Project and has been awarded several grants for research on the social dimensions of women. Her publications include *Cultural Images of Women in Technology* and *Women in the West: A Bibliography of Resources.*

JOHN G. CLARK is Professor of History at the University of Kansas and had held a number of fellowships, including appointment as Visiting Scholar at the U.S. Department of Energy and as a Fellow at the National

Humanities Center. Clark is the author of several books, including *Towns and Minerals in Southwestern Kansas,* many articles, and is completing a book on federal fuels management.

EDWARD W. CONSTANT II is Associate Professor of History at Carnegie Mellon University. He has been awarded a grant by the National Science Foundation for his work on the regulation of the oil industry in Texas, 1910-1950. Constant is the author of papers, articles, and a book, *The Origins of the Turbojet Revolution.*

GEORGE H. DANIELS is Associate Professor of Science, Technology, and Society at Michigan Technological University. He is the author of a large number of articles and books, including *American Science in the Age of Jackson.* Daniels is currently at work on a study of economic policy and technology during the post-World War II era.

AUGUST W. GIEBELHAUS, Associate Professor of History in the School of Social Sciences at Georgia Tech, teaches courses in economic, emergy, and technological history. He is the author of *Business and Government in the Oil Industry: A Case Study of Sun Oil, 1876-1945* and co-editor of *Energy Transitions: Long-Term Perspectives.* From 1977 through 1981, he served as first assistant editor and then associate editor of the journal, *Technology and Culture.*

JACK M. HOLL is Chief Historian in the U.S. Department of Energy, where his duties have included responsibility for the Visiting Scholar Program, contract research, and the *Energy History Report.* Holl's research has focused on the history of federal initiatives in energy development and management, particularly the efforts of the Atomic Energy Commission (with Richard G. Hewlett). He is editor of *Institutional Origins of the Department of Energy* (Washington, D.C., 1982), and of articles and books on energy history and the history of penology.

KENNETH E. KOONS is a Ph.D. candidate in the Doctor of Arts Program in History at Carnegie-Mellon University.

MARTIN V. MELOSI is Associate Professor of History at Texas A & M University. He had held a number of grants and fellowships, including one most recently from the National Endowment for the Humanities, and has published several books, including *Garbage in the Cities: Refuse, Reform and the Environment, 1880-1980.* Currently, he is at work on a book focused on energy and the environment in industrial America since 1830.

BONNIE MAAS MORRISON is Associate Professor in the Department of Human Environment and Design at Michigan State University. She was a Visiting Scholar at the U.S. Department of Energy and has served as project coordinator and consultant for a large number of contemporary energy projects focused on families and housing. She is the author of books and articles on this subject, including the forthcoming *Family Lifestyles and Energy,* and has also prepared numerous technical papers and reports.

JOSEPH A. PRATT is Assistant Professor of History at Texas A & M University. He has served as Visiting Scholar at the U.S. Department of Energy and as Research Assistant for the Papers of Dwight D. Eisenhower at Johns Hopkins University. He is the author of *The Growth of a Refining Region* and of articles on energy and regional economic growth. He is presently at work on a history of the American Petroleum Institute.

MARK H. ROSE is Associate Professor of Science, Technology, and Society at Michigan Technological University. He is the author of articles, papers, and a book, *Interstate: Express Highway Politics, 1941-1956.* Rose is currently at work on a study of energy choices and the social and geographic development of several western cities, 1900-1950.

JOEL A. TARR is Professor of History and Public Policy, Director of the Program in Technology and Society, and Co-Director of the Program in Applied History and Social Science at Carnegie-Mellon University. His main interests are in applying history to contemporary problems, urban studies, and the impacts of technology on the city. He has authored several books, including *The Impact of Transportation Innovation on Changing Spatial Patterns: Pittsburgh, 1850-1934,* and has published articles in many journals. He is currently preparing a National Science Foundation-supported study on energy and the environment in American cities.

LANGDON WINNER is Visiting Associate Professor of Politics and Technology at the University of California, Santa Cruz. He is the author of *Autonomous Technology: Technics-out-of-Control as a Theme in Political Thought* and of numerous articles on politics, technology, and social change. His present work focuses upon ways in which choices about technological design affect the quality of public life.